COMPUTER STUDIES SERIES

PROGRAMMING IN SQL
WITH ORACLE,® INGRES™ AND dBASE™

John Carter MSc MBCS, Grad IMA
Department of Systems and Computing Studies
Polytechnic of East London

OXFORD
BLACKWELL SCIENTIFIC PUBLICATIONS
LONDON EDINBURGH BOSTON
MELBOURNE PARIS BERLIN VIENNA

To Robert and Mary Carter

© John Carter 1992

Blackwell Scientific Publications
Editorial Offices:
Osney Mead, Oxford OX2 0EL
25 John Street, London WC1N 2BL
23 Ainslie Place, Edinburgh EH3 6AJ
3 Cambridge Center, Cambridge,
  Massachusetts 02142, USA
54 University Street, Carlton
  Victoria 3053, Australia

Other Editorial Offices:
Librairie Arnette SA
2, rue Casimir-Delavigne
75006 Paris
France

Blackwell Wissenschafts-Verlag
Meinekestrasse 4
D-1000 Berlin 15
Germany

Blackwell MZV
Feldgasse 13
A-1238 Wien
Austraia

First published 1992

Printed and bound in Great Britain by
Hartnolls, Bodmin, Cornwall

DISTRIBUTORS

Marston Book Services Ltd
PO Box 87
Oxford OX2 0DT
(*Orders:* Tel: 0865 791155
       Fax: 0865 791927
       Telex: 837515)

USA
Blackwell Scientific Publications, Inc.
3 Cambridge Center
Cambridge, MA 02142
(*Orders:* Tel: 800 759-6102
        617 225-0401)

Canada
Oxford University Press
70 Wynford Drive
Don Mills
Ontario M3C 1J9
(*Orders:* Tel: 416 441-2941)

Australia
Blackwell Scientific Publications
(Australia) Pty Ltd
54 University Street
Carlton, Victoria 3053
(*Orders:* Tel: 03 347-0300)

British Library
Cataloguing in Publication Data

A catalogue record for this book is
available from the British Library.

ISBN 0–632–03136–0

Library of Congress
Cataloging in Publication Data

Carter, John (John R.)
    Programming in SQL with Oracle,
Ingres, and dBase IV/John Carter
        p.   cm. — (Computer studies series)
    Includes bibliographical references and
index.
        ISBN 0–632–03136–0
    1. SQL (Computer program language)
2. Oracle (Computer file)   3. Ingres
(Computer file)   4. dBase IV (Computer
program)
I. Title.   II. Series: Computer studies
series (Oxford, England)
QA76.73.S67C37   1992
005.75′6—dc20   92-8218
                                       CIP

Contents

Preface

Many books have been and are being written about SQL. The emphasis in this book is not only to give a large number of programming examples (there are over 270) illustrating each syntactic feature of the language, but also to explore the kinds of situations and problems the programmer or end user is likely to encounter in writing SQL queries in a practical situation, and to answer the question most often asked by programmers coming to a new language : 'How do I ... ?'.

For this reason, every SQL query example starts with a statement of the original query in English, so that the reader can not only find examples of particular SQL command usage, but also find a problem that looks like his or her own and get the right SQL.

Many readers of this book will be students trying to find a method or an example to help them with an assignment, a project, or with exam revision. Most of the examples and the associated explanations in this book have been derived from my experience, gained over four years of using and teaching SQL, of what students find helpful, what they find difficult and what they find interesting.

While SQL examples can be found in the Language manuals for your DBMS, and these must be the final arbiter on questions of precise syntax, the examples and explanations may be too few, too brief, or too technical.

The chapters in this book have been arranged so that self-teaching is made easy. Language features are first explained using simple examples with a gradual progression to 'problem situations'.

Lecturers and teachers of SQL should find that the sequence of chapters given is logical and requires the minimum of 'forward reference'. Later chapters build on and reinforce earlier content. Chapter 9 contains five larger case studies which give a context to several interesting queries and could easily form the basis for further exercises.

It is thought that the absolute beginner in SQL will want to read this book through sequentially. For readers in a hurry, or those wishing to obtain a quick introduction to SQL, I would recommend reading and working through the first few examples following each new language feature. These examples are graded, and start with simple and typical applications of the feature, and progress gradually to more involved usage. The language features are shown in CAPITALS in the Contents pages.

Those who already have some experience of SQL will probably be looking for an example of a particular usage of a given language feature. For such readers, I have included as many non-trivial examples as possible, aiming always to cover and clarify potential problem areas.

For the SQL connoisseur, sections towards the end of each chapter and parts of Chapter 9 attempt to explore the limits of SQL applicability. There are even two examples (Case Studies 5 and 6) where SQL is thought *not* to be immediately applicable.

SQL is portable, so that knowledge gained from reading this book will allow you to query and update databases from many different DBMS (Database Management System) vendors. There are minor variations between SQLs from different vendors. The subtitle of this book highlights ORACLE, INGRES and dBASE IV, and all the query examples have been tested on these three SQLs and any differences noted.

There are usually alternative methods of realizing an SQL query (many subqueries can be replaced by joins for example) and these have been investigated and their relative merits discussed.

In this book, SQL Programming has not been divorced from the wider issues of Systems Analysis and Design. Entity Analysis and Normalization are given a straightforward treatment using diagrams and simple examples, and I trust this will enable the reader to easily understand these techniques so that he or she will be rewarded with a better-designed database and easier-to-write queries and programs.

It is hoped that the reader will find learning SQL with this book interesting, informative and profitable.

John Carter

Acknowledgements

I would like to thank Mr. Francois Taty for the Embedded C examples, and Mr. Michael Everitt for several of the Case Studies.

I would also like to thank the ORACLE organization for the speedy and reliable help I obtained from the on-line help desk on several occasions during the preparation of this book.

I also wish to acknowledge the following trademarks.

ORACLE and SQL*PLUS are registered trademarks of Oracle Corporation.

INGRES is a trademark of Relational Technology.

dBASE and dBASE IV are trademarks of Ashton-Tate Corporation.

Chapter 1

Introduction

1.1 THE RELEVANCE OF SQL

SQL (Structured Query Language) is rapidly becoming the standard query language for accessing data on relational databases. With its simple, powerful syntax, SQL represents a leap forward in database access for all levels of management and computing professionals.

SQL appears in two forms, *interactive* SQL and *embedded* SQL. Embedded SQL usage is close to traditional programming in third generation languages. It is the interactive use of SQL which makes it most applicable for the rapid answering of ad hoc queries. With an interactive SQL query you just type in a few lines of SQL and you get the database response immediately on the screen.

For managers, retrieval of vital information and summary data to aid strategic and operational decision making can be performed almost instantaneously with interactive SQL, without having to wait for programs to be designed, written and tested in the Data Processing department.

For systems analysts and programmers, SQL allows complex data retrieval operations to be programmed in shorter programs whose operation can often be understood totally with just a few minutes of inspection. This is due to the *set oriented* nature of SQL as compared to the record-by-record processing characteristic of 3GLs (Third Generation Languages). Since SQL programs are quicker to write, programming backlogs can be removed, documentation efforts reduced, and program alterations simplified.

Well-designed SQL queries which contain the bulk of the logic of a program can be confidently embedded in a 3GL or 4GL *host program* after being developed and tested interactively at the terminal. The host program can provide the user interface and the embedded SQL can provide the powerful and easy-to-understand logic for navigating the database to retrieve the various combinations of data required.

1.2 WHAT THIS BOOK CONTAINS

Chapter 2 describes how to design a database logical schema and how to design and create the database tables in which data will be stored. This chapter has been included to encourage 'good' database design practice which will result in a database with an absence or a controlled degree of data redundancy and easier-to-write SQL queries throughout the life of the database. It includes simple descriptions of entity analysis and normalization.

Chapter 3 introduces all the basic functions of SQL including GROUP BY, ORDER BY and HAVING. Chapters 4 and 5 show how queries involving two or more tables are implemented using joins and subqueries and shows that while these are often alternatives to each other, there are some situations in which either one or the other must be used.

Chapter 6 illustrates the basic set operations of UNION, INTERSECT and MINUS and how they are used in practical queries. Chapter 7 discusses EXISTS and NOT EXISTS, features which are sometimes found difficult by newcomers to SQL. Their use is compared with that of IN and the appropriate application of each is discussed.

In Chapter 8, the uses of views are explored and the examples show how views can be used to enhance database security and to simplify some SQL programming tasks by acting as programmers' 'stepping stones' between shorter queries and by presenting to the programmer a *view* of a part of the database that is tailored to the needs of specific applications. Examples are given which indicate the *necessity* of using views (or temporary tables) in some situations.

Chapter 9 contains several case studies, each of which highlights typical or 'difficult' SQL queries. These case studies can be made the basis of further exercises. 'Difficult' here does not mean lengthy; rather an attempt has been made to explore the limitations of interactive SQL by finding examples under the heading 'Easy to Say but Hard to Do'. The case study is clear, the query is clear and simple, but the required SQL takes a bit of thought, looks 'interesting', or illustrates a useful SQL programming technique. There are even two examples where SQL is probably *not* the right tool. This is done in a partial attempt to define SQL's 'domain'.

Chapter 10 describes how INSERTs and UPDATEs are performed.

Chapter 11 gives examples of embedded SQL in C, COBOL and dBASE and discusses the concept and use of the *cursor*, which can be used to provide the traditional 'record-by-record' procedural style of programming with SQL. A discussion of when and when not to use embedded SQL is included.

Chapter 12 shows how a DBA (Database Administrator) can control access privileges to different sections of the database for different classes of user. In this chapter, the issues surrounding the uses of database indexes are also discussed. Exercises are provided where appropriate in the text. The Appendix lists all the tables used throughout the text.

1.3 SQL IN CONTEXT

When you purchase a DBMS such as ORACLE, INGRES or dBASE IV, you get several distinct software modules which can all be used for database access. Typically these will include the following :

1. A *screen painter*, which allows data to be input into database tables with some degree of input validation possible.

2. A *report writer*, which can be used to generate formatted reports from database tables and views.

3. The *database manager*, which controls and co-ordinates the creation of and access to database tables, views indexes etc., and allows security features to be added.

4. A *program generator*, which, given simple report formats or input and query screen designs, can automatically generate program code which can then be tailored by the programmer for particular requirements.

5. A *host language* particular to that DBMS; INGRES and dBASE IV have their own *built-in* host languages. These are procedural languages (sometimes called 4GLs) which allow the programmer to embed reports, screens and SQL into the usual IF-ELSE-ENDIF and DOWHILE-ENDWHILE procedural constructs. *External* host languages such as C, COBOL and FORTRAN are also often facilitated by the provision of a *pre-processor* for the language.

6. A Query Language (nowadays usually SQL) which provides the immediate access to and control over the database.

This book concentrates on 5. and 6., that is, the interactive and embedded use of SQL. The relationship of *interactive* SQL to the database is illustrated in Fig. 1.1.

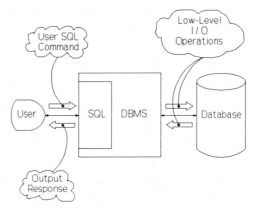

Fig. 1.1 SQL is an Interface Between the User and the Database

The user types in SQL commands which are interpreted by the SQL *query interpreter* into low-level commands to the DBMS which performs the necessary retrieval and update operations on the database. The results of these I/O (Input/Output) operations are passed back to the query interpreter for presentation to the user.

For the *embedded* use of SQL there are several more steps which must be gone through to produce output and these are described in detail in Chapter 11.

1.4 SQL STANDARDS

When any language becomes as popular as SQL is, it is useful to define a 'standard' syntax for the language so that a user knows pretty well what to expect when he or she goes from using SQL at one installation to using it at another. Standards generally define a common 'core' of the language which can perform most if not all of the data processing operations considered appropriate to the language. If a programmer were to stick exclusively to using only the command syntax used in one of the standards then the commands would be portable, that is they could be used unchanged in any database with an SQL interpreter which conformed to that standard.

As the SQL standards become more established, we can expect all major vendors of DBMSs that use SQL to implement a standard 'core' SQL with individual extensions that they consider useful. These will be tested by the market over a number of years and those extensions considered useful will be incorporated into subsequent standards and so on. SQL, being still a relatively new language, has *several* standards, so vendors ought to state explicitly which standard is being adhered to.

The origin of SQL can be traced back to work done in IBM in the mid-1970s which aimed to produce a new high-level language for database queries which would be simpler and more powerful than existing approaches. This resulted in the definition of a language SQUARE and then SEQUEL. IBM produced a prototype DBMS called System R built around SEQUEL and then in 1982 produced its first commercial relational DBMS SQL/DS which used a refinement of SEQUEL called SQL (some people still pronounce SQL as SEQUEL).

Also in 1982 ANSI (American National Standards Institute) began a survey of existing relational database products and by 1983 were concentrating on SQL. In the same year the ISO (International Standards Organisation) began work on standardizing SQL and worked in parallel with ANSI to produce its standard in 1986. Roughly speaking, ISO calls their standard 'The SQL Standard' and the ANSI standard is called ANSI-86 or SQL-86. To be more precise, the ISO standard is described as *'ISO 9075 Database Language SQL'*. The working groups who produced this definition of SQL were ISO TC97/SC21/WG3 and ANSI X3H2. References [1] and [2] describe these standards respectively.

ISO 9075 differs in minor ways from ANSI-86 in terminology and features but they are at about the same 'level'. Since then, ANSI has produced ANSI-89 with referential integrity enhancements and ISO and ANSI are working together to produce SQL2, a single internationally recognized standard.

This book concentrates on three actually existing SQLs which conform fairly closely to ISO 9075 and ANSI-86 but with enhancements. These SQL standards are useful as a general guideline of what to look for in current SQLs and also give the following useful terminology for classifying the SQL commands.

1.5 SQL COMMAND CATEGORIES

There are three basic ANSI categories of command: DDL, DML and DCL. The ISO standard includes the DCL commands under DDL and has a new category 'Module Language'.

1.5.1 DDL (Data Definition Language) Commands

These commands are used for creating, altering and dropping (deleting) database tables. All data on a relational database is stored in these tables. In a large shared ('corporate') database, the use of DDL commands is usually restricted to someone appointed as the *database administrator (DBA)*. In small experimental databases, such as those created by students and individual programmers, there will usually be no such restriction. These commands are described in Chapter 2.

Typical DDL commands are CREATE TABLE, ALTER TABLE, DROP TABLE, CREATE VIEW, DROP VIEW, CREATE INDEX and DROP INDEX.

1.5.2 DCL (Data Control Language) Commands

DCL commands are for general control over the database and include the GRANT command, which is used by the DBA to grant and limit the *privileges* (the powers of connection, creation and those of a DBA) that database users may have; the REVOKE command, which is used to remove privileges; the COMMIT command, which is used to commit (write) any changes that have been made by programs or interactive DML commands to the physical disk-based database and thus make them 'permanent'; and the ROLLBACK command which, if used before a COMMIT, will reverse the set of changes the program has provisionally made in the current program run, and is often used in response to an error condition that later arises.

1.5.3 DML (Data Manipulation Language) Commands

These commands are used (unlike the DDL commands which are used for setting up data *structures*), for inserting, modifying, deleting and querying data *values* on the database. A DDL CREATE command might set up a new database table called INVOICE. After the CREATE command has been executed, there will be no *data* in the table. A DML command INSERT will be used to put rows of data into the table. Application programmers and other SQL users consequently spend most of their time with SQL entering DML commands. Typical DML commands are INSERT, DELETE, and UPDATE. Embedded DML commands (i.e. DML commands placed inside 3GL programs) include DECLARE CURSOR, EXEC SQL, OPEN and CLOSE. Embedded SQL is covered in Chapter 11.

1.5.4 Module Language

As already mentioned, ISO SQL categorizes the commands slightly differently; the ANSI categories above have been inherited largely from the earlier CODASYL type of *network* databases and are thus in current and widespread usage. In ISO SQL, a *module* is a stored collection of *procedures*, each of which is a DML command. Modules can be called up interactively or from within another program. This latter is analogous to embedded SQL but is a more general concept. This terminology is *not* currently in widespread use.

Chapter 2

Table Design and Creation

2.1 INTRODUCTION

This chapter shows how to design and create the database tables that store data in a relational database. The description of all the database tables and their columns constitutes the database *schema*. The schema is a kind of model of that part of the real world that an organization is interested in storing data about. The process of designing the schema is to start from a clear understanding of that part of the real world you wish to model, to produce a diagrammatic model of it (*entity relationship modelling* is the method used here), and then a *relational model*, which is a set of tables. An Entity Relationship diagram is a graphical construct made out of boxes and lines, representing entity types and relationships, and the relational model is a tabular form where each table represents one of the entity types and shows the *attributes* of each entity and the *relationships* between entities. This methodology is becoming the most popular one and it can yield good results. A well-designed Entity Relationship diagram can make the *normalization* checks which are performed on the relational model much simpler. Normalization is described later in this chapter.

2.2 WHAT IS A 'GOOD' DATABASE DESIGN?

2.2.1 'Reality Check'

The 'goodness' of the model is decided by how well the set of database tables that result from the modelling process described actually model the real world and how easily and naturally the tables will support the set of queries and reports that are expected. The full set of queries and reports that will be required will not be known in advance, that is at database design time, so it is not desirable to design the database with *just* the known outputs in mind. The alternative is to turn to the 'real world' and try to produce a model of it as it actually exists. You should be able to answer *any* forthcoming query on the database in an analogous manner to the way you would do it if you had the actual objects you are trying to model in front of you.

However, the designer usually has in mind a number of 'core' processes which are to be run and this set will be useful in testing the paper database design and future prototypes. This first criterion for database 'goodness' I will call the 'reality check' - how well does the database design model the real world?

Have you got things in there (such as 'linkers' or 'pointers' or 'flags') that don't actually exist in the original problem area and which rightfully belong at a much lower, more detailed, more 'physical' machine-oriented level of implementation? If so, perhaps you should think less at this stage about the computer and its software and try to concentrate on the problem itself, the system or situation you are trying to model, describing it in the language normally associated with that situation.

2.2.2 Consistency and Accuracy

Another test of 'goodness' for a database schema is that the resulting database should not contain any duplicate 'facts'; for example it should be stated only once on the entire database that the address of customer X is Y. Limiting or eliminating data redundancy will ensure data consistency, since if a fact is stated only once, then there can be no contradictions. This is no guarantee of course that the 'fact' is correct, just that there will be consistency. Everyone using the database will be obtaining the same 'facts' from it, no matter how they are using it in various queries and reports in various sections and departments of the organization or community of users. The accuracy of the data stored is governed by other factors such as the thoroughness of the manual and computer validation procedures and the frequency of update. This criterion could be called 'consistency and accuracy'.

2.2.3 Transparency

The ease of understanding of the database by novice, regular and expert users is also very important. Everything on the database is intended to 'mean' something and it augers well for its usability that this meaning is actually there on the database and not just in the head of the designer or hidden away in documentation. In designing new programs that are going to process data on the database, or writing SQL queries to answer a specific English (or other spoken language) query, it is imperative that the significance of the attributes that a database object displays are fully understood, as well as the relationships between the objects.

For example the fact that a certain database table is found to contain the attributes employee_number and registration_number does not indicate whether the vehicle is owned, serviced or occasionally driven by that employee. A simple inspection of the table definition will often not suffice in obtaining such semantic information. The Entity Relationship model may help explain the significance of an attribute if the association of attributes in the table is brought about by a foreign key relationship from another table and that relationship is *named* on the Entity Relationship diagram.

Otherwise, one must depend on well-named attributes which announce their own significance, or the documentation the designer has seen fit to produce. CASE (Computer Aided Software Engineering) tools may help here, and it is noticeable that they are becoming more and more integrated into database software. ORACLE*CASE is one example. The CASE tool not only helps to design and generate the database and its applications but also aids understanding of the database by future users. In most CASE tools however, the obligation to describe the 'meaning' of the tables and attributes is voluntary and in any case the utility of such a description depends on the insight and descriptive ability of the designer.

Misunderstanding the significance or meaning of the data held on the database may lead to incorrect strategic decisions being made by, for example, managers using the database as part of a Decision Support or Management Information system, or by senior operational staff making *ad hoc* queries to aid in day-to-day decision making and quality control.

A good database can be understood by its users. We might call this criterion 'transparency'.

2.2.4 Speed

Finally, a good database should be *fast*. Answers to queries should ideally be output immediately but of course there will in practice be some delay between typing in an SQL query and obtaining the response on the screen or printer. Speed can sometimes be improved using database *indexes*, which are additional tables set up by the database designer or administrator (DBA) and maintained by the DBMS itself. They allow relevant database records to be found faster but must themselves be updated when records are inserted or deleted, which may worsen response time for some updates. The probablilty of achieving most of the criteria of a 'good' database, in particular of producing an 'understandable' database with minimal redundancy, can be enhanced by adopting the design approaches described below.

2.3 STAGES IN SCHEMA DESIGN

As already stated, it is useful when designing a database schema to have in mind two things:

1. The real world objects (entity types) that you will want to store data about.

2. The processes that your application normally associates with those objects.

In a relational database, the data about entity types will be held in database tables and the processes will be programs that perform queries, updates and reports. The stages involved in designing the database schema and testing it are shown in Fig. 2.1.

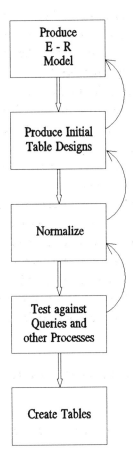

Fig. 2.1 Stages in Developing a Database Schema

Each of these stages is now described. Notice that the process of producing the database design is an iterative one; at every stage there is an iteration loop back to the previous stage. Having normalized the tables for example, it may be necessary to go back and re-draw the Entity Relationship (E-R) diagram to reflect the fact that what was previously considered a single entity type, for example 'statement', has now been split by the normalization process into the three separate entity types 'customer', 'invoice' and 'payment'.

An E-R model is a diagram showing the entity types of interest in the application area of the database and the relationships between them. Each entity type (a box on the diagram) will be *implemented* as a database table containing all the attributes of interest pertaining to that entity type. Provisional table designs are drawn out in the second stage. A *primary key* (an identifier for each entity type) is selected and the tables are subjected to several normalization tests in stage three. Failure in any of these tests results in the table being split, revealing the fact that the table had really represented data about two or more unidentified or 'hidden' entity types.

After the split, the E-R diagram is redrawn to reflect the change in the model (and the enhancement in the designer's understanding of that part of the real-world application area).

The resulting set of tables is tested against a set of major queries and reports that the analyst/designer has collected. This step may reveal the need for changes, including perhaps new entity types and relationships that had not originally occurred to this person.

Finally the table designs are implemented onto the database ('made physical') using the SQL CREATE TABLE command. All of these stages in developing the schema are described below.

2.4 ENTITY RELATIONSHIP MODELLING

2.4.1 What is an Entity Relationship Model?

Entity types are real world objects which we are interested in storing data about. Typical entity types in an accounting application would be 'customer', 'stock item', 'invoice', 'payment', 'delivery' etc. Notice that the name for each type is singular. An entity type name is the name of a class or set of entities, so for example the 'customer' entity type represents or 'is' a set of individual customer entities. Each customer is an entity. (The distinction between the actual living customers and the customer entities as modelled is not often made; the object and the model are treated synonymously and it doesn't seem to cause any problems in the design process described, although the sentiment 'I am not a number' seems fairly apposite in this context).

Each entity type will be represented on our database by a table and the entities within the entity type by rows in the table. Using older terminology, each entity type would be represented by a file and each entity by an individual record in the file. The rows in a table (or records in a file) contain values of the attributes for the individual entity.

At this stage, we concentrate on the production of an E-R diagram which shows entity types represented by boxes and relationships by lines.

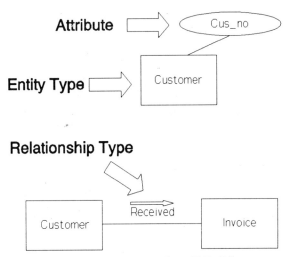

Fig. 2.2 Components of an E-R Diagram

Individual attributes *can* be shown on an E-R diagram (see Fig. 2.2.) but this is not required and for many entity types the number of attributes is too large for them all to be shown. Some designers like to indicate just the primary keys by this method, but in general the idea is that you can show attributes which are of particular interest.

A complete schema diagram for an accounting system may contain ten to twenty entity types. Fig. 2.3 shows an outline Entity Relationship diagram for a simplified accounting system. The Accounts Receivable and Accounts Payable subsystems each use a set of entity types and relationships and processes, both manual and computerized. The processes are of course not shown on the E-R diagram. The set of entity types and relationships associated with a particular subsystem are sometimes called a 'subschema'. The two subschema in Fig. 2.3 overlap - the entity type 'product' is considered to belong to both since sales will decrement stock levels and purchases will increment them. If the diagram were extended, 'product' would probably also be a part of the stock control and perhaps production subschema. Each of these application areas will generally have a different set of users and functions. SQL can restrict the access available

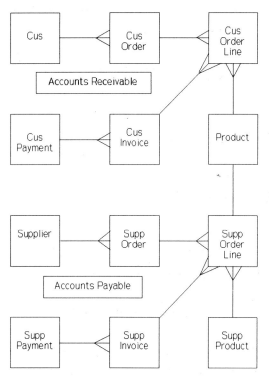

Fig. 2.3 E-R for a Small Accounting System

to certain sets of tables and even to certain columns within tables, to specific sets of account codes protected by passwords. These security aspects are normally the province of the Database Administrator.

2.4.2 Relationships and their Degrees

The relationships between entity types are characterized by a name for the relationship and another name for its inverse (for example 'bought' and 'bought by'), and the 'degree' of the relationship. The degree of a relationship is one of the following:

```
One-to-Many      1 : N
Many-to-One      N : 1
One-to-One       1 : 1
Many-to-Many     M : N
```

This designation refers to the relationship's 'maximum' degree, and indicates the maximum number of entities linked by the relationship. The 'minimum' degree concerns the minimum number of entities linked by the relationship. The maximum degree may be called the *cardinality* and the minimum degree the *optionality* of the relationship. Fig. 2.4 shows how the maximum and minimum degrees can be represented in an entity relationship diagram. All the relationships in Fig. 2.4 are *binary* relationships because they link two entity types. Relationships which link or relate entities within the same single entity type are called *unary* or 'recursive' or 'involuted'. Relationships involving three entity types are called *ternary*, four, *quartenary* and so on.

The degree of a relationship has a profound effect on how the relationship is to be represented in the database tables and it is worthwhile spending some time carefully naming and specifying the degree of each relationship.

Because of the importance of relationship degree, a prospective database schema designer must be clear on what 'degree' means. The second relationship R in Fig. 2.4 is a one-to-many relationship. This means TWO things: firstly, that each of the entities in A can be related by R to 'many' entities in B, and secondly that each of the entities in B can be related by the inverse relationship to just 'one' entity in A. It is important that both of these sentences are stated, as other descriptions of what maximum degree means lead to error. The idea of maximum degree is quite a simple one, but it must be properly understood if the E-R diagram and hence the database table designs are to be correct. Fig. 2.5 extends the idea by introducing two examples with minimum degrees (optionalities) shown. A relationship with zero minimum degree is called *optional* and one with a minimum degree of one (the only other possibility) is called *mandatory*.

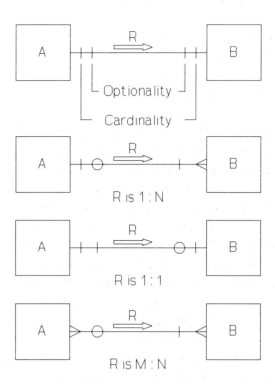

Fig. 2.4 Relationship Degree

In the first relationship in Fig. 2.5, *each* entity in the entity type A is related by relationship R to any number of B entities: 'any number', because the minimum number is shown as zero (the circle), and the maximum number is shown as many (the crowsfoot). Looking at the relationship the other way around, from B to A, that is, looking at the inverse relationship S, then *each* entity in the entity type B is related by S to precisely one (neither more nor less) entity in A because both the minimum and maximum number are shown as one (single lines). In my own experience, when deciding on the degree of a relationship it is important to use the word *each* twice as in the paragraph above, otherwise the incorrect degree is apt to be put on the entity-relationship diagram

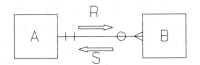

R relates one A to zero or more B 's
S relates one B to one A
S is the inverse of R
R is a one:many relationship
S is a many:one relationship
R is optional
S is mandatory

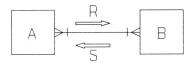

R relates one A to one or more B 's
S relates one B to one or more A 's
S is the inverse of R
R and S are many:many relationships
R and S are mandatory

Fig. 2.5 Degree and Optionality

with unfortunate consequences for the design of the database tables. A common error when deciding the degree of the relationship is to use the statement 'many A's are related to many B's' and then to infer that the relationship in question is a many-to-many. This statement would be true of even a one-to-one relationship! Take for example a one-to-one relationship 'has' between person and birth certificate. It would certainly be true to say that 'many people have many birth certificates' but the conclusion that it was a many-to-many relationship would clearly be incorrect. Similarly, the fatherhood relationship from father to child is clearly one-to-many, but if the question were to be decided on the basis of the (true) statement 'many fathers have many children', the incorrect decision would be made to make it a many-to-many relationship.

The correct procedure in the birth certificate case would be to reason as follows. *Each* person has a maximum of *one* birth certificate, so place a single line for the maximum degree at the birth certificate end of the relationship 'has'. And *each* birth certificate is 'owned by' a maximum of *one* person, so place a single line in the maximum degree position at the person end of the relationship. This is the procedure for determining the maximum degree (cardinality) of a relationship. Notice that *two* questions have to be answered, one for each 'direction' of the relationship. A similar procedure yields the correct minimum degrees (optionalities). The stages in this example are shown in Fig. 2.6. Because this is such an important topic and a frequent source of error, another example follows.

Fig. 2.6 Deriving a One-to-One Relationship

Consider the relationship 'received' between the entity type 'customer' and the entity type 'invoice'. Each customer has received a maximum of 'many' invoices and a minimum of zero invoices, so a crowsfoot is placed in the maximum position and a zero in the minimum position at the

(a)

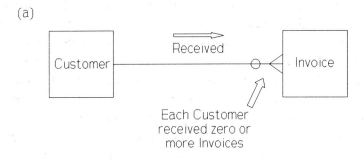

(b)

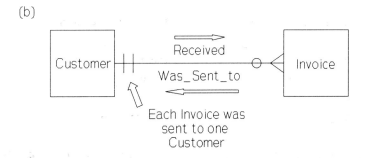

Fig. 2.7 Deriving a One-to-Many Relationship

'invoice' end of the relationship. See Fig. 2.7(a). Now consider the inverse relationship 'was sent to' between 'invoice' and 'customer'. Each invoice was sent to a maximum of one customer and also a minimum of one customer so a single line goes into both positions at the 'customer' end of the relationship. The resulting E-R diagram is Fig. 2.7(b).

2.4.3 Splitting M:N Relationships

Notice that in Fig. 2.3 there are no many-to-many relationships. There is in fact a way of removing all many-to-many relationships and replacing them with a set of one-to-many relationships and new entity types. The advantage of this is that more than one new entity type may emerge, indicating that the original many-to-many was 'hiding' relevant entity types. In Fig. 2.8 the relationship R has been replaced by some new entity types and two or more new relationships. In many cases there will be just one new entity type and two new one-to-many relationships, with the 'many' sides of the new relationships attached to the new entity type.

There is a certain skill required in *naming* the new entity type. In many cases it is just a matter of replacing a verb phrase with a noun. The verb phrase would have been the name associated with the many-to-many relationship, and the noun will be the name of the new entity type. A few examples are given below.

```
M:N Relationship Name        New Entity Type Name
--------------------         --------------------

Works_On                     Job or Assignment
Has_Purchased                Purchase
Drives                       Journey
Was_Prescribed               Prescription
```

This list is meant to give an idea of the sort of replacement that can be made. Sometimes it is difficult to think of a name for the new entity type. Persevere, because it is a part of the real world that actually exists. Resist the temptation to call the new entity type a name like 'Employee-Project' (Assignment) or 'Customer-Product' (Purchase) or 'Driver-Vehicle' (Drives) since such names do not indicate the nature of the relationship (or the entity type that is to replace it).

There may be more than one relationship between the two entity types. In Fig. 2.9 there are *two* many-to-many relationships of interest between the entity types 'Employee' and 'Vehicle'. They can't *both* be called 'Employee-Vehicle'. In fact 'Drives' should be replaced by a relevant entity type that is related to just one employee and one vehicle and is associated with the idea of driving. This is probably the entity type 'Journey'. 'Services' should be replaced by 'Service_Item', meaning a record of servicing operations each of which is related to one employee and one vehicle.

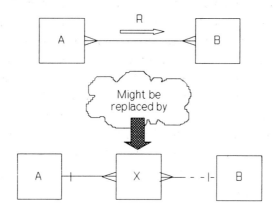

Fig. 2.8 Splitting M:N Relationships

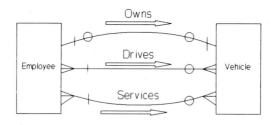

Fig. 2.9 More than One Relationship Between Two Entity Types

There may be more than one entity type 'hidden' in a many-to-many relationship. An example of this is shown in Fig. 2.10. The original relationship 'Purchased' between the Customer and Product entity types is replaced by the entity type 'Order' because that is the appropriate entity type concerning the purchase of our products by customers. When the two new relationships 'Placed' and 'Requested' are drawn in and named, it turns out that 'Requested' is again a many-to-many and hence a candidate for further splitting. This eventually results in the discovery of the *two* new entity types shown. This example demonstrates clearly the benefit of splitting many-to-many relationships. Every one of the entity types will result in a table on the database, as is discussed in the next section. If any entity types are missing from the Entity Relationship diagram then tables will be missing from the database and it will be found that certain queries which will arise in the application area cannot be answered using the database as it stands.

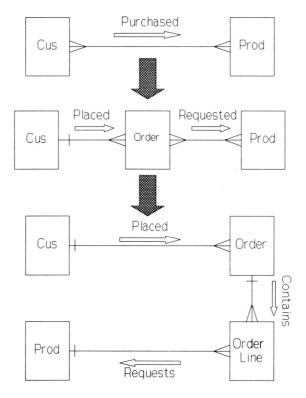

Fig. 2.10 Two Entity Types Hidden in One Relationship

2.5 PRODUCING INITIAL TABLE DESIGNS

2.5.1 Attributes and Keys

After the initial Entity Relationship diagram has been produced, and quite often during its production, the *attributes* of each entity type are considered. These are the qualities of each entity that we want to record. For example, for a customer entity type we may wish to store his or her name, address, balance etc. These are the customer's attributes which will be stored on the database in the *rows* and *columns* of *tables*. In a relational model, every entity has the same set of attributes (name, address etc.) but generally different attribute *values* (John, 10 Downing St. etc.). See Fig. 2.11. An entity type is represented in relational databases as a table ('relation') and the entities as rows ('tuples'). The attributes are represented as column names and the attribute values as column values.

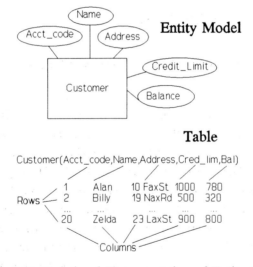

Fig. 2.11 Relational Representation of Entity Types

One of the most important attributes of any entity type is its *primary key*. This is the attribute (sometimes a collection of attributes) that is used to *identify* each entity. A primary key is thus an identifier. It corresponds to our everyday notion of an *ID*. In an accounting system, a customer ID may be CUS_NO, i.e. customer number. C_NO would be the primary key for the CUSTOMER table (which represents the customer entity type on the database). The concept and name 'primary key' has a long and varied history in computing and you will find that people use the term in different ways. The term 'primary key' is used here, and in most other modern database books, to mean a collection of one or more attributes used to identify entities. Used this way, the term has nothing to do with how data is accessed in tables and nothing to do with indexes.

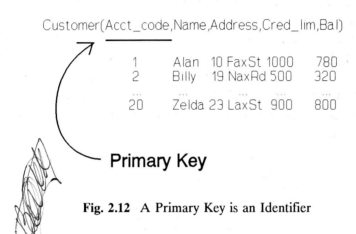

Customer(Acct_code,Name,Address,Cred_lim,Bal)

1	Alan	10 Fax St	1000	780
2	Billy	19 Nax Rd	500	320
...	...	...	...	...
20	Zelda	23 Lax St	900	800

Primary Key

Fig. 2.12 A Primary Key is an Identifier

Because a primary key is an entity identifier and each entity is represented as a row, no two rows in the table can have the same value for the primary key. In the CUSTOMER table of Fig. 2.12, each customer is allowed to have just one value of column ACCT_CODE, since in this table ACCT_CODE is the primary key. The value of ACCT_CODE identifies the customer. (In this simple example each customer can have only one account). This property of the primary key, that is a given value can occur only once in the table, is often called its 'uniqueness' property. In the case where the primary key consists of more than one attribute, the primary key is a *composite key*.

There can often be more than one candidate for being the primary key among the attributes of an entity type, that is different attributes or sets of attributes could be used to identify entities. Each of these possible identifying keys is called a *candidate key*. One of the candidate keys is selected to be the primary key. In Fig. 2.13, which shows an Employee entity type and corresponding table design, both the employee number EMP_NO and national insurance number NI_NO are candidate keys since no two employees in the EMPLOYEE table could have the same value of either of these attributes. Every employee has a value for each of these attributes. Employee to EMP_NO and employee to NI_NO are both one-to-one. Either attribute could be chosen as the primary key. Driving licence number and passport number are also both one-to-one to employee but not every employee will have a driving licence and not every employee will have a passport, so DRIV_LIC_NO and PSPT_NO are not satisfactory candidate keys.

For an attribute set (here, our examples have used single attributes) to qualify for being a primary key, the relationship between it and the entity type must be one-to-one with mandatory optionality in both directions. This is illustrated in Fig. 2.14. Every entity must have one value of key and every value of key currently in force must relate to one entity.

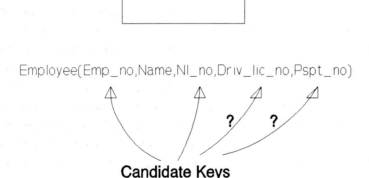

Employee(Emp_no,Name,NI_no,Driv_lic_no,Pspt_no)

Candidate Keys

Fig. 2.13 There May Be More than One Candidate Key

The mapping between the entity type and the primary key is not usually named (neither is the mapping between the entity type and *any* attribute).

One-to-One Mapping

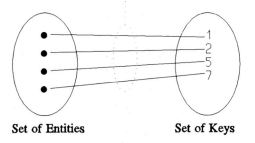

Set of Entities   Set of Keys

The mapping between the entities and
the set of key values should have
cardinality and optionality both 1:1

Fig. 2.14 Primary Keys are 1:1 Mandatory to the Entity Type
they Identify

2.5.2 Foreign Keys

Having a primary key for each entity type (and so for the corresponding
database table) allows us to usefully distinguish individual entities from
each other and to enforce the requirement of relational database tables
that no two rows should be entirely identical (at least the primary key
value will be different). Probably more important than either of these
uses, the primary key gives us a way to represent *relationships* between
entities. In a relational database relationships between entities are
represented using *foreign keys*. That is, the relationships between rows in
tables are represented using foreign keys. Usually the relationships of
interest are binary relationships, so that they relate rows in two different
tables. They could also be unary relationships (using the style of
terminology adopted in section 2.4), so that rows within the *same* table
could be related.

To show a relationship using foreign keys in a one-to-many relationship,
the primary key from the 'one' side of the relationship emigrates to
become a foreign key in the 'many' side. In Fig. 2.15, the attribute

ACCT_CODE is a foreign key from the CUSTOMER table into the INVOICE table. The relationship 'Received' is thus being modelled using a foreign key. The value of the primary key ACCT_CODE in the CUSTOMER table is placed into the INVOICE table to show the customer that received each invoice. So here, ACCT_CODE is the primary key in CUSTOMER and a foreign key in INVOICE. Whenever there is a one-to-many relationship in a relational database, there will be a foreign key from the 'one' side of the relationship into the table on the 'many' side.

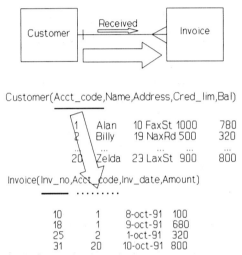

Fig. 2.15 Foreign Key Models 1:N Relationship

A database table can contain more than one foreign key. There will be one foreign key from each table that is related to it by a 1:N relationship. In Fig. 2.16 the CANDIDATE table contains foreign keys from both the CONSTITUENCY table and the PARTY table, since each has a one-to-many relationship to CANDIDATE. In the CANDIDATE table, CONS_NO is a foreign key from the CONSTITUENCY table showing which constituency the candidate is standing in, and the column PARTY_NO in CANDIDATE is a foreign key from the PARTY table showing which party the candidate is aligned to.

In a one-to-one relationship, there is often a choice about where the foreign key is to be placed. Do we place the primary key of the first table

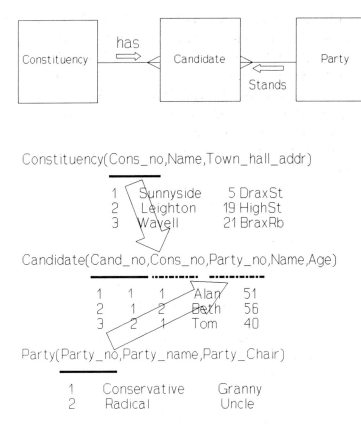

Fig. 2.16 The Table CANDIDATE has Two Foreign Keys

into the second, or that of the second into the first? Or do we in fact combine the attributes of the two tables into one new table? The answer to this question depends mostly on the *optionality* of the relationship. If each entity in the first ('leftmost') entity type is *always* related to one entity in the second ('rightmost') entity type, then the foreign key can move right-to-left. If each entity in the second entity type is *always* related to one in the first, then the foreign key can move left-to-right. If this rule is not followed, then some *null values* may be necessary in the tables. See Fig. 2.17. Employee number 2 does not have a driving licence. If LIC_NO had been placed into EMPLOYEE as a foreign key, then for employee 2, there would have to be a special value (probably NULL) in the row to

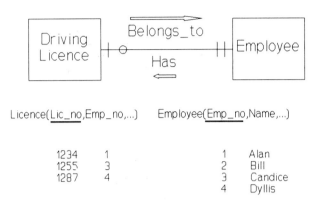

Licence(Lic_no,Emp_no,...)   Employee(Emp_no,Name,...)

1234	1
1255	3
1287	4

1	Alan
2	Bill
3	Candice
4	Dyllis

Fig. 2.17   Foreign Keys in a 1:1 Relationship

show this; there would be no licence number to put there. By putting the foreign key the other way around so that EMP_NO is a foreign key in LICENCE, no special values are required. Notice that EMP_NO is in this example also a candidate key in LICENCE. One alternative that might occur to the designer is to eliminate LICENCE completely by combining the two tables. This would exacerbate the situation in EMPLOYEE since *every* licence attribute in EMPLOYEE would then be null. Since licence-holding employees constitute a *subset* of employees, we place the employee number in licence (always applicable) rather than the licence number in employee (not always applicable).

Fig. 2.18 shows how a *unary* ('involuted') relationship can be represented by a table. A unary relationship is one which concerns entities in just one entity type. There are individual relationships between entities within the same entity type. For example in an employee entity type there may be a 'manages' relationship between employee entities. The 'Managed_By' relationship is optional since there is one employee e1 who has no manager. His MGR_NO column is therefore blank. The hierarchical organization chart shown can be represented simply in relational form and the EMPLOYEE table shows how. MGR_NO is a foreign key from EMPLOYEE to itself. The inverse relationship 'Manages' is also optional since several of the employees manage nobody (the 'leaves' of the tree).

There are several other variants of entity model and corresponding table variants possible, but most of the likely situations have now been covered.

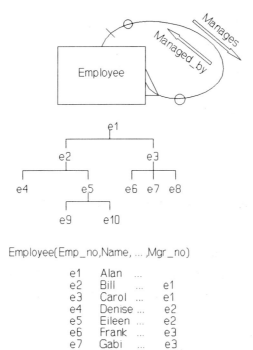

Employee(Emp_no,Name, ... ,Mgr_no)

e1	Alan	...	
e2	Bill	...	e1
e3	Carol	...	e1
e4	Denise	...	e2
e5	Eileen	...	e2
e6	Frank	...	e3
e7	Gabi	...	e3
e8	Helen	...	e3
e9	Iris	...	e5
e10	Janet	...	e5

Fig. 2.18 Foreign Keys in a Unary Relationship

2.5.3 Other Attributes

Apart from the key attributes already discussed, any other attributes 'of interest' are selected for each entity type and placed in the corresponding tables. This is a fairly straightforward process. The analyst/designer has various sources for this information, including the normal methods of observing existing documents, interview, questionnaire, existing file designs etc. The inclusion of each attribute needs to be justified however.

There are, apart from efficiency (storage and speed) considerations, ethical and legal questions which may act as a constraint on what is stored on the database. In this connection, the provisions of the Data Protection Act may be consulted.

2.6 NORMALIZATION

2.6.1 Introduction

Once the provisional set of table designs has been produced, they should be checked using the process of Normalization. Normalization tends to be a rather technical subject but it is possible to present it in a fairly straightforward manner. Normalizing a table involves the application of several tests to the tables to ensure that they cannot contain duplicate data - that is the main objective. It acts as a check on the process of entity analysis and modelling and some consider it an alternative. On the whole, normalization is a more precise and less intuitive means of producing table designs. In practice, using both methods seems to produce the best results fastest. In a normalized database every table contains data facts about just *one* entity type and every row contains data facts about *one* entity. This of course is also the objective of the entity analysis above.

There are three basic Normal Forms, First Normal Form (1NF), Second Normal Form (2NF), and Third Normal Form (3NF) [3]. If the entity analysis above has been performed well, it may emerge that all the initial table designs are already in 3NF and no further changes are required. The general effect of normalization however is to *split* existing table designs (the literature calls these tables 'relations'). This reveals the fact that before the split, the table was representing data from more than one entity type. Normalization can thus be viewed as a fairly deterministic method of 'discovering' hidden entity types.

2.6.2 First Normal Form

The effect of First Normal Form is to remove *repeating groups*. A repeating group is a group of one or more columns which can appear a different number of times from record to record. Repeating groups thus result in different records in a file having a different number of fields. In relational databases this is not possible; every row must have the same number of columns. Fig. 2.19 gives an example of the removal of a repeating group under the provisions of 1NF.

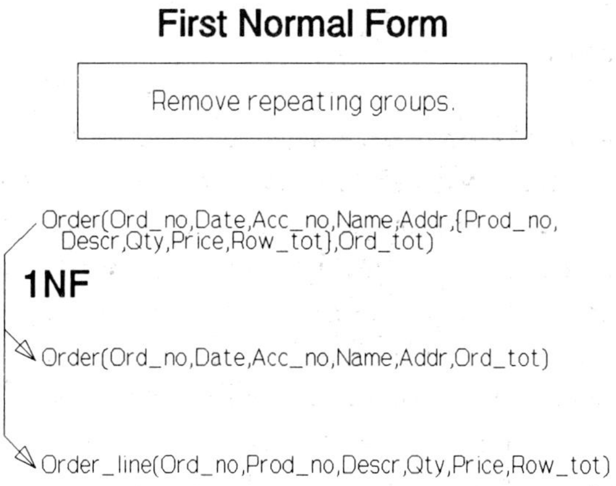

First Normal Form

Remove repeating groups.

Order(Ord_no,Date,Acc_no,Name,Addr,{Prod_no,
Descr,Qty,Price,Row_tot},Ord_tot)

1NF

Order(Ord_no,Date,Acc_no,Name,Addr,Ord_tot)

Order_line(Ord_no,Prod_no,Descr,Qty,Price,Row_tot)

Fig. 2.19 File Split by First Normal Form

1NF normalization is performed by placing each repeating group in a separate relation (table). In Fig. 2.19 there is a single repeating group, shown between curly brackets { }. You have to make up the name of the new table yourself; the 1NF procedure doesn't say how to do this. Looking at the repeating group, it seems to be about an individual product purchased in an order, so I have called the new table ORDER_LINE. This split will then need to be reflected in the entity model by introducing a new entity type ORDER_LINE, so as to keep the model up-to-date.

Make sure that the relationship between ORDER and ORDER_LINE is maintained by using a foreign key. Otherwise it would not be possible to ascertain which order the order line was from. In this example, the probable primary key from the original ORDER file, namely ORD_NO, is placed into ORDER_LINE as a foreign key. Since there is clearly a one-to-many relationship between ORDER and ORDER_LINE, the foreign key placement is pretty obvious. However, if the placement had been incorrectly made the other way, the next normalization step (2NF) would have removed the problem by an additional split.

In fact any remaining problems in the table designs will be resolved by subsequent normalization steps.

2.6.3 Second Normal Form

Second normal form turns on the idea of *functional dependency*, so it is
necessary to first define this before considering the provisions and
operation of 2NF. Fortunately it is the relatively familiar idea of a
mathematical function, that is, a many-to-one mapping. See Fig. 2.20.

Functional Dependency

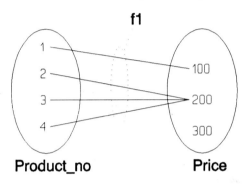

Fig. 2.20 Price is Functionally Dependent on Product Number

The set of product numbers and the set of prices are shown, as is an un-
named mapping f1 between the two sets. This mapping indicates what the
price of each product is. For example the price of product 1 is 100
pounds. The mapping f1 is a *function* because for every value of product
number there is just one value of price. This is analogous to the familiar
mathematical functions such as sin and square etc. For every value of a
number X there is just one value of sin(X) for example. Sin is not a one-
to-one function because for a given value of sin(X) there can be more
than one value of X that will give that value. In the same way, our un-
named function f1 is many-to-one. The fact that f1 is un-named indicates
the interesting point that the relationship between individual attributes
and between the attributes and the entity type *are* in general un-named.
Perhaps the name of f1 is 'has'.

The idea of second normal form is to *remove functional dependencies on
parts of composite keys*. See Fig. 2.21. This continues the earlier example
concerning sales orders, that is orders for our products sent by customers.

Second Normal Form

Remove functional dependencies on *parts* of composite keys.

Order(Ord_no,Date,Acc_no,Name,Addr,{Prod_no, Descr,Qty,Price,Row_tot},Ord_tot)

1NF

Order(Ord_no,Date,Acc_no,Name,Addr,Ord_tot)

Order_line(Ord_no,Prod_no,Descr,Qty,Price,Row_tot)

2NF

Order_line(Ord_no,Prod_no,Qty,Row_tot)

Product(Prod_no,Descr,Price)

Fig. 2.21 Second Normal Form Splits Order Line Further

The position after 1NF is shown in the top half of the diagram and is the point reached in Fig. 2.19. Looking at the ORDER_LINE table, it can be seen that the primary key is composite (both ORD_NO and PROD_NO are underlined). The reason for using this composite key is that neither ORD_NO nor PROD_NO on their own would be a satisfactory primary key since there could be several order lines with the same order number and there could be several order lines with the same product number, so neither of these attributes is 'unique'. However, it is considered true that any *combination* of values of order number and product number would be unique because no customer would order the same product twice in the same order. (If they did we could simply add the quantities). Thus order number and product number together is a composite candidate key and is in fact the chosen primary key.

Having chosen a primary key, it is discovered that this table is not in second normal form because there is a functional dependency between PROD_NO and DESCR, that is the product number and its description, (each product number has *one* description) and also between PROD_NO and PRICE (each product number has *one* price). So both DESCR and PRICE are functionally dependent on PROD_NO which is just *part* of the primary key, and this breaks the provisions of 2NF.

The reason this is a problem is that if the table were left in this non-2NF condition, duplicate data facts could appear. Every time any customer purchased a particular product, both the description and price would appear in the row. This duplication represents a waste of storage space and can lead to update problems if, for example, the price of a certain product were suddenly to change; a search of all occurences of this duplicate fact would be required in order to update each one. It is the aim of normalization to have each fact stored on the database once only.

The remedial action taken is to split the ORDER_LINE table so that all the attributes that are functionally dependent on PROD_NO alone are 'hived off' into a new table PRODUCT where all the attributes of products can be stored. Some attributes remain in the ORDER_LINE table - these are the attributes that *are* functionally dependent on the *whole* primary key. For example QTY (quantity of that product ordered in that order) is functionally dependent on the composite key ORD_NO with PROD_NO because if you were to ask me 'What was the quantity ordered?' I would have to ask you to tell me 'Which order number *and* which product number?' Another way is to demonstrate that QTY is not functionally dependent on either part of the composite key. For example QTY is not functionally dependent on PROD_NO since for a particular product there can be lots of different quantities in the table, and for a given quantity there can be lots of different product numbers in the table. This indicates that PROD_NO to QTY is many-to-many and is hence not functional (many-to-one or one-to-one).

The tables that emerge from the 2NF step are the new ORDER (produced by 1NF) and the new ORDER_LINE and PRODUCT (produced by 2NF). It turns out that even after these normalization steps, there is still a potential for the duplication of data facts in the design of these three tables.

2.6.4 Third Normal Form

In third normal form (3NF), we remove *functional dependencies between non-key attributes* from the tables by further splitting. See Fig. 2.22. The ORDER table that emerged from 1NF processing was not effected by

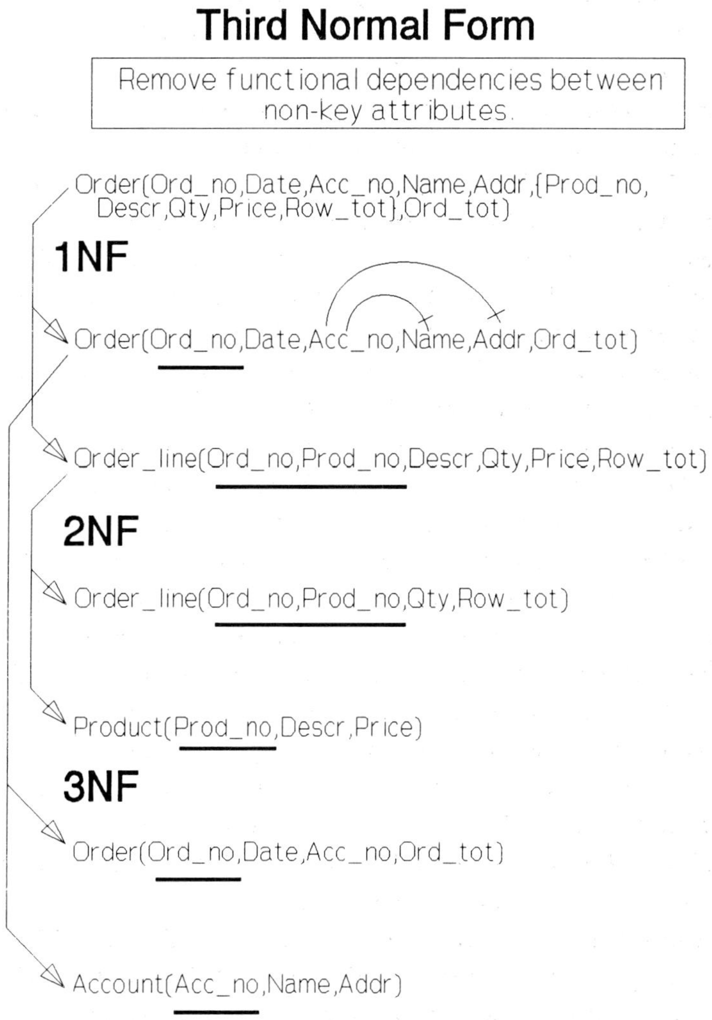

Third Normal Form

> Remove functional dependencies between non-key attributes.

Order(Ord_no,Date,Acc_no,Name,Addr,{Prod_no, Descr,Qty,Price,Row_tot},Ord_tot)

1NF

Order(Ord_no,Date,Acc_no,Name,Addr,Ord_tot)

Order_line(Ord_no,Prod_no,Descr,Qty,Price,Row_tot)

2NF

Order_line(Ord_no,Prod_no,Qty,Row_tot)

Product(Prod_no,Descr,Price)

3NF

Order(Ord_no,Date,Acc_no,Ord_tot)

Account(Acc_no,Name,Addr)

Fig. 2.22 Third Normal Form Splits Order Further

2NF processing since it does not have a composite key. It is therefore already in 2NF (does not break the 2NF provisions). However, data duplication can still occur in ORDER. Every time a given customer sends in an order, the account number, name and address will be repeated. This is because NAME and ADDRESS are functionally dependent on ACC_NO, and ACC_NO is not a candidate key so a given value of ACC_NO could quite reasonably appear more than once in the table (every time that customer sends in an order).

Consequently, ORDER is split and all those attributes which depend on ACC_NO are placed in a new table, appropriately called ACCOUNT, and all attributes dependent on ORDER_NO are retained in ORDER. If an ACCOUNT table had already existed and contained NAME and ADDR then of course there would be no need to create a new one; NAME and ADDR would just be removed from ORDER. All resulting tables should now be re-checked for being in 3NF.

It is quite interesting to interpret the effects of the normalization described above on the original ORDER table in terms of entity models. What has happened is that ORDER has been replaced by ORDER and ORDER_LINE under the provisions of 1NF. ORDER_LINE was then replaced by a new ORDER_LINE and PRODUCT using 2NF, and ORDER was then split into a new ORDER and ACCOUNT by 3NF. This is illustrated in Fig. 2.23.

There are other normal forms including BCNF, 4NF, 5NF and DKNF. Each seeks to remove the potential for data redundancy from the database design by pointing out new features of table designs that could result in such redundancy. The interested reader is referred to books on database theory (Reference 1 for example) for descriptions of these normal forms. If the steps described above have been conscientiously applied to all tables then very few, if any, data duplication problems will arise in practice.

As indicated in Fig. 2.1, after normalization and the possible discovery of new entity types, the designer should now go back and modify the entity model to bring it into line with the normalized table designs. This is important, because the entity model will be used frequently by all technical database users to design queries, updates and reports throughout the life of the database.

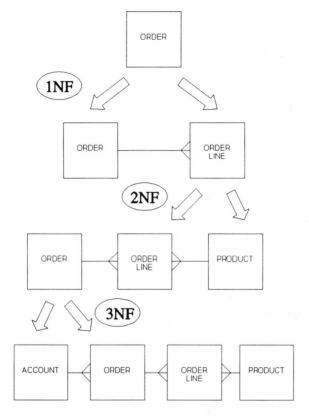

Fig. 2.23 Normalization Discovered New Entity Types

2.7 DESK CHECKING THE DATABASE DESIGN

It has been mentioned in a previous section how useful it is to have available a representative set of queries and report descriptions with which to test the correctness of the database design that has now emerged from our entity modelling and normalization stages. This should be done before the actual database tables are created on the database to further minimize the chances of database design errors. A short example of this type of checking will be given here, but in practice some time should be spent ensuring that all sections of the database are checked.

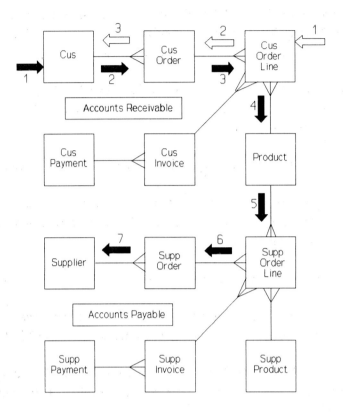

Fig. 2.24 Desk Checking Two Queries

Query 2.1 'What is the address of the customer that invoice number
         1234 was sent to?'

The query path is shown in Fig. 2.24 in the clear arrows:

1. Start by retrieving any CUS_ORDER_LINE   row for INV_NO 1234.
Looking at the diagram, it is not necessary to start at the
CUS_INVOICE   table since we already know the INV_NO   which is
clearly a foreign key in CUS_ORDER_LINE   because of the 1:N
relationship between these two entity types.

2. Inspect this CUS_ORDER_LINE row to find the appropriate CUS_ORDER_NO, which is a foreign key from the CUS_ORDER table. Retrieve the relevant CUS_ORDER row.

3. Inspect the CUS_ORDER row to find the CUS_NO, which is a foreign key from the CUS table. Retrieve the relevant CUS row and display the customer's address.

Query 2.2 'Who is the main supplier of products that ABC Ltd buys?'

This query is a bit more involved. It is merely necessary at this stage to determine that the query *can* be answered. The query path is shown in the black arrows in Fig. 2.24.

1. Retrieve the row in CUS for ABC Ltd.

2. Inspect this CUS row to find the C_NO and using this retrieve *all* the ORDER rows for this C_NO. C_NO is a foreign key in ORDER.

3. Inspect each CUS_ORDER row retrieved and obtain its ORD_NO. For each ORD_NO retrieve *all* rows in CUS_ORDER_LINE with that ORD_NO.

4. Inspect each CUS_ORDER_LINE row retrieved and obtain its PROD_NO. For each PROD_NO retrieve the row in PRODUCT with that PROD_NO.

5. Inspect each PRODUCT row retrieved and retrieve all the correct SUPP_ORDER_LINE rows with that PROD_NO.

6. Inspect each SUPP_ORDER_LINE retrieved to find the appropriate SUPP_ORDER with that supplier ORD_NO.

7. Inspect each SUPP_ORDER row to find the SUPP_NO and retrieve the corresponding SUPPLIER row. You have now retrieved sufficient data to be able to calculate, for each supplier, the total expenditure on

goods made by ABC Ltd (if that is going to be the criterion), so it is possible to generate a report with the following columns:

```
Supplier        Total Expenditure
--------        -----------------
```

This list can then be searched to find the supplier with the largest number against it.

  While these two examples do not give a detailed description of the processing required, the above at least suggests that there is an *access path* via which the queries can be answered.

2.8 CREATING THE DATABASE TABLES

2.8.1 Syntax of the SQL CREATE TABLE Command

At this stage we have a fully normalized and desk-checked paper database design which we can now proceed to implement using the SQL CREATE command. The basic syntax forms of the CREATE command are as follows:

```
CREATE TABLE table-name
   (column-name  data-type  [NULL | NOT NULL], ... )
```
and
```
CREATE TABLE table-name
   (column-name  [NOT NULL], ... )
     AS query
```

Fig. 2.25 Basic Syntax of CREATE TABLE

The ellipsis (...) indicates that the preceding items can be repeated. In dBASE IV only the first form of the command is available. The data types available are summarized in Fig. 2.26 for ORACLE, INGRES and dBASE IV. The NOT NULL option specifies that when data is being

INSERTed into that column, or when its value is being UPDATEd, the NULL value is not allowed. This forces the user or application program to specify a value for the field. One column at least must not be null, that is the column used as the primary key since, as discussed, it will be used as a foreign key to link the row to other rows in the database and it also serves as the row's identifier. So always specify NOT NULL for primary keys and any other columns which you want to ensure will always have an 'actual' value. The *uniqueness* property of primary keys is enforced using CREATE INDEX (Chapter 12). In the ISO 9075 and ANSI-86 standards it *is* enforced in CREATE TABLE with CREATE TABLE UNIQUE.

In the second form of the command, the AS clause allows the new table to be defined in terms of columns from tables that already exist on the database. The columns' types and sizes are copied from the result of the AS query. If all the columns in the query have well-defined and unique names, (column, ...) may be omitted. The major difference between this form and the first form however is that here the CREATE TABLE actually writes rows into the new table. The main use I have found for this second form of the command is to produce temporary tables during the execution of complex queries. This is discussed in Chapters 7 and 8.

ORACLE	INGRES	dBASE IV	Note
CHAR(size)	CHAR(size)	CHAR(size)	1
CHAR(size)	VARCHAR(size)	CHAR(size)	2
LONG			3
LONG RAW			4
NUMBER	FLOAT	FLOAT(X,Y)	5
INTEGER	INTEGER	INTEGER	6
INTEGER	SMALLINT	SMALLINT	7
NUMBER(X,Y)	FLOAT	NUMERIC(X,Y)	8
NUMBER(size)			9
RAW(size)			10
DATE	DATE	DATE	11
		LOGICAL	12

Fig. 2.26 Approximate Equivalences Among Data Types

Notes on Data Types

1. Maximum size in ORACLE is 240, INGRES and dBASE IV 254 characters.

2. INGRES VARCHAR allows a maximum length of 2000 characters.

3. ORACLE LONG allows a maximum length of 65,535 characters. Cannot be used in subqueries, functions, expressions, WHERE clauses or indexes. Only one LONG column per table. Good for comment text.

4. ORACLE LONG RAW stores up to 65,535 bytes of binary data. Useful for foreign codes, small pictures or anything else.

5. ORACLE is 40 digits, INGRES is 8 bytes. For dBASE, x is 20 and y is 8 maximum. All allow 'scientific' notation like -1.23E46.

6. ORACLE is same as 'NUMBER', INGRES -2E9 to +2E9, dBASE is 11 digits with sign.

7. INGRES is -32,768 to +32767, dBASE is 6 digits with sign.

8. Fixed point decimal. ORACLE limit like 'NUMBER', dBASE limits are like FLOAT(x,y).

9. ORACLE fixed length integers.

10. ORACLE raw binary limited to 240 bytes (c.f. LONG RAW).

11. Dates in the form 24-dec-91 for ORACLE and INGRES, mm/dd/yy default for dBASE IV.

12. dBASE allows 'true' =.T., .t., .Y., .y. equivalently, and 'false' =.F., .f., .N., .n. equivalently.

13. INGRES has a data type MONEY which automatically displays the currency sign.

Example 1

```
 1  CREATE TABLE CUS
 2  (C_NO     NUMBER(2)  NOT NULL,
 3  TITLE     CHAR(5),
 4  SNAME     CHAR(10),
 5  INITS     CHAR(4),
 6  STREET    CHAR(10),
 7  CITY      CHAR(6),
 8  POSTC     CHAR(7),
 9  CRED_LIM  NUMBER(5,0),
10  BALANCE   NUMBER(7,2) ) ;
```

This is how the CUS table, which is used in many of the examples throughout this book, was created. Since C_NO is the primary key it has been defined as NOT NULL. Any combination of the other columns may be null. The *default* is NULL. CRED_LIM is a five-digit integer. BALANCE can have maximum value 9999.99 since the number 7 in the column data type description shows the maximum total width including the decimal point.

Example 2

```
1  CREATE TABLE TEMP2 AS
2  SELECT SUM(NO_OF_VOTES)   T
3  FROM CANDIDATE ;
```

In this example line numbers have been shown. These are not typed when you enter SQL commands but are used in this book just to help the explanations of the queries and other commands.

Here, in line 1, the AS indicates that the second form of the CREATE TABLE command is being used. Lines 2 and 3 constitute an SQL SELECT command, the descriptions of which form a large part of this book. In this very simple example, a single-column, single-row table called TEMP2 is being created which will contain the sum of the votes from table CANDIDATE.

2.8.2 Dropping Tables

Tables can be removed from the database (provided the user has the appropriate database privileges - See Chapter 12) using the simple syntax:

```
DROP TABLE table ;
```

For example we could remove all the CUS table data and its definition in the data dictionary from the database by:

    1 DROP TABLE CUS ;

2.8.3 Altering Table Definitions

The descriptions of columns in a table can be modified, and extra columns can be added to a table in ORACLE using the ALTER TABLE command. The methods used in INGRES and dBASE IV are shown later. The syntax forms of the ALTER TABLE command are:

```
ALTER TABLE table
ADD (column-name data-type [NULL|NOT NULL], ... )
```

and

```
ALTER TABLE table
MODIFY (column-name [data-type] [NULL|NOT NULL], ... )
```

Both these forms can be used without any interference with the data already in the table. The first form adds one or more new columns which can be entered in the same way as the CREATE TABLE command above. In the second form of the command either the data type, or the 'nullability' of the column, or both can be altered for one or more columns.

Example 1

        1 ALTER TABLE CUS
        2 ADD (COMPANY_NAME   CHAR(30));

This ALTER TABLE command adds a new column COMPANY_NAME to the CUS table and places NULL in it throughout. NULL is the default value for ADD. A NOT NULL column can be added only to a table that has no rows since if you attempted to add a NOT NULL column to a table *with* existing rows, the system would not know what values to put in the column (clearly NULL would be no good). If you want to add a NOT NULL column, first add it as the default, then fill in values for every existing row, then use the MODIFY form of ALTER TABLE to make it NOT NULL.

Example 2

```
1  ALTER TABLE CUS
2  MODIFY
3  (INITS  CHAR(6),
4    STREET NOT NULL) ;
```

This command modifies two things in the table. First, the INITS column is expanded to 6 characters (it was 4). This is presumably because longer initial strings, such as 'A.J.P.' can be accommodated. Second, the STREET column of CUS is now specified as NOT NULL. You had better ensure that no existing STREET values *do* contain the value NULL before you execute this command.

Adding extra columns in INGRES is slightly more involved. Firstly it is necessary to create the definition of a temporary table containing the new column:

```
1  CREATE TABLE TEMP    < --- New Temporary Table
2  (C_NO      SMALLINT  NOT NULL,
3   TITLE     VCHAR(5),
4   SNAME     VCHAR(10),
5   INITS     VCHAR(4),
6   STREET    VCHAR(10),
7   CITY      VCHAR(6),
8   POSTC     VCHAR(7),
9   CRED_LIM  MONEY,
10   BALANCE   MONEY,
11   COMPANY_NAME   VCHAR(30) ) ;  < --- New Column
```

This step can be performed in SQL itself using this CREATE TABLE command or more quickly outside of SQL using the INGRES CREATE NEW TABLE menu option and then the GetTableDef option to save having to retype existing column names.

Having created the new table definition, the rows in the existing CUS table are copied into it using the SQL INSERT command:

```
1  INSERT INTO TEMP
2  SELECT *
3  FROM CUS ;
```

The new COMPANY_NAME column will of course remain blank. The next step is to DROP the old CUS table and CREATE the new from TEMP:

```
1  DROP TABLE CUS ;   <---'DROP CUS' for INGRES V 5.0
```

```
1  CREATE TABLE CUS AS
2  SELECT *
3  FROM TEMP ;
```

Finally DROP the temporary table:

```
1  DROP TABLE TEMP ;
```

A similar procedure is performed in dBASE IV, except that the data types will be different in the CREATE TABLE step. See Fig. 2.26.

Chapter 3

SELECT with a Single Table

3.1 INTRODUCTION

The purpose of the SQL SELECT statement is to retrieve and display data gathered from one or more database tables. SELECT is the most frequently used SQL command and can be used interactively to obtain immediate answers to queries, or embedded in a program written in a host language such as C or COBOL for more complex data retrieval and reporting. Interactive use of SELECT is where the power of SQL is most readily demonstrated, with many complex data retrieval operations often requiring just a few well-chosen lines of SQL.

This chapter illustrates the basic features and options of the SELECT command when used interactively with a single database table. Queries involving two or more tables are covered in subsequent chapters and embedded SQL is discussed in Chapter 11. Descriptions of all of the tables used in the examples are given in the Appendix.

3.2 SELECT SYNTAX

```
SELECT      [DISTINCT | ALL { * | col-exprn [,col-exprn]...}
FROM        table-name alias [, table-name alias]...
[WHERE      condition]
[GROUP BY   col-name [,col-name]...]
[HAVING     condition]
[ORDER BY   [ordering]...]
```

Fig. 3.1 Basic SELECT Syntax

The basic syntax of the SELECT statement is shown in Fig. 3.1.
Square brackets show non-mandatory items. Braces {} and bars show alternative items, and three dots... mean the preceding item may be

repeated. Additional clauses in the SELECT statement are covered in subsequent chapters. The syntax may vary slightly from one implementation of SQL to another but all versions should contain at least this minimum set. Variations in the syntax between ORACLE, INGRES and dBASE IV SQL are noted throughout the text.

The sequence of processing in a SELECT command is :

```
FROM        Specifies the table(s) to be accessed
WHERE       Filters the rows on some condition
GROUP BY    Forms groups of rows with the same column values
HAVING      Filters the groups on some condition
SELECT      Specifies which results will be output
ORDER BY    Determines the order of the output results
```

The examples in this chapter illustrate the usage of each of these clauses.

3.3 SELECTING COLUMNS

The simplest SELECT statement it is possible to enter will retrieve all columns from every row of a table. Remember that 'column' is SQL's name for what is commonly called a field or attribute and 'row' is the term used in SQL for what is often called a record. Similarly, the terms 'table' and 'file' are often used interchangeably. The SQL 'table-row-column' terminology will be used here. For example to list the entire CUS table the following SQL command would be entered:

Query 3.1 'List all details stored on every customer.'

```
1  SELECT *
2  FROM CUS ;
```

Lines 1 and 2 show what would be typed in. The line numbers themselves are not actually typed in and are just shown here for purposes of explanation. The semi-colon at the end of the line simply informs the SQL interpreter that command input has finished and to execute the command immediately.

Following the word SELECT in line 1 is the list of columns that are to be retrieved. Here, the asterisk means that *all* columns are required. In line 2, the FROM clause states the database tables the retrieved columns are to come from. In this SELECT, the table is the CUS table. So the command means 'Select all columns from the CUS table and since no WHERE clause is specified, do this for every row i.e. list all rows'. The command could alternatively have been typed in a single line:

    1 SELECT * FROM CUS ;

Assuming the CUS table is as shown in the Appendix, the output resulting from this SELECT command is thus:

C_NO	TITLE	SNAME	INITS	STREET	CITY	POSTC	CRED_LIM	BALANCE
1	Mr	Sallaway	G.R.	12 Fax Rd	London	WC1	1000	42.56
2	Miss	Lauri	P.	5 Dux St	London	N1	500	200
3	Mr	Jackson	R.	2 Lux Ave	Leeds	LE1 2AB	500	510
4	Mr	Dziduch	M.	31 Low St	Dover	DO2 9CD	100	149.23
5	Ms	Woods	S.Q.	17 Nax Rd	London	E18 4WW	1000	250.1
6	Mrs	Williams	C.	41 Cax St	Dover	DO2 8WD		412.21

All columns and all rows in the CUS table have been retrieved. Notice that there is no value shown for CRED_LIM for C_NO 6. This field value is as yet unknown and contains NULL. NULL is a special value provided by SQL. You can use it in a variety of ways, to mean a variety of things. Be clear on what it is going to mean in your own application. In the present example we have used NULL to mean 'as yet unknown'. You might want to use it to mean 'not applicable' (this customer doesn't have a credit limit) or to have some other meaning. SQL treats NULL in a special way. For example you can retrieve all rows containing a column with the value NULL. The other properties of NULL are indicated in context in later examples.

If only a subset of the columns is wanted, then a list of the required column names is placed after the SELECT. In relational algebraic terminology this process is called *projection*. A subset of columns is said to be 'projected out' of a table. Alternatively the phraseology 'Table X's projection onto columns A,B,C or A X B X C' (which simply means columns A,B,C from table X, with any duplicate rows removed, are to be output) may be used. Duplicate output rows may potentially arise because rows that are in other ways different may hold similar values of the projected columns. A project operation removes those duplicates. In SQL you can choose to have the duplicates removed or leave them in. Query 3.2 contains a projection because only two of the columns in the table are required to be output.

Query 3.2 'List out the customer account numbers and the invoice
              amounts of all customers who have outstanding invoices'.

Here it is assumed that the database table INVOICE contains only outstanding invoices, i.e. those that have not been paid in full or for which a payment has been received in the current month. All fully-paid invoices from previous months have been removed to an archive file. The full table definition is shown in the Appendix. The SQL query is:

```
1  SELECT C_NO, AMOUNT
2  FROM INVOICE ;
```

Instead of listing all columns from INVOICE, only columns C_NO and AMOUNT are required and so they are specified in line 1. These column names are the usual form of the 'column expressions' shown in Fig 3.1. Column expressions can also contain arithmetic and various functions. In this query the column expressions are simply column names and this is often the case.

The output from this command would be:

```
C_NO    AMOUNT
----    ------
   1      26.2
   4    149.23
   1     16.36
   2       200
   3       510
   5     250.1
   6    412.21
```

There is no standard way of specifying the required columns negatively, for example 'All columns except the third and the fifth'; all columns required must be explicitly stated. So if you wanted to list out all columns except *one* from a table with many columns, you would have a fair amount of typing to do.

In some queries you may want to remove any duplicate output rows that could be displayed as a result of an SQL query. For example consider the query:

Query 3.3 'List out the account numbers of all customers with outstanding invoices'.

1 SELECT C_NO
2 FROM INVOICE ;

This SQL command would produce the following output:

```
C_NO
----
   1
   4
   1
   2
   3
   5
   6
```

The C_NO 1 has appeared twice in the output because it appeared twice on the INVOICE table. In some queries these duplicates may be considered a nuisance and in others may give misleading results. Duplicate output rows can be removed when required using the DISTINCT option in the SELECT statement:

Query 3.4 'List out the account numbers of all customers with outstanding invoices (each account number to appear only once)'.

```
1  SELECT DISTINCT C_NO
2  FROM INVOICE ;
```

The output now has the duplicate row removed.

```
C_NO
----
   1
   4
   2
   3
   5
   6
```

The option ALL shown in Fig. 3.1 is the opposite to DISTINCT and it allows duplicate rows to be displayed. Since it is the default option ALL is not normally typed.

It is important to note that DISTINCT does not refer to individual columns, but to the complete column list that appears after the SELECT. Its only effect is to prevent duplicate *rows* appearing in the output as a result of a projection.

There should of course be no duplicate rows in the original table since that would contravene one of the fundamental integrity constraints of relational databases, which should contain no duplicate rows. When only a subset of the columns is output however, duplicate rows could quite legitimately occur and it is the job of DISTINCT to remove these.

Whether or not DISTINCT is typed depends on the application and its individual requirements.

The effect of using DISTINCT in Query 3.2 would be to produce the same output as shown above since for this data there are no duplicate output rows. However, if the INVOICE table had contained two rows for C_NO 1 with the same value for AMOUNT, only ONE row would have appeared in the output since as far as the output was concerned that would have been a duplicate output row. This might be incorrectly construed as indicating only one invoice for C_NO 1. See Section 3.5 for the use of DISTINCT with aggregate functions such as COUNT. Column expressions may be more than simply column names. Arithmetic expressions and string operations involving columns can also appear. Query 3.5 shows arithmetic and Query 3.7 gives an example of output column concatenation, a string operation.

Query 3.5 'For each product, list out the percentage by which the
current stock level exceeds minimum stock level'.

```
1 SELECT PROD_NO, DESCR, 100 * (QIS - MINQ)/ MINQ
2 FROM PRODUCT ;
```

The third column expression is an arithmetic expression involving two column names QIS and MINQ (quantity in stock and minimum stock level respectively) and the constant 100. In ORACLE SQL*PLUS, the output will appear like this:

PROD_NO	DESCR	100*(QIS-MINQ)/MINQ
1	Bat	100
2	Ball	0
3	Hoop	-40
4	Net	-60
5	Rope	-90

In INGRES SQL Version 5 the third column is given the heading 'sql1' and subsequent columns involving calculated expressions are designated sql2, sql3 etc. In ORACLE SQL*PLUS, columns may be given aliases so that we could use the command:

```
1 SELECT PROD_NO, DESCR, 100*(QIS-MINQ)/MINQ EXCESS
2 FROM PRODUCT ;
```

This command uses the alias EXCESS for the arithmetic expression preceding it. An SQL alias is an alternative name for a column expression or table name. In this example a column alias is being used to make the output appear more attractive, but aliases have other uses as we shall see. The current query produces the output:

PROD_NO	DESCR	EXCESS
1	Bat	100
2	Ball	0
3	Hoop	-40
4	Net	-60
5	Rope	-90

The command is the same for INGRES Version 6 except that the keyword AS precedes the column alias. This is also true for INGRES *table* aliases.

3.4 SELECTING ROWS USING WHERE

The WHERE clause in the SQL SELECT statement syntax is used to limit the number of rows that will be delivered to the output. It uses a test condition to 'filter' the rows of the table so that only a specified subset of rows will appear at the output. The 'condition' shown in Fig 3.1 is a test which involves one or more columns of the table. The test is applied to each row of the table in turn and if the condition in the WHERE clause is true for a row, then the row will be passed to the output. In relational algebraic terminology this operation is known as a *select* or *restrict*. Unlike the 'Project' where only some of the columns appear at the output, with a 'Select' only some of the rows appear. In practice of course Select and Project are often used together so that after the WHERE clause has decided whether the row passes the test, the list of column-expressions decides which column data will be output.

3.4.1 Simple Conditions

Query 3.6 'List all products whose price is greater than five pounds'.

```
1 SELECT PROD_NO, DESCR, PRICE
2 FROM PRODUCT
3 WHERE PRICE > 5 ;
```

Here we have both a Project and a Select operating. Line 1 projects out the columns PROD_NO, DESCR and PRICE, and line 3 contains the simple condition 'PRICE > 5' which says that the only rows in the table PRODUCT that will be output are those where the value of the PRICE column in the row is greater than 5. The output is:

```
PROD_NO   DESCR   PRICE
-------   -----   -----
      1   Bat        12
      4   Net        20
      5   Rope        6
```

In SQL the following simple comparison operators are available:

=	equals
<	is less than
>	is greater than
< =	is less than or equal to (i.e. not greater than)
> =	is greater than or equal to (i.e. not less than)
< >	is not equal to

! =	is sometimes used instead of '< >'.

All operators work with character and date as well as numeric data types. With inequality tests involving character data, the alpha-numerical order (i.e. the collating sequence) of the data is used and for dates, chronological sequence is used. Note that any of these operators used to compare a value with a field containing the value NULL will fail. The only test that will succeed with NULL is 'IS NULL'. The following example queries illustrate these points.

Query 3.7 'List the names of all customers with surnames
          beginning with letters up to and including "J" '.

```
1  SELECT TITLE, INITS, SNAME
2  FROM CUS
3  WHERE SNAME < 'K' ;
```

The output will be:

```
TITLE  INITS  SNAME
-----  -----  -----
Mr     R.     Jackson
Mr     M.     Dziduch
```

If line 3 had been:

```
3 WHERE SNAME < = 'J' ;
```

then no names starting with J would ever be included, except for the unlikely surname of 'J' itself.

Incidentally, to improve the appearance of the output, the three output columns TITLE, INITS and SNAME could be concatenated using the concatenation operator '||'as follows:

```
1  SELECT TITLE||' '||INITS||SNAME CUSTOMERS
2  FROM CUS
3  WHERE SNAME < 'K' ;
```

This produces the more presentable output:

```
CUSTOMERS
- - - - - - - - -
Mr R.Jackson
Mr M.Dziduch
```

Note also in line 1 the use of the ORACLE-style column alias to improve the appearance of the heading. In INGRES, insert an 'AS' before the alias. Comparison operators can also be used with date fields:

Query 3.8 'List details of all invoices sent out before 1st Jan 1991'.

```
1  SELECT *
2  FROM INVOICE
3  WHERE DATE < '1-jan-91' ;
```

Line 3 selects out all rows where the invoice date is before 1st Jan 1991. The resulting output will therefore be:

```
INV_NO  C_NO  INV_DATE    AMOUNT
- - - - - -   - - - -   - - - - - - - -    - - - - - -
   940     1  05-DEC-90    26.2
```

All the appropriate arithmetic operators can be used with dates, so that it is possible for example to add days to a date and to subtract dates to get a number of days.

Query 3.9 'List details of all customers not living in London'.

```
1  SELECT *
2  FROM CUS
3  WHERE CITY < >'London' ;
```

This shows the inequality operator '< >', which can also be written '! ='.

The WHERE condition can involve more than one column, as the following query illustrates. Both BALANCE and CRED_LIM are columns in the CUS table.

Query 3.10 'List out the details of all customers who have
                exceeded their credit limit'.

    1 SELECT *
    2 FROM CUS
    3 WHERE BALANCE > CRED_LIM ;

This gives the following output:

C_NO	TITLE	SNAME	INITS	STREET	CITY	POSTC	CRED_LIM	BALANCE
3	Mr	Jackson	R.	2 Lux Ave	Leeds	LE1 2AB	500	510
4	Mr	Dziduch	M.	31 Low St	Dover	DO2 9CD	100	149.23

Note that the row for C_NO 6 was not output. No comparisons involving a NULL value will succeed, apart from IS NULL. Query 3.5 could be modified so that only stock items that had low stock levels were output:

Query 3.11 'List out the percentage shortfall in stock of all items that
                need to be reordered'.

    1 SELECT PROD_NO, DESCR, 100 * (QIS - MINQ)/ MINQ
    2 FROM PRODUCT
    3 WHERE QIS < MINQ ;

which gives:

PROD_NO	DESCR	100*(QIS-MINQ)/MINQ
3	Hoop	-40
4	Net	-60
5	Rope	-90

Query 3.12 'Produce a simple Reorder Report'

```
1  SELECT PROD_NO,  DESCR, REORDQ
2  FROM PRODUCT
3  WHERE QIS < MINQ ;
```

This query requires little comment, except to say that it is probably frequently used and illustrates the simplicity of SQL syntax.

3.4.2 The LIKE Operator

One very useful feature used in WHERE conditions is the LIKE operator. It works with character fields and allows 'fuzzy matching'. The query contains an approximation to the spelling of the required column contents and all rows where the corresponding characters match up are retrieved. The general form of an SQL command containing LIKE is:

```
1  SELECT ...
2  FROM ...
3  WHERE A LIKE B
   ...
```

A will generally be a column name and B is a 'mask' containing a combination of known characters and one or more of:

%   which matches with zero, one or more characters, and
_   the underscore character, which matches with just one
     character.

Query 3.13 'List out the customer account details of all customers whose name starts with "Dz" '.

```
1  SELECT *
2  FROM CUS
3  WHERE SNAME LIKE 'Dz%' ;
```

The % sign will match with any number of characters following the 'Dz'.

Query 3.14 'What's the address of that Czech customer. I can't
           remember the account number or how to spell his name, but I
           think the second letter was a "z" '.

    1 SELECT *
    2 FROM CUS
    3 WHERE SNAME LIKE '_z%' ;

In both cases the following output would result:

C_NO	TITLE	SNAME	INITS	STREET	CITY	POSTC	CRED_LIM	BALANCE
4	Mr	Dziduch	M.	31 Low St	Dover	DO2 9CD	100	149.23

The LIKE operator can sometimes be used to advantage with postcodes:

Query 3.15 'List the customers living in the general area of this
           Milton Keynes address at MK2 6EF'.

    1 SELECT SNAME, STREET
    2 FROM CUS
    3 WHERE POSTC LIKE 'MK2 6EF' ;

    1 SELECT SNAME, STREET
    2 FROM CUS
    3 WHERE POSTC LIKE 'MK2 6__' ;

    1 SELECT SNAME, STREET
    2 FROM CUS
    3 WHERE POSTC LIKE 'MK2 %' ;

Each SELECT in this sequence selects a larger catchment area than the previous one. The LIKE phrase in the last SELECT has a space before the '%' so as to prevent postcodes like MK20 ..., MK21 ... etc. being output.

Query 3.16 'List all the female customers'.

```
1  SELECT *
2  FROM CUS
3  WHERE TITLE LIKE '%s' ;
```

This depends on the observation (or hope?) that the title of every female customer ends with an 's' and that the title of no male customer does. In practice one would hope that the database designers would have foreseen the need for this query and included a gender column in the CUS table. For another solution to this query using the IN operator see Section 3.4.4.

3.4.3 The BETWEEN Operator

BETWEEN can be used in a WHERE clause in which it is required to select rows where the value of a specified column is within a given range:

Query 3.17 'List out details of all sales invoices with an invoice date
          between 1st Dec 1990 and 13th Jan 1991'.

```
1  SELECT *
2  FROM INVOICE
3  WHERE INV_DATE  BETWEEN  '1-dec-90'  AND  '13-jan-91';
```

Note that the invoice rows with dates between 1st Dec 90 and 13th Jan 91 *inclusive* will be output. With the INVOICE table shown in the Appendix, the output will be:

```
INV_NO  C_NO  INV_DATE      AMOUNT
------  ----  --------      ------
   940     1  05-dec-90       26.2
```

```
1002    4  12-jan-91    149.23
1003    1  12-jan-91     16.36
```

Query 3.18 'List details of all customers with surnames starting
             with letters from "E" to "L" '.

1 SELECT *
2 FROM CUS
3 WHERE SNAME BETWEEN 'E' AND 'M' ;

or

1 SELECT *
2 FROM CUS
3 WHERE SNAME BETWEEN 'E' AND 'Lzz' ;

These are different ways of retrieving precisely those records required. See
Query 3.7 for further discussion of character string comparisons.

3.4.4 The IN Operator

In situations where it is required to test the value of some column against
a given *set* of values, the IN operator can be used. In this chapter where
queries involving only a single database table are being considered, the set
of values are literals, that is, the WHERE clause of the SQL SELECT
command contains a list of the actual values that will be searched for in
the table. Chapter 5 shows that the set of values can also be obtained
from somewhere else on the database as a result of a *subquery* and this
ability is one of the factors that makes SQL a truly powerful fourth
generation programming language.

   The basic operation of IN is quite straightforward. As with all examples
of the WHERE clause, every row in the table is inspected to see if it
passes the test contained in the 'condition' of Fig 3.1. The test will involve
one of the columns in the row so that if the value of the column
corresponds to one of the values in the set of values of the IN list, the

row passes the test and will appear at the output. NOT IN can be used, in which case the row passes the test if the value is *not* in the list.

Query 3.19 'List the details of all deliveries of product numbers
1, 3 and 5'.

```
1  SELECT *
2  FROM DELIVERY
3  WHERE PROD_NO  IN (1,3,5) ;
```

In line 3, each row in the DELIVERY table (See Appendix) is checked to see if its PROD_NO value is in the list (1,3,5). If it is, the row is output, resulting in:

```
C_NO   PROD_NO   QTY    DEL_DATE
----   -------   ---    --------
  3        1      3     03-NOV-90
  5        3      4     12-NOV-90
  3        3      1     12_NOV_90
```

For each of these records, PROD_NO is either 1, 3 or 5.

Query 3.20 'List the account numbers of customers who have purchased products other than product numbers 2, 4 and 5'.

```
1  SELECT DISTINCT C_NO
2  FROM DELIVERY
3  WHERE PROD_NO  NOT IN (2,4,5) ;
```

This query assumes that DELIVERY shows all the purchases that have occurred. The WHERE clause tests each row and if the product number is not 2 and not 4 and not 5 (i.e. it is not a member of the set (2,4,5)) then the row passes the test and its C_NO is output.

The DISTINCT option is used here to prevent the repeated output of customer account numbers for customers who have purchased more than one product which is not in the list, for example C_NO 3 in the current table extension. (The term 'extension' simply means the actual rows in the table, which can of course vary with time due to database updates, as distinct from the column names and characteristics (the 'intension') which define the structure of the table and are not subject to regular alteration). The output for this query is thus:

```
C_NO
----
  3
  5
```

Note that this query

  'Customers who have purchased products not in the list (2,4,5)'

    is quite different from the query

  'Customers who have not purchased products in the list (2,4,5)'.

Despite the superficial resemblance between them, the second query has a different meaning, a different result (usually) and an entirely different SQL SELECT command. In the second query two tables have to be consulted - CUS is consulted to access each customer, and DELIVERY is consulted for each customer to check whether he or she has purchased the listed products. The reason that consulting DELIVERY alone is not satisfactory for the second query is that the table shows what *has* been purchased; it cannot show what has *not* been purchased. There is in fact more than one interpretation that people will (correctly) make of the second query. It can mean either:

  'Customers who have not purchased all products in the
    list (2,4,5)'
or

  'Customers who have not purchased one or more products in the
    list (2,4,5)'

It also seems likely that if the word 'all' in the former is replaced by 'any', then an ambiguity again appears to some people. These questions of interpretation should be identified by the Systems Analyst who should ideally have a firm grounding in the grammar and semantics of his or her spoken language, and a reasonable command of logic and set theory. Chapters 4 and 5 give SQL SELECT commands for all the above queries involving more than one table. Here is another single-table query using IN:

Query 3.21 'List all the female customers'.

This is the same query as Query 3.16 but this time using IN. The idea is that all female customers have the title Miss, Ms or Mrs.

```
1  SELECT *
2  FROM CUS
3  WHERE TITLE IN ('Miss','Ms','Mrs') ;
```

3.4.5 Compound Conditions using AND, OR and NOT

So far in this chapter, all the WHERE clauses used simple conditions, that is the conditions involved only one type of test per row. To perform two or more tests in a single WHERE clause, the AND and OR operators, together with round brackets () and NOT can be used to string several conditions together to form a *compound condition*.

Query 3.22 'List out the details of all overdrawn London customers'.

There are two conditions that must be met here.

To be output, customers must:

(Cond 1) have a debt greater than their credit limit

AND

(Cond 2) be based in London.

The SELECT command is:

    1 SELECT *
    2 FROM CUS
    3 WHERE BALANCE > CRED_LIM
    4 AND   CITY = 'London' ;

Query 3.23 'List out customers who are overdrawn or live in London'.

To be output, customers must:

(Cond 1) have a debt greater than their credit limit

    OR

(Cond 2) be based in London.

The SELECT command is:

    1 SELECT *
    2 FROM CUS
    3 WHERE BALANCE > CRED_LIM
    4 OR   CITY = 'London' ;

The output for this query is:

C_NO	TITLE	SNAME	INITS	STREET	CITY	POSTC	CRED_LIM	BALANCE
1	Mr	Sallaway	G.R.	12 Fax Rd	London	WC1	1000	42.56
2	Miss	Lauri	P.	5 Dux St	London	N1	500	200
3	Mr	Jackson	R.	2 Lux Ave	Leeds	LE1 2AB	500	510

| 4 | Mr | Dziduch | M. | 31 Low St | Dover | DO2 9CD | 100 | 149.23 |
| 5 | Ms | Woods | S.Q. | 17 Nax Rd | London E18 4WW | | 1000 | 250.1 |

Note that the row for C_NO 6 (See Appendix) is not present since the customer is neither a London customer nor is the BALANCE (= 412.21) greater than the CRED_LIM (=NULL). NULL is a special value that an SQL column can take. It can 'mean' whatever the database designer wants it to mean. 'Missing value', 'not yet known' and 'not applicable in this case' are possibilities. The database designer should make it clear in all documentation what it means in each case. SQL has its own rules relating to NULL. This query illustrates one of those rules: when a number is compared with NULL, the result is NULL. Query 3.27 discusses NULL further.

'OR' as defined in SQL and in other programming languages is an 'inclusive' OR which means that in compound conditions such as the one shown in lines 3 and 4 above, the CUS row will be output if the line 3 condition alone is true, or if the line 4 condition alone is true, or if they are *both* true. It is called an 'inclusive OR' because it includes the case where both individual conditions are true. An 'exclusive' OR does not produce output if both conditions are true. This would correspond to listing those customers who were either overdrawn or London based but not both. See Query 3.25 for an example using exclusive OR.

Note that care must be taken in choosing the correct operator. In practice people are not always clear whether it is an AND or an OR that is required. If the current query had been written in the form:

'List out the details of all overdrawn and all London customers'

some people would produce the same SQL code as that for Query 3.22, whereas the correct SQL is in fact identical to that for Query 3.23. The former group are probably misled by the appearance of 'and' in the query, simply transcribing it from the English sentence into the SQL command. One way to arrive at the proper choice between AND and OR is to imagine each individual row of the table being tested, and asking, in effect, 'What conditions need to be fulfilled to let this individual row through?'. In the example above the customer should be either overdrawn *or* London based (or both) so an OR would be used in the SQL command. In Query 3.22 the customer should be both overdrawn AND London based so an AND is used. An alternative view is to think of the query conditions in terms of sets and set operations. See Reference [4] for a tutorial on sets. For example our universal set (i.e. the set of objects under consideration) may be our set of customers represented by the table CUS. The elements of the set are (represented by) the rows of CUS. The first subset of interest is the set of overdrawn customers and the second subset is the set of London based customers. See Fig 3.2.

Each of these subsets 'of interest' is represented in the Venn diagram by a circle. In the current example there are two subsets of interest so there are two circles in the Venn diagram. Inside the left circle is the set of customers for whom the first condition ('overdrawn') is true (T) and outside the circle the set of customers for whom the condition is false (F). Similarly the customers in the right circle are London based (second condition is true (T)) and those outside it are not London based (second condition false (F)).

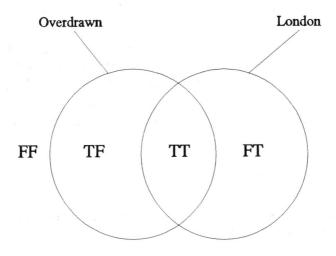

Fig. 3.2 Venn Diagram for Query 3.22

Notice that the circles overlap so that all four combinations of the two conditions are included in the Venn diagram:

Overdrawn	London Based
F	F
F	T
T	F
T	T

Fig. 3.3 Truth Table for Two Conditions

If there had been three conditions each with two values T (True) and F (False), then there would be eight ($=2^3$) distinct areas in the Venn diagram and eight rows in the truth table.

Now the set of people of interest in the query could be any combination of the four distinct areas shown in Fig 3.2, for example:

'Overdrawn'   (TF or TT)

'Overdrawn or London based'   (TF or TT or FT)

In fact, since each of the four distinct areas in the Venn diagram of Fig. 3.2 may be highlighted or not highlighted, selected or not selected for output, then the total number of possible queries involving these two conditions is $2^{(2^2)}$.   In general, the total number of queries Q involving N conditions each of which can have two values T or F is given by:

$$Q = 2^{(2^N)}$$

so that for three conditions the total number of logically different queries it is possible to make is 256.

Query 3.24 'List out details of customers who are overdrawn but
            not living in London'.

    1 SELECT *
    2 FROM CUS

```
3 WHERE BALANCE > CRED_LIM
4 AND   CITY ! =   'London' ;
```

Query 3.25 'List out details of customers who are overdrawn or
living in London but not both'.

```
1 SELECT *
2 FROM CUS
3 WHERE (BALANCE > CRED_LIM
4 OR CITY = 'London')
5 AND NOT (BALANCE > CRED_LIM AND CITY = 'London');
```

This is the 'exclusive OR' condition and corresponds to TF or FT in the
truth table of Fig 3.3.

The query could be written equivalently as:

```
1 SELECT *
2 FROM CUS
3 WHERE (BALANCE > CRED_LIM AND CITY ! =   'London')
4 OR    (BALANCE < = CRED_LIM AND CITY = 'London');
```

There are thus often several equivalent ways of casting the same query
using combinations of AND, OR and NOT and Reference [4] describes
some simple logical techniques for showing equivalences and in some
cases simplifying the query and making it more clearly correct. In cases of
three or more conditions it is often beneficial to draw up the truth table
and tick the rows where output is required. The resulting expression can
then often be simplified using a Karnaugh map. The only real alternative
to checking the internal logic of the query in this way is the more
pragmatic approach of writing the query using a combination of common
sense and experience, running the query against test database tables
containing an exhaustive set of condition combinations, one row for each
combination, and then desk checking the results. The only problem with
this technique is that it may not always be clear what to do if the output
from the query is incorrect. In practice a combination of checking the

query logic and test runs is the most reliable policy for non-trivial queries.

Query 3.26 'List out details of all non-overdrawn customers not
living in Bradford, Leeds or London'.

```
1 SELECT *
2 FROM CUS
3 WHERE BALANCE < = CRED_LIM
4 AND CITY NOT IN ('Bradford', 'Leeds', 'London') ;
```

is a shorter equivalent of

```
1 SELECT *
2 FROM CUS
3 WHERE BALANCE < = CRED_LIM
4 AND CITY ! = 'Bradford'
5 AND CITY ! = 'Leeds'
6 AND CITY ! = 'London' ;
```

Query 3.27 'List out details of all customers where the credit
limit is unknown'.

Assuming that in this database as-yet unknown values are represented by
the special SQL value NULL, the query would be as follows:

```
1 SELECT *
2 FROM CUS
3 WHERE CRED_LIM IS NULL ;
```

Line 3 evaluates to TRUE for C_NO 6, giving :

C_NO	TITLE	SNAME	INITS	STREET	CITY	POSTC	CRED_LIM	BALANCE
6	Mrs	Williams	C.	41 Cax St	Dover	DO2 8WD		412.21

To list details of all customers with non-null CRED_LIM, use:

```
1  SELECT *
2  FROM CUS
3  WHERE CRED_LIM  IS NOT NULL ;
```

Line 3 evaluates to FALSE for C_NO 6.

Note that in all other cases than the two queries above, wherever a column X has a NULL value and is involved in a comparison, the condition itself evaluates to NULL. The truth table below shows the result of compound conditions involving two conditions X and Y, where one or both evaluate to NULL.

```
---------------------------------

X      Y           X AND Y    X OR Y
---------------------------------

NULL   NULL        NULL       NULL
NULL   TRUE        NULL       TRUE
NULL   FALSE       FALSE      NULL



-----------

X      NOT X
-----------

NULL   NULL
```

Fig. 3.4 Truth Table for Compound Conditions with NULL Values

Query 3.28 'List customers who have a balance over 400 pounds or a credit limit over 500 pounds'.

```
1  SELECT *
2  FROM CUS
3  WHERE BALANCE  >  400
4  OR    CRED_LIM  > 500 ;
```

The output from this query is:

C_NO	TITLE	SNAME	INITS	STREET	CITY	POSTC	CRED_LIM	BALANCE
1	Mr	Sallaway	G.R.	12 Fax Rd	London	WC1	1000	42.56
3	Mr	Jackson	R.	2 Lux Ave	Leeds	LE1 2AB	500	510
5	Ms	Woods	S.Q.	17 Nax Rd	London	E18 4WW	1000	250.1
6	Mrs	Williams	C.	41 Cax St	Dover	DO2 8WD		412.21

For C_NO 6, the test in line 3 evaluates to TRUE and the test in line 4 evaluates to NULL since CRED_LIM is NULL. By line 2 of the main table of Fig 3.4, the result is TRUE, so the row is output. Now consider this query:

Query 3.29 'List out the account details of all customers who have a balance of over 400 pounds and a credit limit of over 500 pounds'.

```
1  SELECT *
2  FROM CUS
3  WHERE BALANCE  >  400
4  AND   CRED_LIM  >  500 ;
```

The result of this query is to produce the following output:

```
NO RECORDS SELECTED
```

For C_NO 6, the test in line 3 evaluates to TRUE and the test in line 4 evaluates to NULL since CRED_LIM is NULL. By line 2 of the main table of Fig. 3.4, the result is NULL, so the row is not output. Rows are only output if the compound condition evaluates to TRUE. Care must be taken with tables where NULL values are allowed. Consider the following query:

Query 3.30 'List the account number and balance of customers whose credit limit is not equal to 500 pounds'.

```
1  SELECT C_NO, BALANCE
2  FROM CUS
3  WHERE CRED_LIM != 500 ;
```

This output would be:

```
C_NO        BALANCE
----        -------
  1          42.56
  4         149.23
  5         250.1
```

The record for C_NO 6 would not be output even though her credit limit is NOT 500 pounds. This is because any comparison other than IS NULL and IS NOT NULL with a NULL field yields a NULL result and records are only output for TRUE results. In the present example the records for customers with NULL credit limits will only be output if the extra condition shown in line 4 is added:

```
1  SELECT C_NO, BALANCE
2  FROM CUS
3  WHERE CRED_LIM != 500
4  OR CRED_LIM IS NULL ;
```

3.5 AGGREGATING DATA

It is often necessary to obtain summary or aggregate results from database tables. For example a manager may want to know the number of employees in each department or the average salary of a particular grade. Implicit in this idea is the concept of a group. A number of rows in a table are considered as a group and some summary data extracted, such as the number of rows in the group or the maximum, minimum or average salary in the group of rows. The 'group' can be the whole table, in which case a single result will be output or the group can be a group of rows which have a common attribute such as the same value in the 'department' column of an employee table in which case there will be one result for each department group.

Groups are specified in the SQL SELECT command by the GROUP BY clause. After the groups have been formed there is the possibility of further filtering the results with the HAVING clause which acts on the group results in a similar way to the action of the WHERE clause on the table itself so that only data from selected groups will be output.

It is perhaps worthwhile to repeat here the sequence of execution of the clauses in the SELECT command.

```
FROM        Specifies the table(s) to be accessed
WHERE       Filters rows on some condition
GROUP BY    Forms groups of rows with same column value
HAVING      Filters groups on some condition
SELECT      Specifies what results will be output
ORDER BY    Determines the order of the output results
```

3.5.1 Aggregate Functions

The following functions in SQL are used to produce summary or aggregate results from groups of rows in database tables:

```
AVG(X)    Average value of numeric column X in the group of rows
COUNT(X)  Number of rows where X is non-null in the group of rows
MAX(X)    Maximum value in numeric column X in the group of rows
MIN(X)    Minimum value in numeric column X in the group of rows
SUM(X)    Sum of values in numeric column X in the group of rows
```

ORACLE SQL*PLUS also has the statistical functions:

```
VARIANCE(X) The variance (measure of spread) of numeric column
            X in the group of rows
STDDEV(X)   The standard deviation (measure of spread) of
            numeric column X in the group of rows
```

How to obtain the statistic Mode (most popular value of X) is shown in

Query 3.42 below. This statistic may or not be numeric. Note that in calculating these results, all rows with a NULL value of X are ignored, so that for example the AVG of the set of numbers (2,4,null,6,8) is 5 since there are considered to be four numbers in the set, not five.

The DISTINCT option can be used with all of these functions to ignore duplicates so that AVG(DISTINCT X) for the set of column X values (2,4,4,6,0) is (2+4+6+0)/4 = 3 whereas AVG(X) is (2+4+4+6+0)/5 = 3.2.

Query 3.31 'What is the total amount owed by our customers?'

```
1  SELECT SUM(BALANCE)
2  FROM CUS ;
```

giving   SUM(BALANCE)

               1564.1

Here the aggregate function SUM ranges over the whole table (the 'group' is the whole table) to obtain the single value.

Query 3.32 'What is the total amount owed by our London customers?'

```
1  SELECT SUM(BALANCE) LONDON_TOTAL
2  FROM CUS
3  WHERE CITY ='London' ;
```

Here the CUS table is pre-filtered by the WHERE clause in line 3 to consider only London customers in the calculation. Note also the use of the column alias LONDON_TOTAL which simply improves the appearance of the output.

```
LONDON_TOTAL
------------
    492.66
```

Query 3.33 'How many customers have a balance over 400 pounds?'.

```
1  SELECT COUNT(*) BALANCE_OVER_400
2  FROM CUS
3  WHERE BALANCE > 400 ;
```

```
BALANCE_OVER_400
----------------
               2
```

Since it is the number of rows that is wanted, there is no need to name an individual column in the COUNT function. COUNT(*) simply means the count of the number of rows. The answer would have been the same if any column name had been used instead.

It is possible to use the DISTINCT option when duplicate values are to be ignored in an aggregate function.

Query 3.34 'How many different cities are there in the
                 CUS file?'

```
1  SELECT COUNT(DISTINCT CITY)
2  FROM CUS ;
```

```
COUNT(DISTINCTCITY)
-------------------
                  3
```

As a temporary change from customers, balances etc., here is another example of DISTINCT being used with COUNT. We have a database table called CITATION which is part of a database containing data about fossils. The CITATION table shows the species of living things (plant or animal) mentioned in various documents. The sequence number gives the order in which a given species is cited in a particular document.   The structure of the table is thus:

```
CITATION
--------


DOCUMENT   SEQ_NO    GENUS     SPECIES    AGE    LOCATION
--------   ------    -----     -------    ---    --------
       1        1    Felis     Tigris     10000    India
       1        2    Vulpes    Vulpes     20000    Thailand
       1        3    Felis     Tigris     20000    Thailand
```

etc.

The query is:

Query 3.34a 'How many different species are there on the
database?'

> 1 SELECT COUNT(DISTINCT GENUS||SPECIES)
> 2 FROM CITATION ;

The reason for having to use the concatenation operator ||is due to a
quirk in the naming convention that biologists use. When asked the
species of a living thing the biologist mentions two words (generally). The
first word is known as the genus and the second word as the species. So
a species 'consists of' a genus and a species. This is an example of the kind
of muddle we must avoid in database design wherever possible. To return
to our customers:

Query 3.35 'What percentage of customers have a balance
over 400 pounds?'

```
The formula is    100*(no of customers with balance over 400)
                  -----------------------------------------
                            (no of customers)
```

Surprisingly the SQL for this query is not as straightforward as it seems.
To calculate the numerator of the expression a WHERE clause is

required i.e. WHERE BALANCE > 400. To calculate the denominator a count of ALL rows is required, indicating that a WHERE is not required. Consequently a separate scan of the table is required for each term and a solution to this query must be postponed until Chapter 5 where subqueries are considered.

Query 3.36 'Calculate the maximum, minimum, range and average credit limit of our customers'

```
1  SELECT MAX(CRED_LIM)  A, MIN(CRED_LIM)  B,
2  MAX(CRED_LIM) - MIN(CRED_LIM)  C, AVG(CRED_LIM)  D
3  FROM CUS ;
```

A	B	C	D
1000	100	900	620

It is perhaps worth repeating here that in calculating all these results the NULL value of CRED_LIM is ignored, as the following query clearly shows:

Query 3.37 'Demonstrate how COUNT works with NULL values'.

```
1  SELECT COUNT(CRED_ LIM), COUNT(BALANCE), COUNT(*)
2  FROM CUS ;
```

COUNT(CRED_LIM)	COUNT(BALANCE)	COUNT(*)
5	6	6

3.5.2 Forming Groups with GROUP BY

So far, the 'group' on which the aggregate functions operated to obtain their numeric results was the whole table. In many queries the result of an aggregate function will be required on each of several groups, where groups are identified or obtain their group identity by sharing some common attribute values, that is by sharing common values of some columns. If the SELECT command contains the code '... GROUP BY DEPARTMENT' then there will be just one row output for each department.

Query 3.38 'List out the average age of employees in each department'.

Assuming an EMPLOYEE table of the form:

```
EMP_NO  NAME       AGE  DEPARTMENT
------  ----       ---  ----------
  1     Judy        23  Billing
  2     Madge       27  Accounts
  4     Karen       19  Billing
  3     Terence     42  Billing
  5     Grace       25  Accounts
```

The query is:

```
1 SELECT DEPARTMENT, AVG(AGE)
2 FROM EMPLOYEE
3 GROUP BY DEPARTMENT ;
```

The output will be:

```
DEPARTMENT   AVG(AGE)
----------   --------
Billing         28
Accounts        26
```

In line 3 of the query the GROUP BY clause forms intermediate groups of rows, one for each department. These groups of rows are said to be 'intermediate' because they do not last and are never displayed. They exist only temporarily for the purpose of calculating the results of the aggregate function. Since there are only two departments mentioned in the table, there will be two groups of intermediate rows formed.

```
EMP_NO  NAME      AGE  DEPARTMENT
------  ----      ---  ----------

The first group is:

  1     Judy       23  Billing
  4     Karen      19  Billing
  3     Terence    42  Billing

The second group is:

  2     Madge      27  Accounts
  5     Grace      25  Accounts
```

There is one group of rows for each department. Now the SELECT in line 1 of the query asks for the department and the average age to be output for each group and the output is as shown above. It is possible to output A SINGLE department value for each group since every member of the group has the same value in the DEPARTMENT column. It is also possible to output a single value of average age for each group.

It would not be possible to output a single value of EMP_NO for each group because there may be more than one employee number in each department. Similarly, it would not be possible to output a single value of NAME for each group because there are several values of NAME in each value of the GROUP BY variable DEPARTMENT. Although the idea of GROUP BY is fairly straightforward once the notion of a group is understood, its misuse is a common source of error.

Thus the following queries would be *incorrect* because some of the columns in the SELECT line (line 1) could have more than one value per group:

```
1  SELECT EMP_NO,  AVG(AGE)      < ----- Incorrect Queries
2  FROM EMPLOYEE
3  GROUP BY DEPARTMENT ;
```

```
1  SELECT NAME, AVG(AGE)
2  FROM EMPLOYEE
3  GROUP BY DEPARTMENT ;
```

Query 3.39 'List out the number of employees and the maximum, minimum and average age of employees in each department'.

This query can be successfully accomplished because for each department there is a single value of each output item.

```
1 SELECT DEPARTMENT, COUNT(*), MAX(AGE), MIN(AGE),
2  AVG(AGE)
3  FROM EMPLOYEE
4  GROUP BY DEPARTMENT ;
```

The output is:

```
DEPARTMENT  COUNT(*), MAX(AGE), MIN(AGE), AVG(AGE)
----------  --------  --------  --------  --------
  Accounts      2        27        25        26
  Billing       3        42        19        28
```

Note the secondary effect of GROUP BY of presenting the departmental groups in alphabetical order.

Query 3.40 'List out the average age of employees in each department. Only consider those whose age is over twenty'.

```
1  SELECT DEPARTMENT, AVG(AGE)
2  FROM EMPLOYEE
3  WHERE AGE > 20
4  GROUP BY DEPARTMENT ;
```

Remembering that the filtering process carried out by WHERE occurs before GROUP BY (See Section 3.2), the intermediate groups of rows by department will be:

```
EMP_NO  NAME      AGE  DEPARTMENT
------  ----      ---  ----------
The first group is:

  1      Judy      23  Billing
  3      Terence   42  Billing


The second group is:

  2      Madge     27  Accounts
  5      Grace     25  Accounts
```

Notice that the 19-year-old has been removed prior to the formation of the groups. The resulting output from the query is thus:

```
DEPARTMENT   AVG(AGE)
----------   --------
Accounts         26
Billing        32.5
```

Note that in ORACLE SQL*PLUS it is not necessary to have the GROUP BY variable in the SELECT line, so that the following query is valid:

```
1  SELECT  AVG(AGE)
2  FROM EMPLOYEE
3  GROUP BY DEPARTMENT ;
```

The output will be simply:

```
AVG(AGE)
--------
      28
      26
```

Query 3.41 'List out from the CUSTOMER table the total amount outstanding by city.

```
1  SELECT CITY, SUM(BALANCE)
2  FROM CUS
3  GROUP BY CITY ;
```

The output is:

```
CITY        SUM(BALANCE)
----        ------------
Dover         561.44
Leeds            510
London        492.66
```

In ORACLE SQL*PLUS (not in INGRES or dBASE), it is possible to nest the aggregate functions, so that the following query is possible:

Query 3.42 'What is the maximum total outstanding balance?'

```
1  SELECT  MAX(SUM(BALANCE))
2  FROM CUS
3  GROUP BY CITY ;
```

And the output is:

```
MAX(SUM(BALANCE))
-----------------
          561.44
```

Query 3.43 'Which is the city with the maximum total outstanding
        balance?'

Despite the similarity with query 3.42, this query must be left until
Chapter 5 because it requires the use of subqueries. It is sometimes
necessary to group on two or more columns at once. Consider the
following table EMPLOYEE1:

DEPARTMENT	EMPLOYEE_NO	JOB_DESCRIPTION
1	12	Fitter
1	19	Turner
1	14	Fitter
1	20	Miller
2	6	Turner
2	17	Miller
2	21	Miller

Query 3.44 'List out the number of employees in each job by
        department'.

```
1  SELECT DEPARTMENT, JOB_DESCRIPTION,  COUNT(*)
2  FROM EMPLOYEE1
3  GROUP BY DEPARTMENT, JOB_DESCRIPTION  ;
```

The output is:

DEPARTMENT	JOB_DESCRIPTION	COUNT(*)
1	Fitter	2
1	Miller	1
1	Turner	1
2	Miller	2
2	Turner	1

It would not have been any good grouping on just JOB_DESCRIPTION because then COUNT(*) would have contained, for example, the number of turners across ALL departments. If the GROUP BY had been on DEPARTMENT, then COUNT(*) would have contained the total number of employees of ANY description for each department.

It is possible to group by an expression rather than simple columns. The expression may be string or numeric and usually involves columns in the table. The expression must appear as a column expression in the SELECT line of the SELECT statement. Consider the GROUPS table (see Appendix) which shows the student membership of workshop groups in each of two terms:

TERM	GROUP_NO	MEMBER
1	1	1
1	1	2
1	1	3
1	2	4
1	2	5
1	2	6
2	1	5
2	1	7
2	10	2
2	10	3

Query 3.45 'List out the number of members in each group for both terms'.

Notice that there is a composite key consisting of TERM with GROUP_NO which identifies a group.

The SQL SELECT command is:

```
1  SELECT TERM*100+GROUP_NO, COUNT(*)
2  FROM GROUPS
3  GROUP BY TERM*100+GROUP_NO ;
```

which results in the output:

```
TERM*100+GROUP_NO     COUNT(*)
-----------------     --------
              101        3
              102        3
              201        2
              210        2
```

An alternative formulation is:

1 SELECT TERM, GROUP_NO, COUNT(*)
2 FROM GROUPS
3 GROUP BY TERM, GROUP_NO ;

which has the equivalent output:

```
TERM      GROUP_NO      COUNT(*)
----      --------      --------
   1          1            3
   1          2            3
   2          1            2
   2         10            2
```

3.6 SELECTING GROUPS WITH HAVING

After the groups have been formed using GROUP BY, the group data that would be output can itself be filtered using the HAVING clause of SQL. HAVING thus acts towards groups in the same way that WHERE acts towards table rows. Instead of a result being output for every group, only selected groups pass through the filtering effect of HAVING.

The HAVING clause is particularly powerful when it is used with subqueries. This is what is required to answer query 3.43. Subqueries are discussed in Chapter 5.

Query 3.46 'List from the EMPLOYEE table all departments where
the average age is under 27'.

    1 SELECT DEPARTMENT, AVG(AGE)
    2 FROM EMPLOYEE
    3 GROUP BY DEPARTMENT
    4 HAVING AVG(AGE) < 27 ;

results in:

```
DEPARTMENT    AVG(AGE)
---------  ----------
Accounts        26
```

Query 3.47 'Which cities have a total customer balance of over
500 pounds?'

    1 SELECT CITY, SUM(BALANCE)
    2 FROM CUS
    3 GROUP BY CITY
    4 HAVING SUM(BALANCE) > 500 ;

results in:

```
CITY    SUM(BALANCE)
------  ------------
Dover       561.44
Leeds        510
```

Query 3.48 'Which workshop groups have more than two members
and how many members do these groups have?'

    1 SELECT TERM, GROUP_NO, COUNT(*)
    2 FROM GROUPS
    3 GROUP BY TERM, GROUP_NO
    4 HAVING COUNT(*) > 2 ;

which results in:

TERM	GROUP_NO	COUNT(*)
1	1	3
1	2	3

Note that the HAVING clause does not have to involve the aggregate function but since this is the only value newly calculated in the GROUP BY operation, it is most likely that it will.

The query:

```
1 SELECT TERM, GROUP_NO,  COUNT(*)
2 FROM GROUPS
3 GROUP BY TERM, GROUP_NO
4 HAVING TERM = 2 ;
```

which only allows through term 2 groups by filtering AFTER the groups have been formed, has the same effect as the query:

```
1 SELECT TERM, GROUP_NO,  COUNT(*)
2 FROM GROUPS
3 WHERE TERM = 2
4 GROUP BY TERM, GROUP_NO  ;
```

which only allows through term 2 groups by filtering BEFORE the groups have been formed. The output in both cases is:

TERM	GROUP_NO	COUNT(*)
2	1	2
2	10	2

If it is not required to output the results of the aggregate functions, they can be calculated in the HAVING clause itself. For example:

Query 3.49 'Which workshop groups have more than two members?'

```
1  SELECT TERM, GROUP_NO
2  FROM GROUPS
3  GROUP BY TERM, GROUP_NO
4  HAVING COUNT(*) > 2 ;
```

gives as output

TERM	GROUP_NO
1	1
1	2

Grouping may on occasion be performed without using any aggregate function at all. The effect is simply to list out each group just once. For example in the workshop groups example, the query:

Query 3.50 'List out all the workshop groups'

can be implemented by:

```
1  SELECT TERM, GROUP_NO
2  FROM GROUPS
3  GROUP BY TERM, GROUP_NO ;
```

resulting in:

TERM	GROUP_NO
1	1
1	2
2	1
2	10

The same effect can be obtained using DISTINCT:

```
1  SELECT DISTINCT TERM, GROUP_NO
2  FROM GROUPS ;
```

Query 3.51 'List the number of employees and the average age in
each department with three employees and an average
age over 27'.

This requires a compound condition in the HAVING clause of the query
and the required SQL is:

```
1  SELECT DEPARTMENT, COUNT(*), AVG(AGE)
2  FROM EMPLOYEE
3  GROUP BY DEPARTMENT
4  HAVING COUNT(*) > 3
5  AND AVG(AGE) > 27 ;
```

The resulting output is:

```
DEPARTMENT    COUNT(*)    AVG(AGE)
----------    --------    --------
Billing          3          28
```

Query 3.52 'List the average age of employees in each department
with more than one employee'.

```
1  SELECT DEPARTMENT, AVG(AGE)
2  FROM EMPLOYEE
3  GROUP BY DEPARTMENT
4  HAVING COUNT(*) > 1 ;
```

This query again illustrates that the aggregate function used in the
HAVING clause need not be output.

3.7 SORTING THE OUTPUT WITH ORDER BY

The purpose of the ORDER BY clause is to present the output in either
ascending or descending order of an expression involving columns of the
table. The expression that the output will be sorted on may alternatively
be indicated by an integer which specifies the position in the SELECT line
of the expression . The order of the rows in the table in the database is
not altered; ORDER BY simply changes the order in which the results
of a query are displayed. The syntax of the ORDER BY clause is:

SELECT ...
     ORDER BY {expr|posn} [ASC|DESC], ...

Query 3.53 'List out the contents of the CUSTOMER table in
             alphabetical order of surname'.

1 SELECT *
2 FROM CUS
3 ORDER BY SNAME ;

Ascending order is the default, so the output appears in alphabetical
order as expected.

Query 3.54 'List out the customer surname and balance, in descending
             order of balance'.

1 SELECT SNAME, BALANCE
2 FROM CUS
3 ORDER BY 2 DESC ;

Line 3 requests that the second output column (BALANCE) be chosen
as the sort key, and that the output rows appear in descending order of
BALANCE. The row with the highest balance will thus appear first.

Query 3.55 'List out the customer file in descending order of
balance (i.e. highest first) within ascending order
of city name'.

The SQL for this is simply:

```
1  SELECT *
2  FROM CUS
3  ORDER BY CITY, BALANCE DESC ;
```

Note that the 'major sort key' CITY uses the default ASCending.

3.8 EXERCISES

Using the ELECTION schema shown in the Appendix, write SQL
SELECT commands to perform the following:

1. List the details of all candidates not in the Labour party.

2. List the total number of votes in constituency 1.

3. List the total number of votes for each party.

4. List the total number of votes for each party having a total
vote of over 100.

5. List the total number of votes for each party in descending
order of number of votes.

6. List the maximum number of votes.

7. List the number of votes for each party with more than 200 votes
total, best first.

8. List the party with the maximum number of votes.

Chapter 4

SELECT with Joined Tables

4.1 INTRODUCTION

All the queries in Chapter 3 involve the use of only one table. In many practical situations it will be necessary to access information from two or more tables in order to find the answer to database queries. For example suppose it was required to list out the name and address of all customers who had purchased a particular product. This would probably involve accessing a CUSTOMER table, a DELIVERY table and a PRODUCT table. Or in a medical situation it might be required to list all patients who had been prescribed a certain drug, which would probably involve accessing PATIENT, PRESCRIPTION and DRUG tables.

The idea of joining tables in SQL (and in other database software) is that individual rows in one table are 'attached' to some 'corresponding' rows in another table. This creates a set of rows that contain columns from both tables. The rows are joined horizontally. The original tables are not altered and the joined rows exist only for the duration of the SELECT command containing the join. It is possible to save the joined rows in a new table but this is usually not necessary, the purpose of the join being only to answer the immediate query. Chapter 8, which discusses VIEWs, shows how to make it appear to the user that the tables have been permanently joined and in Chapter 9 there is an example where joined rows are stored in a temporary table which is subsequently DROPped. Temporary tables of this type ought not to remain on the database since they take up space and in any case represent duplicate data which goes against the ideals of the database approach described in Chapter 2.

The criteria for joining rows are decided by the SQL user; for example in the medical example mentioned above where three tables are being joined, rows from the PATIENT table will be joined to rows from the PRESCRIPTION table 'on' matching patient_no and rows from DRUG

96

will be joined to rows from PRESCRIPTION on matching drug_no. In this case the 'join criteria' are the identical values of columns which are foreign keys in one of the tables and primary keys in the other. This is not necessarily the case and there are several examples below where columns other than primary and foreign keys are involved as join criteria. It is possible to join on criteria other than equality and it is also possible to join a table to itself, meaning that some of the rows of the table are joined to other rows from the same table. Examples of all these variations are given below.

4.2 THE DIFFERENT TYPES OF JOIN

Some writers on database query languages use special terminology for the various types of join that can occur.

4.2.1 Equijoin

An 'equijoin' corresponds to the situation in which the join condition is based on equality between values in a common column which both tables contain.

4.2.2 Greater Than Join

A 'greater than' join is used where the value of a column in the first table is greater than the value of the corresponding column in the second table. 'Less than', 'not equal' and similar types of join can be likewise defined.

4.2.3 Natural Join

According to the definition of equijoin, two columns with the same name would appear at the output. Since they would always contain the same value for a particular row, one of the duplicated columns is clearly redundant. In a 'natural join', one of the duplicate columns is removed.

4.2.4 Cartesian Product Join

The 'cartesian product' join is one where there are no join criteria, so that every row of the first table is joined to every row of the second table. This 'join' will have little value in practice but it may be considered a useful idea for two reasons. Firstly, it gives the idea of the extreme case in which the maximum number of rows it is possible to generate from a number of tables is calculated by the product of the number of rows in each joined table. Secondly, a practical join containing some join criteria can be conceived of as simply being a subset (a 'select') of the cartesian product join. However, this would be a very inefficient way for a real SQL translator to proceed; clearly the 'selects' should be performed before the 'joins'.

4.2.5 Outer Join

Of the three DBMSs being considered here the outer join is explicitly implemented only in ORACLE SQL*PLUS. This form of the join is useful where it is required to include rows in the output from one table where there is no 'corresponding' row in the second table, together with all the rows that do correspond; for example an SQL user might wish to list out details of all departments and their employees even if some departments have no employees, in which case just the departmental details are required for those departments. The outer join is used in this situation. In contrast to this, all of the previously-mentioned joins would remove from the output details of any department with no employees because the join criteria would find no match. To highlight this point, all of the non-outer joins are collectively designated as *inner* joins. It is possible to simulate an outer join in DBMSs where none is explicitly defined in the language using UNION and NOT EXISTS. This is covered in Chapter 7.

4.2.6 Inner Join

As mentioned above the inner join is the collective name for all joins which are not outer joins.

4.2.7 Self-Join

It is sometimes necessary to join a table to itself to answer an SQL query. This is the case when it is required to compare some of the rows of the table with other rows in the same table. For example a user might want to obtain a list of all employees who obtain a higher salary than their managers, where both salaries are shown in a single table EMPLOYEE. Or it might be desired to list out pairs of residents who live in the same street. In these cases the table appears twice in the FROM clause of the SELECT command and rows in the two 'copies' of the table are distinguished from each other by using a different table alias. There are also cases where the table may need to be joined to itself more than once. Examples of the SQL for self-joins are shown later in this chapter.

There is often more than one way of programming an SQL SELECT command and in many cases a join can be replaced by a subquery. Subqueries are discussed in Chapter 5. In this chapter the earlier examples concern the joining of two tables. This is followed by examples where more than two tables are joined.

4.3 SELECTING DATA FROM TWO TABLES

The main differences between selecting data from one table and selecting data from two tables are:

1. The FROM clause contains reference to the *two* tables to be joined.

2. The WHERE clause must contain one or more additional conditions

stating the criteria for deciding which rows from the two tables are to be joined. These are the 'join criteria'.

Query 4.1 'List the names, addresses and invoice details of all customers who have outstanding invoices'.

Here the output will contain information from the two tables CUS and INVOICE. Name and address will come from CUS and 'invoice details' will come from INVOICE.

```
1  SELECT TITLE, INITS, SNAME, STREET, CITY, POSTC,
2     INV_NO, INV_DATE, AMOUNT
3  FROM CUS, INVOICE
4  WHERE CUS.C_NO  = INVOICE.C_NO;
```

The descriptions of tables CUS and INVOICE are contained in the Appendix. In line 1, the list of column names required in the output is given. Note that this is a combination of column names from the two tables CUS and INVOICE; the first five columns come from CUS and the other three from INVOICE. If there is a large number of column names as here, the column list can be continued onto subsequent lines. Line 3 shows the two tables from which data values are to be drawn, and line 4 gives the join criterion i.e. that the customer account numbers on the CUS and INVOICE tables should be equal. Notice that the identically named customer account numbers: C_NO in both tables, have to be qualified by prefixing them with their respective table names in order to avoid ambiguity. The output from this query is as follows:

TITLE	INIT	SNAME	STREET	CITY	POSTC	INV_NO	INV_DATE	AMOUNT
Mr	G.R.	Sallaway	12 Fax Rd	London	WC1	940	05-DEC-90	26.2
Mr	G.R.	Sallaway	12 Fax Rd	London	WC1	1003	12-JAN-91	16.36
Miss	P.	Lauri	5 Dux St	London	N1	1004	14-JAN-91	200
Mr	R.	Jackson	2 Lux Ave	Leeds	LE1 2AB	1005	20-JAN-91	510
Mr	M.	Dziduch	31 Low St	Dover	DO2 9CD	1002	12-JAN-91	149.23
Ms	S.Q.	Woods	17 Nax Rd	London	E18 4WW	1006	21-JAN-91	250.1

Mrs   C.   Williams 41 Cax St Dover DO2 8WD   1017 22-JAN-91 412.21

This output contains data from columns of both tables. Note that data for Mr G.R. Sallaway appears twice because he has two outstanding invoices. In general, if M rows of the first table match with N rows of the second table then the number of joined rows output will be M times N.

Instead of using the full table name to qualify identically named column names in the two tables, it is possible to use table 'aliases', that is, alternative names for the tables. The output from the current query would have been the same if the following form of the SQL SELECT command had been used:

```
1  SELECT TITLE, INITS, SNAME, STREET,
2  CITY, POSTC, INV_NO,  INV_DATE,  AMOUNT
3  FROM CUS A, INVOICE B
4  WHERE A.C_NO  = B.C_NO  ;
```

The table alias follows the table name in the FROM clause to establish, for example, that 'A' is an alias for CUS for the duration of the query. Similarly, 'B' is an alias for the INVOICE table. These aliases are used in this query in the WHERE clause to qualify the identically named C_NO columns from both tables. Any name could be used as an alias, although it is usual to use a short alias name. The use of aliases in this example simply reduces the amount of typing necessary. When a table appears more than once in a query, as for example, in a self-join, the aliases are mandatory as a later example will illustrate.

Query 4.2 'List the account numbers, names, addresses and invoice details of all customers who have outstanding invoices'.

```
1  SELECT A.C_NO,  TITLE, INITS, SNAME,
2  STREET, CITY, POSTC, INV_NO,  INV_DATE,  AMOUNT
3  FROM CUS A, INVOICE B
4  WHERE A.C_NO  = B.C_NO  ;
```

The output from this query is identical to that of Query 4.1 except that the account number C_NO is also shown. Since C_NO appears in both tables, ambiguity must be avoided by qualifying the column name with the table name, in this case the alias 'A', otherwise SQL would have reported an error of the form 'Ambiguous column name'. Using 'B' or 'CUS' or 'INV' as the qualifier would have worked just as well.

This query is an example of a natural join, as defined in section 4.2. It is not necessary, from SQL's point of view, to list columns from both tables. Take the following query for example:

Query 4.3 'List the account numbers, names and addresses of all customers who have outstanding invoices'.

```
1 SELECT A.C_NO, TITLE, INITS, SNAME,
2   STREET, CITY, POSTC
3 FROM CUS A, INV B
4 WHERE A.C_NO =B.C_NO;
```

The output is as follows:

C_NO	TITLE	INIT	SNAME	STREET	CITY	POSTC
1	Mr	G.R.	Sallaway	12 Fax Rd	London	WC1
1	Mr	G.R.	Sallaway	12 Fax Rd	London	WC1
2	Miss	P.	Lauri	5 Dux St	London	N1
3	Mr	R.	Jackson	2 Lux Ave	Leeds	LE1 2AB
4	Mr	M.	Dziduch	31 Low St	Dover	DO2 9CD
5	Ms	S.Q.	Woods	17 Nax Rd	London	E18 4WW
6	Mrs	C.	Williams	41 Cax St	Dover	DO2 8WD

All of these columns are from the CUS table, but the second table was necessary in order to eliminate outputting details of any customers who did not have outstanding invoices (in this case every customer had at least one outstanding invoice so that every customer appeared). The idea in this query is to list details of every customer who had at least one outstanding invoice. There is an alternative form of this query using EXISTS, for which see Chapter 7.

Note that G.R. Sallaway has again appeared twice, this time with entirely identical data values. This duplication of output can be eliminated using DISTINCT as follows:

```
1 SELECT DISTINCT A.C_NO, TITLE, INITS, SNAME, STREET,
2   CITY, POSTC
3 FROM CUS A, INVOICE B
4 WHERE A.C_NO  = B.C_NO;
```

giving:

C_NO	TITLE	INIT	SNAME	STREET	CITY	POSTC
1	Mr	G.R.	Sallaway	12 Fax Rd	London	WC1
2	Miss	P.	Lauri	5 Dux St	London	N1
3	Mr	R.	Jackson	2 Lux Ave	Leeds	LE1 2AB
4	Mr	M.	Dziduch	31 Low St	Dover	DO2 9CD
5	Ms	S.Q.	Woods	17 Nax Rd	London	E18 4WW
6	Mrs	C.	Williams	41 Cax St	Dover	DO2 8WD

Remember that DISTINCT does not apply to individual columns; it simply prevents entirely identical rows appearing at the output. If there is any difference between output rows, no matter how small, then both rows will be output.

In Chapter 3, the use of column aliases to improve the appearance of the output was discussed. So there are two types of alias, *table aliases* and *column aliases*. The following form of the current query uses both:

```
1 SELECT DISTINCT A.C_NO  ACCOUNT, TITLE,
2   INITS, SNAME, STREET, CITY, POSTC
3 FROM CUS A, INVOICE B
4 WHERE A.C_NO  =B.C_NO;
```

giving:

ACCOUNT	TITLE	INIT	SNAME	STREET	CITY	POSTC
1	Mr	G.R.	Sallaway	12 Fax Rd	London	WC1
2	Miss	P.	Lauri	5 Dux St	London	N1
3	Mr	R.	Jackson	2 Lux Ave	Leeds	LE1 2AB
4	Mr	M.	Dziduch	31 Low St	Dover	DO2 9CD
5	Ms	S.Q.	Woods	17 Nax Rd	London	E18 4WW
6	Mrs	C.	Williams	41 Cax St	Dover	DO2 8WD

The column alias ACCOUNT replaces C_NO as heading for this column.

Query 4.4 'List the names, addresses and invoice details of all London customers who have outstanding invoices with invoice amounts over 100 pounds'.

```
1  SELECT TITLE, INITS, SNAME, STREET, CITY, POSTC,
2     INV_NO, INV_DATE, AMOUNT
3  FROM CUS A, INVOICE B
4  WHERE A.C_NO  = B.C_NO
5  AND  CITY = 'London'
6  AND  AMOUNT  > 100;
```

This query contains two additional conditions: firstly that only London based customers are to be considered and secondly that only invoices with values over 100 pounds need be considered. Each of the conditions in lines 4 and 5 relates to a column in one of the tables.

Query 4.5 'For each employee, list out the jobs which will give him or her a standard salary higher than his or her current salary'.

```
1  SELECT *
2  FROM EMPLOYEE2, JOB
3  WHERE STD_SALARY  > SALARY;
```

The queries so far have all had a single join criterion involving equality. In the following example a 'greater than' join is performed. Suppose the EMPLOYEE2 and JOB tables are:

| EMPLOYEE2 | | | JOB | |
| --------- | | | --- | |

E_NO	NAME	SALARY	DESCR	STD_SALARY
1	Alan	10000	Clerk	9000
2	Bill	20000	Accountant	18000
3	Carol	30000	Manager	25000

This will give every combination of employee and job details where the STD_SALARY is greater than the current salary for that employee and thus may be of some use to a personnel department in discussions with employees about their possible career paths. The output is as follows:

E_NO	NAME	SALARY	DESCR	STD_SALARY
1	Alan	10000	Accountant	18000
1	Alan	10000	Manager	25000
2	Bill	20000	Manager	25000

Note that no column name qualifiers or aliases are required since there are no common column names in the two tables. The output indicates that Alan has two choices of jobs with higher salaries than his, Bill has just one, and for Carol there is no job with a higher standard salary than her own.

Query 4.6 'For each employee show all employees who are earning a higher salary'.

Assuming the same database as for the previous query, only one table, EMPLOYEE2, needs to be accessed since that is the source of all current salary data. For each employee it is required to inspect the salary of every other employee in the table to see if any of those employees receives a higher salary. The table is being used in two different ways and one way the SQL user can deal with this is to use a 'self-join' where the table is notionally joined to itself - every row to every other row - in the fashion of a cartesian product on a single table, and then only those rows where the second salary is higher than the first are selected for output.

Another way to view what is going on in the SQL self-join, as with all joins, is to imagine a pointer pointing to rows in each table; the pointer to the first table starts by pointing to the first row and while it is there, the pointer to rows in the second table 'scans' the second table row by row, checking to see if the join and all other criteria on the second table have been satisfied and if so putting a copy of the first table's row and a copy of the second table's matching row to the output. With the self-join the 'first' and 'second' tables can be imagined as separate but identical tables although of course there is only one table. The query SQL is as follows:

```
1  SELECT *
2  FROM EMPLOYEE2 A, EMPLOYEE2 B
3  WHERE B.SALARY > A.SALARY;
```

with the resulting output:

E_NO	NAME	SALARY	E_NO	NAME	SALARY
1	Alan	10000	2	Bill	20000
1	Alan	10000	3	Carol	30000
2	Bill	20000	3	Carol	30000

Again, Carol has nobody with a salary higher than hers and is presumably looking for a new job.

Query 4.7 'List out all employees who are earning more than their manager'.

Suppose there is a table on the database like this:

EMPLOYEE3

- - - - - - - - -

EMP_NO	NAME	SALARY	MGR_NO
1	Audrey	10000	3
2	Betty	20000	4
3	Carol	15000	2
4	Denise	15000	7
7	Erica	20000	

The table shows what people are earning and also who their managers are. It is assumed that MGR_NO is the same 'domain' as EMP_NO, so that every manager will have an employee row in this table. For example employee 1 has manager 3 who in turn has an employee row with EMP_NO = 3. In simple terms, the MGR_NO shown is someone's EMP_NO. Note that Erica does not have a manager so MGR_NO in her row is null.

Rows of the table have to be compared with other rows in the same table, i.e. an employee's salary with his or her manager's salary. One way to achieve this is to use a self-join. (Another way is to use a subquery - see Chapter 5). It is helpful to imagine what an ideal table for this query would look like. It would simply contain for each employee his or her salary and the manager's.

EMP_NO	NAME	SALARY	MGR_SALARY
1	Audrey	10000	15000 etc.

It would then be simple to select out the required rows. The following SQL statement does precisely that:

```
1  SELECT A.*, B.NAME, B.SALARY
2  FROM EMPLOYEE3 A, EMPLOYEE3 B
3  WHERE A.MGR_NO = B.EMP_NO
4  AND   A.SALARY > B.SALARY;
```

Line 1 asks for all the A columns and just name and salary of the B 'copy'
of the table, i.e. of the manager. The output is as follows:

EMP_NO	NAME	SALARY	MGR_NO	NAME	SALARY
2	Betty	20000	4	Denise	15000

Suppose the data in the table EMPLOYEE3 had been as follows:

EMPLOYEE3

EMP_NO	NAME	SALARY	MGR_NO
1	Audrey	10000	3
2	Betty	20000	
3	Carol	15000	2
	Denise	15000	7
7	Erica	20000	

Note that MGR_NO for Betty and EMP_NO for Denise are now null.
The effect of the same SQL query would now be that no rows would have
been selected for output. The reason for this was covered in Chapter 3
where it was stated that the effect of comparing a null with another null
is null and rows can only be joined if the join criterion (here,
A.MGR_NO = B.EMP_NO) is TRUE.

4.4 SELECTING DATA FROM MORE THAN TWO TABLES

For more complex queries than those covered so far, it is sometimes
necessary to access data from three or more database tables. The rules are
similar to the situation with two tables. Every table used is mentioned in
the FROM clause of the SELECT command, and join criteria for
matching rows from the tables to be joined must appear in the WHERE

clause. The join criteria often, but not always, involve the use of foreign keys where the value of a primary key in one table is matched with the same value of a foreign key in another table. Many of the examples below involve the tables CUS, INVOICE and PAYMENT, which are detailed in the Appendix and reproduced here for convenience:

CUS

C_NO	TITLE	SNAME	INITS	STREET	CITY	POSTC	CRED_LIM	BALANCE
1	Mr	Sallaway	G.R.	12 Fax Rd	London	WC1	1000	42.56
2	Miss	Lauri	P.	5 Dux St	London	N1	500	200
3	Mr	Jackson	R.	2 Lux Ave	Leeds	LE1 2AB	500	510
4	Mr	Dziduch	M.	31 Low St	Dover	DO2 9CD	100	149.23
5	Ms	Woods	S.Q.	17 Nax Rd	London	E18 4WW	1000	250.1
6	Mrs	Williams	C.	41 Cax St	Dover	DO2 8WD		412.21

INVOICE

INV_NO	C_NO	INV_DATE	AMOUNT
940	1	5-DEC-90	26.2
1002	4	12-JAN-91	149.23
1003	1	12-JAN-91	16.26
1004	2	14-JAN-91	200
1005	3	20-JAN-91	510
1006	5	21-JAN-91	250.1
1017	6	22-JAN-91	412.21

PAYMENT

- - - - - - -

INV_NO	PMT_NO	PMT_DATE	AMOUNT
940	2	12-DEC-90	13
1005	1	14-JAN-91	510
1017	1	30-JAN-91	100
940	3	19-JAN-91	10

Query 4.8 'List the account codes, names, and invoice payments for all customers'.

```
1  SELECT A.C_NO, SNAME, B.INV_NO, B.AMOUNT,
2    PMT_NO, PMT_DATE, C.AMOUNT
3  FROM  CUS A, INVOICE B, PAYMENT C
4  WHERE A.C_NO  = B.C_NO
5  AND   B.INV_NO  = C.INV_NO;
```

The output from this query is as follows:

C_NO	SNAME	INV_NO	AMOUNT	PMT_NO	PMT_DATE	AMOUNT
1	Sallaway	940	26.2	2	12-DEC-90	13
1	Sallaway	940	26.2	3	19-JAN-91	10
3	Jackson	1005	510	1	14-JAN-91	510
6	Williams	1017	412.21	1	30-JAN-91	100

Firstly consider the query itself. In line 1, the table alias qualifiers in A.C_NO and B.INV_NO are necessary because these column names appear in two tables and without them SQL would give an 'ambiguity' error. In the CUS table C_NO is the primary key and in the INVOICE table C_NO is a foreign key indicating the one-to-many relationship between the CUS entity type and the INVOICE entity type as discussed in Chapter 2. One customer can be sent many invoices but a given (one) invoice is sent to only one customer.

There is a similar one-to-many relationship between INVOICE and PAYMENT, because in the company using this database, one invoice can have many payments (instalments) but one payment is allowed to cover (i.e. is allocated to) only one invoice. Hence this relationship between INVOICE and PAYMENT can be shown by the primary key INV_NO in the INVOICE table appearing as a foreign key in PAYMENT.

The reason for the table alias qualifier 'B.' in B.AMOUNT in line 1 of the query is slightly different. There are two identically named AMOUNT columns in the INVOICE and PAYMENT tables. The meanings of the two AMOUNT columns is however different. In the INVOICE table, AMOUNT means the invoice amount, i.e. the value of the bill sent to the customer, whereas AMOUNT in the PAYMENT table is the value of the payment made by the customer in response to the invoice. This double meaning for a column name causes no problems in practice since the column name can always be qualified by the table name to remove any ambiguity and this is the reason for the 'B.' qualifier in line 1 and the 'C.' qualifier for AMOUNT in line 2 of this query. The table alias names A, B and C are established in line 3 (yes, *after* their use in lines 1 and 2) and the join criteria established in lines 4 and 5.

Now referring to the output obtained from this query, notice that customer Sallaway appears twice because he has made two payments (both against invoice number 940) in this accounting period. The other two customers Jackson and Williams appear once because they both have a single invoice with a single payment associated with each. What is interesting about the output is the data that does NOT appear. Firstly, only three of the six customers appear. Secondly, only three of the seven invoices appear. Why? The answer is clear when the mechanism of the inner join is considered.

In line 4, which is used for joining rows from the CUS and INVOICE tables, it is possible to imagine the temporary result before the matching PAYMENT rows are joined on in line 5.

C.NO	SNAME	INV_NO	AMOUNT
1	Sallaway	940	26.2
1	Sallaway	1003	16.36

2	Lauri	1004	200
3	Jackson	1005	510
4	Dziduch	1002	149.23
5	Woods	1006	250.1
6	Williams	1017	412.21

Every customer account appears in this intermediate result because every customer happens to have at least one outstanding invoice. If any customer did not have an outstanding invoice, that customer's details would be eliminated at this stage because the join criterion of line 4 would not have been satisfied. This probably conforms to the sense of the (fairly vague) English version of the query shown above. Customer Sallaway appears twice because he has two outstanding invoices.

The next step in the SQL query is to join the payment details onto this intermediate result and this is performed in line 5. The join criterion in line 5 says that in order for a row from this intermediate result to be passed to the output, B.INV_NO, which is column 3 in the intermediate result, should match with a C.INV_NO in the PAYMENT table. The INV_NO of the first row of the intermediate result matches with the INV_NO of the first row of the PAYMENT table (both equal to 940) so a joined row consisting of the columns mentioned in lines 1 and 2 of the query are passed to the output. The second row of PAYMENT also matches the first row of the intermediate result so the projected columns of these rows are also joined, forming the second row of the output. There are no further payments for invoice 940 so the 'pointer' to the intermediate result table is incremented to point to its second row (INV_NO =1003). There are *no* matches in the PAYMENT table for this intermediate table row so the row is abandoned and produces no output. Thus the invoice details of Sallaway's invoice number 1003 are lost and are eliminated from the output. Similarly, the intermediate data for Lauri, Dziduch and Woods is eliminated from the output because none of them has a payment to his or her credit.

It is not certain whether this was what was wanted when the English query was formulated since it is rather vague. If the query had been put in the form:

'List all current invoice and payment details for all of our customers'

then this SQL form of the query would definitely *not* be correct since:

1. Any customer with no current invoices would not be
   output, and more importantly

2. Invoice details for any customer with current invoices
   having no payments would not be output.

It is easy to see the shortcomings of this SQL query by inspecting the small amount of data in the tables, but as is emphasized elsewhere in this book, spotting errors this way cannot be relied upon when large tables are being queried. The remedy is, as always, found by a combination of:

1. A thorough understanding of the operation of SQL, and

2. Thorough desk checking of the query output using
   carefully chosen test data.

Inspection of important queries by a critical programming colleague can also prove helpful. One of the disadvantages of a powerful programming language like SQL is that more mistakes can be made more quickly. On the positive side, it is usually considerably easier to comprehend the logic of an SQL query than that of a program written in a procedural language such as COBOL, FORTRAN, PASCAL or C, and a good SQL programmer will generally get results faster than a good 3GL programmer.

Getting the *correct* output for this query involves the use of the outer join, which is covered in Section 4.5.

The next example concerns the join of a table to itself twice - a three-way self-join. Consider the table GROUPS which shows the make-up of some computing workshop groups in term 1 and term 2. Each workshop group has three members.

Query 4.9 'Produce a listing showing the composition of each workshop group for terms 1 and 2'.

The GROUPS table is as follows:

GROUPS

TERM	GROUP_NO	MEMBER
1	1	1
1	1	2
1	1	3
1	2	4
1	2	5
1	2	6
2	10	3
2	10	2
2	10	9
2	1	5
2	1	7
2	1	8

```
1 SELECT A.TERM, A.GROUP_NO,
2   A.MEMBER, B.MEMBER, C.MEMBER
3 FROM GROUPS A, GROUPS B, GROUPS C
4 WHERE A.TERM = B.TERM
5 AND   A.GROUP_NO  = B.GROUP_NO
6 AND   B.TERM = C.TERM
7 AND   B.GROUP_NO  = C.GROUP_NO
8 AND   A.MEMBER  <  B.MEMBER
9 AND   B.MEMBER  <  C.MEMBER;
```

The output appears as follows:

TERM	GROUP_NO	MEMBER	MEMBER	MEMBER
1	1	1	2	3
1	2	4	5	6
2	1	5	7	8
2	10	2	3	9

This is similar in principle to the previous 2-way self-join and there should be no surprises in query lines 1 to 7. The purpose of the inequalities in lines 8 and 9 is to prevent duplication of output rows which differ only in having the members in a different order. Otherwise rows like the following would be output:

TERM	GROUP_NO	MEMBER	MEMBER	MEMBER	
1	1	1	2	3	
1	1	1	3	2	etc.

Without the inequalities, identical rows in table GROUPS would also join, giving output rows such as:

TERM	GROUP_NO	MEMBER	MEMBER	MEMBER	
1	1	1	1	1	etc.

because every group member is clearly in the same group as him or herself. The case where there are not always three members in a group presents difficulties in formulating the correct SQL query and is left for a later example. (See Chapter 9, Case Study 2).

4.5 THE OUTER JOIN

Suppose it was required to perform the following query:

Query 4.10 'List out all the departments and their associated
employees'

and the following tables exist on the database:

```
DEPARTMENT                    EMPLOYEE4
- - - - - - - - - -           - - - - - - - - -
```

DEPT_NO	DEPT_NAME
1	Sales
2	R and D
3	Billing

EMP_NO	NAME	DEPT_NO
1	Alan	3
2	Bill	1
3	Corin	3
4	Dennis	1

Assume that if a department at present may have no employees then it is still required to list that department's details. If the following SQL SELECT command were issued:

```
1  SELECT A.DEPT_NO,  DEPT_NAME, EMP_NO, NAME
2  FROM DEPARTMENT A, EMPLOYEE4 B
3  WHERE A.DEPT_NO  = B.DEPT_NO;
```

then the output would be:

DEPT_NO	DEPT_NAME	EMP_NO	NAME
1	Sales	2	Bill
1	Sales	4	Dennis
3	Billing	1	Alan
3	Billing	3	Corin

This is a conventional natural join. Note that there are no details of the R and D department because that row in DEPARTMENT had no rows in EMPLOYEE4 to join with. This is the type of problem that the outer join was designed to deal with. In ORACLE SQL*PLUS there is a built-in outer join which is called up by slightly modifying the join criterion in the WHERE clause. The problem here was that the R and D department had no EMPLOYEE4 row to join up with. The remedy is to add the symbol (+)after the column or columns in the table which might prevent a row join by not having any matching rows. In this example the SQL query is modified as follows:

```
1  SELECT A.DEPT_NO, DEPT_NAME, EMP_NO, NAME
2  FROM DEPARTMENT A, EMPLOYEE4 B
3  WHERE A.DEPT_NO  = B.DEPT_NO  ( + );
```

The symbol (+)has been added to the join column in the EMPLOYEE4 table because this is the table that might have no matches for a given row in the other table. The output produced by this modified query is:

```
DEPT_NO  DEPT_NAME   EMP_NO  NAME
-------  ---------   ------  ----
      1  Sales            2  Bill
      1  Sales            4  Dennis
      2  R and D
      3  Billing          1  Alan
      3  Billing          3  Corin
```

which gives details of the R and D department even though there are no employees in that department. The (+)symbol tells SQL*PLUS to treat the EMPLOYEE4 table as if it contained an additional all-null row and to join this row to any row in DEPARTMENT which cannot find a match.

Query 4.11 'List out all departments with no employees'.

Notice that in the above result all the columns for the R and D department which came from the imaginary null row in EMPLOYEE4 are in fact null. This gives an easy way to answer this query:

```
1  SELECT A.DEPT_NO, DEPT_NAME, EMP_NO, NAME
2  FROM DEPARTMENT A, EMPLOYEE4 B
3  WHERE A.DEPT_NO  = B.DEPT_NO  ( + )
4  AND B.DEPT_NO  IS NULL;
```

Any of the columns in EMPLOYEE4 could have been used in line 4 because they are all null. The output is:

```
DEPT_NO  DEPT_NAME   EMP_NO  NAME
-------  ---------   ------  ----
      2  R and D
```

There is an alternative SQL query which could have been used here which involves the use of NOT EXISTS in a subquery. See Chapter 7 for examples. In query 4.8, which concerns the joining of the three tables CUS, INVOICE and PAYMENT, it was noted that the SQL query used there had the undesirable property of omitting from the output certain vital data. The query is restated here:

Query 4.12 'List all current invoice and payment details for all
of our customers'.

Details of all invoices with no payments were lost from the output. In the case where the only invoices sent to a customer were as yet unpaid, the customer details were also omitted from the output. Since the probable use of the output data would be to prepare monthly Statements of Accounts for customers, that query would result in customers only receiving acknowledgement of their payments and the reminder aspect of the statement would be lost. The remedy for this problem is the outer join with the (+)being applied to the PAYMENT table. To restate the effect of the outer join, an 'all null' row is appended to the PAYMENT table with the special property that it will join to any INVOICE row that can't find a matching PAYMENT. The 'all null' row is of course not actually appended. This is simply a useful way of describing the action of the outer join. See Query 4.8. The modified query is:

```
1 SELECT A.C_NO, SNAME, B.INV_NO, B.AMOUNT,
2   PMT_NO, PMT_DATE, C.AMOUNT
3 FROM  CUS A, INVOICE B, PAYMENT C
4 WHERE A.C_NO  = B.C_NO
5 AND   B.INV_NO  = C.INV_NO  (+);
```

The only change is the addition of the (+). The output from this query is now as follows:

C_NO	SNAME	INV_NO	AMOUNT	PMT_NO	PMT_DATE	AMOUNT
----	-----	------	------	------	--------	------
1	Sallaway	940	26.2	2	12-DEC-90	13
1	Sallaway	940	26.2	3	19-JAN-91	10
1	Sallaway	1003	16.36			
2	Lauri	1004	200			
3	Jackson	1005	510	1	14-JAN-91	510
4	Dziduch	1002	149.23			
5	Woods	1006	250.1			
6	Williams	1017	412.21	1	30-JAN-91	100

All six customers and seven invoices are now accounted for. In the unlikely event of a statement being required for customers with *no* outstanding invoices, a (+) would be appended to line 4.

4.6 EXERCISES

1. Write an SQL statement to list details of all PRODUCTs and their deliveries (DELIVERY table) .

2. Write an SQL statement to list details of all PRODUCTs which have *not* had deliveries. Use an outer join.

3. Write an SQL SELECT statement to find the *median* of a column of numbers.

Chapter 5

SELECT with Subqueries

5.1 INTRODUCTION

SQL contains the facility for nesting one SELECT command within another. The nested SELECT is called a subquery and it appears in parentheses in the WHERE clause of the outer SELECT statement as shown in Fig 5.1.

```
SELECT ...          <---  Outer Query
FROM   ...
WHERE  ...
[AND    ...]...
   (SELECT  ...      <---  Subquery
FROM    ...
WHERE   ... ) ;
```

Fig. 5.1 The Position of an SQL Subquery

The purpose of the subquery is to specify selection criteria for selecting some rows (or groups when used with HAVING) from the table or tables mentioned in the outer SELECT statement. In previous chapters, the selection criteria in the WHERE (and HAVING) clauses were comparisons between column values (and aggregated column values in the case of HAVING) and *constants*.

  The subquery consists of a SELECT statement which will retrieve a set of values from one or more tables in the database. It is *these* values which are then used in the selection criteria of the outer SELECT's WHERE or HAVING clause to determine which rows from the tables in the outer select (or from the intermediate grouped values in the case of HAVING) will appear at the output. Subqueries are in practice, for many programmers, a more 'natural' alternative to the join and there are some situations in which there is no alternative to using a subquery. There are also some situations in which there is no alternative to using a join. Joins and subqueries can be inter-mixed. One important restriction in the use of subqueries is that the values selected by the subquery do not themselves appear at the output; they are simply used as part of the selection criteria of the outer SELECT. Fig. 5.2 gives more detail with regard to the syntax of subqueries. In both Fig. 5.1 and Fig. 5.2, only the WHERE selection criteria are shown; very similar syntax is used when a subquery is used to filter *groups* using HAVING. Examples of both appear below.

```
(a)  SELECT ...
     FROM   ...
     WHERE  col-exprn {comparison [ALL|ANY] | IN | NOT IN }
      (SELECT ...
       FROM   ...
       WHERE  ...
       [GROUP BY ...]
       [HAVING   ...]) ;


(b)  SELECT ...
     FROM   ...
     WHERE  {EXISTS | NOT EXISTS}
      (SELECT ...
       FROM   ...
       WHERE  ... )
     [GROUP BY ...]
     [HAVING  ...]
     [ORDER BY ...] ;
```

Fig. 5.2 The Detailed Format of Subqueries

The second format which uses the EXISTS and NOT EXISTS constructs is covered in Chapter 7. Only the first format (Fig. 5.2(a)) is discussed in the present chapter.

The subquery is considered as part of the WHERE (or HAVING)

clause of the outer SELECT and the outer SELECT may continue after the subquery's closing parenthesis with the usual GROUP BY, HAVING and ORDER BY clauses. An ORDER BY must not be included in the subquery itself. The 'comparison' is '=' or '<' or '>' or '>=' or '<=' or '!='.

If ALL, ANY, IN or NOT IN are included, then the subquery is expected to return a *set* of one or more values from a single column in the subquery. If none of these terms appears, then the subquery must return a *single* value. ORACLE SQL*PLUS has a useful additional feature which allows more than one column to be returned from the subquery and compared to corresponding columns in the outer query. There is an example of this below.

The WHERE and HAVING clauses in the subquery may themselves contain further subqueries. It is usual in most queries for the nesting of subqueries to go no further than four or five deep. Subqueries can be used as an alternative to joins in navigating around a database where the query is required to span several entity types in the logical schema. There are examples of this in Chapter 9 where queries requiring movement between diverse entity types (usually via foreign keys) are discussed. In such cases the utility of having the Entity Relationship schema diagram available cannot be over-emphasized.

The normal procedure is to join adjacent tables in the navigation path by equating the primary key on the 'one' side of a one-to-many relationship with the corresponding foreign key on the 'many' side.

As a matter of interest, the SQL query interpreter, in its attempt to optimize the sequence of database search operations required, may convert SQL subqueries into joins as one of its early translation steps. All of the above points are demonstrated in the following examples.

5.2 SIMPLE SUBQUERIES AND THEIR JOIN EQUIVALENTS

Query 5.1 'List out the employees in the EMPLOYEE table who are in the same department as Karen'.

The EMPLOYEE table is as follows:

```
EMPLOYEE
--------


EMP_NO  NAME     AGE  DEPARTMENT
------  ----     ---  ----------
     1  Judy     23   Billing
     2  Madge    27   Accounts
     4  Karen    19   Billing
     3  Terence  42   Billing
     5  Grace    25   Accounts
```

The answer to this query could be obtained by first querying the EMPLOYEE table to establish which department Karen works in and then querying the same table again:

1 SELECT DEPARTMENT
2 FROM EMPLOYEE
3 WHERE NAME = 'Karen' ;   giving:

```
DEPARTMENT
----------
Billing
```

and then:

1 SELECT NAME
2 FROM EMPLOYEE
3 WHERE DEPARTMENT = 'Billing';

which gives the answer to the query:

```
NAME
----
Judy
Karen
Terence
```

Notice that 'Karen' appears in the output, since she is of course in the same department as herself! Instead of having to type two queries, a single query containing a subquery can be employed:

```
1  SELECT NAME
2  FROM EMPLOYEE
3  WHERE DEPARTMENT =
4   (SELECT DEPARTMENT
5    FROM EMPLOYEE
6    WHERE NAME = 'Karen') ;
```

with identical results.

Lines 4 to 6 are the subquery, which must be enclosed in parentheses as shown. The subquery must be executed before the outer query so that it can deliver the value 'Billing' to the outer query's WHERE clause. This simple example illustrates the basic flavour of SQL subqueries. Note that the value 'Billing' from the subquery never appears at the output; it is simply used in the selection criteria of the outer query. This is true no matter how deep the level of nesting in a query; only the outer query delivers values to the output.

  This is not the only way to implement the query. There are often several ways of formulating SQL code for a given query. The same result could have been obtained here if the following self-join form of the query had been used:

```
1  SELECT B.NAME
2  FROM EMPLOYEE A, EMPLOYEE B
3  WHERE A.DEPARTMENT = B.DEPARTMENT
4  AND   A.NAME = 'Karen' ;
```

This just does a notional self-join on EMPLOYEE on department and then selects out rows where the first name is 'Karen'. The form of the query that is used - either subquery or join - is a matter of programming style. Most SQL programmers seem to prefer the subquery form, probably because the question of what is to be output (outer SELECT) is separated from the question of the selection criteria (inner SELECT). Notice also the absence of table aliases in the subquery version.

Query 5.2 'List out details of all products which have had deliveries'.

The data required is contained in the two tables:

PRODUCT

PROD_NO	DESCR	QIS	MINQ	REORDQ	PRICE
1	Bat	10	5	10	12
2	Ball	5	5	20	2
3	Hoop	3	5	10	3
4	Net	2	5	10	20
5	Rope	1	10	10	6

DELIVERY

C_NO	PROD_NO	QTY	DEL_DATE
3	2	2	3-NOV-90
3	1	3	3-NOV-90
1	4	6	7-NOV-90
5	3	4	12-NOV-90
3	3	1	12-NOV-90

Notice that PROD_NO in the DELIVERY table is a foreign key from PRODUCT. See Fig. 5.3. The query is as follows:

```
1 SELECT *
2 FROM PRODUCT
3 WHERE PROD_NO IN
```

4   (SELECT PROD_NO
5   FROM DELIVERY);

and the result is:

PROD_NO	DESCR	QIS	MINQ	REORDQ	PRICE
1	Bat	10	5	10	12
2	Ball	5	5	20	2
3	Hoop	3	5	10	3
4	Net	2	5	10	20

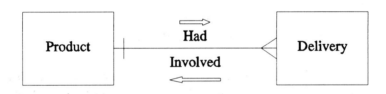

Fig. 5.3 Product-Had-Delivery

In this example the subquery is addressing a different table from the outer query. The IN operator has been covered in Section 3.4.4. It 'expects' a list of values to follow it. These values are used to help select rows in the outer query's table. The subquery is executed first and delivers the list of values (2,1,4,3,3) from the DELIVERY table because this is the set of products that have been delivered. The value of PROD_NO in each row of the PRODUCT table is checked to see if it is contained in this set of values and if it is, the PRODUCT row is output.

(2,1,4,3,3) is not, strictly speaking, a set since it contains a duplicate.

This does little harm in practice and will not affect the output from the query, since if any number is IN (2,1,4,3) then it is also IN (2,1,4,3,3). This duplication within the set can easily be removed using a DISTINCT in the subquery:

```
1  SELECT *
2  FROM PRODUCT
3  WHERE PROD_NO  IN
4   (SELECT DISTINCT  PROD_NO
5    FROM DELIVERY);
```

Note that this query could also have been implemented relatively simply as a join:

```
1  SELECT DISTINCT A.*
2  FROM PRODUCT A, DELIVERY B
3  WHERE A.PROD_NO  = B.PROD_NO;
```

The DISTINCT is necessary here because some products may have been delivered twice (as already discussed) and this would have resulted in those PRODUCT rows being output twice. DISTINCT simply removes any duplicate output rows.

Query 5.3 'List out details of all products which have had no
          deliveries'.

The only change required compared with the previous query is to replace IN with NOT IN since what the query will now need to output is all products in the PRODUCTS whose product number does *not* appear in the list of product numbers in DELIVERY:

```
1  SELECT *
2  FROM PRODUCT
3  WHERE PROD_NO  NOT IN
4   (SELECT PROD_NO
5    FROM DELIVERY);
```

The output is of course:

```
PROD_NO DESCR  QIS MINQ REORDQ PRICE
------- -----  --- ---- ------ -----
      5 Rope     1   10     10     6
```

The join version of this query has to be an outer join:

1   SELECT A.*
2   FROM PRODUCT A, DELIVERY B
3   WHERE A.PROD_NO = B.PROD_NO (+)
4   AND B.PROD_NO IS NULL ;

(+) indicates an *outer* join. All PRODUCT and DELIVERY rows with
matching product number are joined and then (this is the outer join part)
any row in PRODUCT with no corresponding row in DELIVERY is
joined onto nulls and appended to the join result. It is these rows that are
required by this query - the non-matching ones - and they are selected
exclusively for output by line 4. This form of the outer join will work only
in ORACLE SQL*PLUS. INGRES SQL (and SQL*PLUS) could achieve
the same effect using a UNION and a NOT EXISTS (See Chapter 7).
This join version of the query is probably not as obvious in meaning to
most programmers or other SQL users as is the subquery version above.
  It is possible to have subqueries with joins in the outer SELECT. For
example:

Query 5.4 'List the customer names and invoice amounts for
          invoices which have been paid in January'.

Clearly, CUS and INVOICE and PAYMENT must all be consulted to
satisfy this query. See Fig. 5.4.

Refer to the Appendix for the table descriptions of CUS, INVOICE and
PAYMENT if required.

One subquery version of the query is as follows:

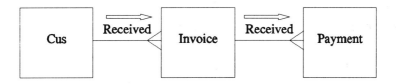

Fig. 5.4 CUS-INV-PMT

1 SELECT INITS, SNAME, AMOUNT
2 FROM CUS, INVOICE
3 WHERE CUS.C_NO = INVOICE.C_NO
4 AND INV_NO IN
5 (SELECT INV_NO
6   FROM PAYMENT
7   WHERE PMT_DATE BETWEEN '1-jan-90' AND '31-jan-91');

The two tables CUS and INVOICE are joined in the outer SELECT *since outputs are required from both tables*. If any PAYMENT details, such as the payment amount for example, had been required to be output then all the tables would have had to be joined since no data from a subquery can be output, as already mentioned. This is a situation in which a join must be used instead of a subquery.

  The subquery in lines 5 to 7 specifies the set of invoice numbers to be considered by inspecting the payment dates. The relevant set of invoice numbers delivered by the subquery is (940, 1005, 1017). The 'owners' of these invoices are Sallaway, Jackson and Williams. The output from the whole query is thus:

```
INITS  SNAME      AMOUNT

-----  -----      ------

Mr     Sallaway    26.2

Mr     Jackson     510

Mrs    Williams   412.21
```

It is also possible to have joins in the subquery part:

Query 5.5 'List the names of all customers who have made a
       payment before the invoice was sent'.

The general strategy in this query is to join the INVOICE and
PAYMENT tables in the subquery so that the invoice and payment dates
can be compared. The selected customer numbers are then fed to the
outer query so the customer names can be output from the CUS table.
The resulting SQL query is thus:

```
1  SELECT SNAME
2  FROM CUS
3  WHERE C_NO  IN
4   (SELECT C_NO
5    FROM INVOICE, PAYMENT
6    WHERE INVOICE.INV_NO  =  PAYMENT.INV_NO
7    AND PMT_DATE  <  INV_DATE);
```

The subquery uses a join (equijoin) of tables INVOICE and PAYMENT
on INV_NO so that the invoice and payment dates can be compared, and
it delivers to the outer query the set of customer numbers (3) since this
is the only customer who has paid before he was asked. The output is:

```
SNAME
- - - - -
Jackson
```

because the payment date of payment number 1 of invoice number 1005
is earlier than its invoice date. The join in this example could have been
replaced by another nested subquery.

   Note that, as in query 5.4, if it was required to output the invoice and/or
payment details relating to this query, this would not be possible using a
subquery since, as already stated, data retrieved in the subquery cannot
be output. The only data that can be output comes from the outer query.
There would be no such restriction in the case of the full join version:

```
1 SELECT SNAME, B.INV_NO,  INV_DATE,  PMT_DATE
2 FROM CUS A, INVOICE B, PAYMENT C
3 WHERE A.C_NO  =  B.C_NO
4 AND   B.INV_NO  =  C.INV_NO
5 AND   INV_DATE  >  PMT_DATE;
```

which gives:

```
SNAME           INV_NO  INV_DATE    PMT_DATE

-----           ------  --------    --------

Jackson           1005  20-JAN-91   14-JAN-91
```

It is sometimes useful to be able to return *more* than one column from
the subquery:

Query 5.6 'List employees in the EMPLOYEE1 table who have the
       same job in the same department as employee 12'.

The EMPLOYEE1 table contains the following data:

```
EMPLOYEE1

---------


DEPARTMENT   EMPLOYEE_NO   JOB_DESCRIPTION

----------   -----------   ---------------

        1            12    Fitter
        1            19    Turner
        1            14    Fitter
        1            20    Miller
        2             6    Turner
        2            17    Miller
        2            21    Miller
```

The SQL query is:

```
1  SELECT *
2  FROM EMPLOYEE1
3  WHERE (DEPARTMENT, JOB_DESCRIPTION)  =
4    (SELECT DEPARTMENT, JOB_DESCRIPTION
5     FROM EMPLOYEE1
6     WHERE EMPLOYEE_NO  =  12);
```

The resulting output is:

```
DEPARTMENT  EMPLOYEE_NO  JOB_DES
----------  -----------  -------
         1           12  Fitter
         1           14  Fitter
```

In this query the subquery returns two columns, which are then compared with the respective columns in the outer query.

This ability to return more than one column in a subquery is available only in ORACLE SQL*PLUS. However it is possible to obtain the same result without using this implementation-specific feature by utilizing a join, in this case a self-join:

```
1  SELECT A.DEPARTMENT, A.EMPLOYEE_NO,
2    A.JOB_DESCRIPTION
3  FROM EMPLOYEE1 A, EMPLOYEE1 B
4  WHERE A.DEPARTMENT = B.DEPARTMENT
5  AND   A.JOB_DESCRIPTION  = B.JOB_DESCRIPTION
6  AND   B.EMPLOYEE_NO  = 12 ;
```

5.3 ANY and ALL

These options are best demonstrated by examples.

Query 5.7 'List out the details of all employees in EMPLOYEE3 who are not receiving the maximum salary'.

The idea is that a given employee's details will be output if it is possible to find ANY employee who receives a higher salary. The data is:

EMPLOYEE3

EMP_NO	NAME	SALARY	MGR_NO
1	Audrey	10000	3
2	Betty	20000	4
3	Carol	15000	2
4	Denise	15000	7
5	Erica	20000	

One way of writing the SQL version of this query is:

```
1  SELECT *
2  FROM EMPLOYEE3
3  WHERE SALARY < ANY
4  (SELECT SALARY
5    FROM EMPLOYEE3);
```

which gives the following result:

EMP_NO	NAME	SALARY	MGR_NO
1	Audrey	10000	3
3	Carol	15000	2
4	Denise	15000	7

Betty and Erica are removed from the output because there are no employees who receive a lower salary than they do. The operation of the ANY is to output a row from the outer query wherever there is AT LEAST ONE row in the subquery which makes the selection criterion TRUE. Here, for Audrey, for example, there is at least one employee (e.g. Betty but also Carol and Denise) who receives a higher salary.

In spoken language the phrase 'less than any' may be given a similar meaning to 'less than all'. Care must be taken in formulating SQL queries using ANY and ALL that their precise meaning in SQL is understood. It can be argued that one of the responsibilities of an analyst-programmer is to clarify this type of imprecision in normal language.

Since the difference between the functioning of the SQL versions of ANY and ALL is often misunderstood (probably, as stated, because of fuzziness of their usage in spoken language), another example of the use of ANY follows.

Query 5.8 'List details of all employees in EMPLOYEE3 for whom there is AT LEAST ONE employee who does not receive the same salary'.

The SQL query is:

```
1  SELECT *
2  FROM EMPLOYEE3
3  WHERE SALARY ! =   ANY
4   (SELECT SALARY
5    FROM EMPLOYEE3);
```

The resulting output is:

EMP_NO	NAME	SALARY	MGR_NO
1	Audrey	10000	3
2	Betty	20000	4
3	Carol	15000	2
4	Denise	15000	7
5	Erica	20000	

which is the whole EMPLOYEE3 table. The reason is of course that unless all salaries are the same, there will always be *at least one* employee who does not receive the same salary as a given employee. Returning now to Query 5.7 (reproduced here as Query 5.9), it is probably worthwhile demonstrating an alternative SQL formulation.

Query 5.9 'List out the details of all employees in EMPLOYEE3
who are not receiving the maximum salary'.

```
1  SELECT *
2  FROM EMPLOYEE3
3  WHERE SALARY ! =
4  (SELECT MAX(SALARY)
5    FROM EMPLOYEE3);
```

which has identical output to Query 5.7's SQL command but seems a
clearer formulation. It is difficult to see how this query could be
implemented using a join instead of a subquery. This is left as an exercise
for the reader.

ALL is quite different in its operation from ANY and is more intuitively
obvious in its function. Staying with the EMPLOYEE3 table, consider the
following query.

Query 5.10 'List details of all employees in table EMPLOYEE3
who earn the maximum salary'.

The SQL is:

```
1  SELECT *
2  FROM EMPLOYEE3
3  WHERE SALARY > = ALL
4  (SELECT SALARY
5    FROM EMPLOYEE3);
```

with the output:

```
EMP_NO  NAME    SALARY  MGR_NO
------  ----    ------  ------
     2  Betty   20000       4
     5  Erica   20000
```

Betty and Erica earn the maximum salary. For each of them, their salary is greater than or equal to ALL employees in the table. If the ' > = ' had been replaced by a ' > ', no rows would have been selected because in order to have a salary higher than ALL employees in the table, they would have had to earn a higher salary than themselves! An alternative formulation for this query is of course:

```
1  SELECT *
2  FROM EMPLOYEE3
3  WHERE SALARY =
4   (SELECT MAX(SALARY)
5    FROM EMPLOYEE3);
```

Query 5.11 'List details of the employee in table EMPLOYEE3
              who earns more than anyone else'.

This query is clearly different from Query 5.10, since considering the EMPLOYEE3 table, there is no-one who receives a salary higher than all the rest, since Betty and Erica both receive the maximum. Consequently the correct output would be:

NO RECORDS SELECTED

Unfortunately, to convert the logic of Query 5.10 to that of Query 5.11, it would not be satisfactory to simply replace the ' > = ALL' with a ' > ALL', since, as explained above, this would entail an employee earning more than herself.

The question arises then of what the correct SQL query *should* be. Whatever the SQL query is, it must work in all realistic situations, in particular the cases where the highest salary is unique, and where it is not.

Suppose the existence of the table overleaf called EMPLOYEE5, which clearly contains very similar data.

Now Erica has been removed, Betty clearly earns more than anyone else and must appear at the output of the SQL query as the person who receives more than anyone else.

EMPLOYEE5

EMP_NO	NAME	SALARY	MGR_NO
1	Audrey	10000	3
2	Betty	20000	4
3	Carol	15000	2
4	Denise	15000	7

The correct query would have to output *no rows at all* for EMPLOYEE3 and Betty's row for EMPLOYEE5. Using '> = ALL' as in the above query would give incorrect results for the EMPLOYEE3 table since both Betty and Erica would be output. Using '> ALL' in the query would give incorrect results in the EMPLOYEE5 table since Betty does not earn more than herself. Another SQL query that might be tried is:

1 SELECT *
2 FROM EMPLOYEEn
3 WHERE SALARY >=
4   (SELECT MAX(SALARY)
5   FROM EMPLOYEEn);

'EMPLOYEEn' stands for either EMPLOYEE3 or EMPLOYEE5; the query must work correctly on both tables.

This SQL statement would output both Betty and Erica for table EMPLOYEE3, which is wrong because *no* rows should be selected. Replacing the '> =' with a '> ' would never output any rows for *any* table of this description because nobody can receive a higher salary than the maximum. This problem can be overcome by using a *correlated subquery*. See Section 5.4.

There are certain equivalences that exist between IN and ANY and ALL:

	IN	can be replaced by	=	ANY
and	NOT IN	can be replaced by	!=	ALL

So for example Query 5.2 could be written equivalently as:

```
1  SELECT *
2  FROM PRODUCT
3  WHERE PROD_NO  =  ANY
4   (SELECT PROD_NO
5    FROM DELIVERY) ;
```

and Query 5.3 could be rewritten as:

```
1  SELECT *
2  FROM PRODUCT
3  WHERE PROD_NO  != ALL
4   (SELECT PROD_NO
5    FROM DELIVERY) ;
```

5.4 CORRELATED SUBQUERIES

In all the queries in the previous section, the subquery was executed *once* to return a set of one or more values. In the case of Query 5.10 for example the set of salary values returned was (10000, 20000, 15000). The problem arose with Query 5.11 which is reproduced here:

Query 5.11 'List details of the employee in table EMPLOYEEn
            who earns more than anyone else'.

To provide a correct SQL query formulation for Query 5.11, it is necessary to scan the table in the subquery once for *each* row in the outer query so that the row for every employee other than the current outer-query employee is tested. In a correlated subquery, the subquery is executed repeatedly, once for each candidate row considered for selection by the outer query and its WHERE clause.

The correct SQL SELECT command for Query 5.11 is the correlated subquery:

```
1  SELECT *
2  FROM EMPLOYEEn A
3  WHERE SALARY > ALL
4  (SELECT SALARY
5   FROM EMPLOYEEn B
6   WHERE B.EMP_NO != A.EMP_NO);
```

For each row in the outer query, the subquery inspects *all other* rows (line 6 does the 'other') to check that none has a higher salary.

The way to recognize the *need* for a correlated subquery is:

For each row in the outer query, all rows in the subquery must be inspected.

The way to recognize the *existence* of a correlated subquery is to look for:

A table alias which appears in both the outer query and the subquery.

Here, the table alias A appears in both the outer query and the subquery. The B alias in lines 5 and 6 is not strictly necessary; the query would work just as well without it. For the data in table EMPLOYEE3, the SQL query outputs:

```
NO RECORDS SELECTED
```

and for the data in table EMPLOYEE5, it outputs:

```
EMP_NO  NAME     SALARY    MGR_NO
------  ----     ------    ------
     2  Betty    20000
```

These are the correct results.

A join equivalent of this query is possible and it is the following outer self-join.

```
1 SELECT A.*
2 FROM EMPLOYEE3 A, EMPLOYEE3 B
3 WHERE A.EMP_NO != B.EMP_NO (+)
4 AND   A.SALARY <= B.SALARY (+)
5 AND   B.SALARY IS NULL;
```

This version of the query joins together all rows of unlike employee number (line 3) so that everyone's salary can be compared with everyone else's. Line 4 checks that A's salary is less than or equal to B's, but the effect of the outer join and line 5 is to ensure that in fact A's salary is less than or equal to nobody else's salary. The output is the same as for the correlated subquery version for both tables. In the view of the present author, this formulation of the query engenders less confidence than the correlated subquery version because it is less intuitive. In any situation in which one is not sure if the SQL query is correct, as may be the case in the last query, the procedure the programmer should follow is to test the query thoroughly using a greater range of test data. Further examples of correlated and uncorrelated subqueries will occur in subsequent chapters.

It is now possible to return to a problem encountered in Chapter 3 with Query 3.43, which could not be answered with a simple select. The query is reproduced here:

Query 5.12 'Which is the city in CUS with the maximum total outstanding balance?'

The CUS table is reproduced here for convenience:

C_NO	TITLE	SNAME	INITS	STREET	CITY	POSTC	CRED_LIM	BALANCE
1	Mr	Sallaway	G.R.	12 Fax Rd	London	WC1	1000	42.56
2	Miss	Lauri	P.	5 Dux St	London	N1	500	200
3	Mr	Jackson	R.	2 Lux Ave	Leeds	LE1 2AB	500	510
4	Mr	Dziduch	M.	31 Low St	Dover	DO2 9CD	100	149.23
5	Ms	Woods	S.Q.	17 Nax Rd	London	E18 4WW	1000	250.1
6	Mrs	Williams	C.	41 Cax St	Dover	DO2 8WD		412.21

It is necessary to perform two scans of the CUS table; one to establish the maximum total balance for a city, and a second scan to list the city having that total balance.

```
1  SELECT CITY, SUM(BALANCE)
2  FROM CUS
3  GROUP BY CITY
4  HAVING SUM(BALANCE) =
5   (SELECT MAX(SUM(BALANCE)))
6    FROM CUS
7    GROUP BY CITY) ;
```

The output from this query is:

```
CITY        SUM(BALANCE)
----        ------------

Dover          561.44
```

Note the use of the nested aggregate functions in line 5. Lines 5 to 7 establish the maximum total outstanding balance across all cities. Having established this figure, it is necessary to link this up with the city in the outer query. The outer query table does not immediately have this data available since there is no single row containing the total for the whole city. Consequently the outer query needs to recalculate the total balance for each city and match it with the figure delivered by the subquery. The interested reader might like to try the following SQL code as an alternative:

```
1  SELECT CITY, SUM(BALANCE)
2  FROM CUS
3  GROUP BY CITY
4  HAVING SUM(BALANCE) > =  ALL
5   (SELECT SUM(BALANCE)
6    FROM CUS
7    GROUP BY CITY);
```

Query 5.13 'Which customers have made payments on all their
            outstanding invoices?'

Here it is advisable to break down the query into two parts. Firstly, it can
be established which customers have invoices which have had no
payments, with the query:

```
1  SELECT C_NO
2  FROM INVOICE
3  WHERE INV_NO  NOT IN
4   (SELECT INV_NO
5    FROM PAYMENT) ;
```

which yields:

```
C_NO
----
   4
   1
   2
   5
```

The next step is to retrieve details of all customers who do not appear in
this list. The above SQL can be used as a subquery to 'feed' these C_NOs
to an outer query which will provide the required data:

```
1  SELECT *
2  FROM CUS
3  WHERE C_NO  NOT IN
4   (SELECT C_NO
5    FROM INVOICE
6    WHERE INV_NO  NOT IN
7    (SELECT INV_NO
8     FROM PAYMENT)) ;
```

which insists (in line 3) that a customer's details will only be output if his or her customer number is not in the list shown above. The output is then:

C_NO	TITLE	SNAME	INIT	STREET	CITY	POSTC	CRED_LIM	BALANCE
3	Mr	Jackson	R.	2 Lux Ave	Leeds	LE1 2AB	500	510
6	Mrs	Williams	C.	41 Cax St	Dover	DO2 8WD		412.21

5.5 EXERCISES

1. Using the CANDIDATE table, write an SQL SELECT statement to find the candidate with the maximum number of votes.

2. Using the same table, write a SELECT statement to find the candidate with the maximum number of votes *and* his or her number of votes.

3. Given the following tables, write an SQL query to answer the query 'Who has purchased something that is not an instrument?':

```
PURCHASE                INSTRUMENT
--------                ----------


CUS      PROD           PROD      PRICE
---      ----           ----      -----
Alan     Violin         Violin    100
Betty    Book           Piano     500
```

You might try using ANY or ALL. The correct output is of course:

```
CUS
---
Betty
```

Chapter 6

UNION, INTERSECT and MINUS

6.1 INTRODUCTION

UNION, INTERSECT and MINUS are set oriented SQL commands. They are the SQL counterparts of the 'union', 'intersection' and 'complement' operations traditionally associated with mathematical sets. The notion of sets is important in database work and is fortunately quite simple and intuitive for most database users. The basic ideas of union, intersection and complement are briefly described here. Reference [4] contains a more detailed treatment.

Imagine there are two or more sets. The UNION of the sets will contain all the elements from each of these sets, with any duplicates removed. The INTERSECTION of the sets will contain all the elements which appear in every set. If any element does not exist in every set, it will not appear in the intersection of the sets. The 'complement' of a set with respect to another set is all the elements which exist in the first set but not in the second. Complements are achieved in SQL by the MINUS operator, so called because in some ways the idea of a complement can be thought of as 'all these minus all these'.

Of course this is not the first time sets have been mentioned in this text. An SQL table can be considered as a set of rows. When a simple SELECT statement with a WHERE condition accesses a single table, data from a subset of the rows in the table is delivered to the output. If an AND condition is used, indicating two selection criteria, the resulting set of rows output is the intersection of the two sets of rows which would have resulted had the two conditions been entered separately in two SELECT statements. The same kind of relationship exists between OR and UNION, and AND NOT and MINUS.

It is also possible to view the operation of some joins (See Chapter 4) as similar in some ways to the intersection of the sets of rows from two or more tables, or even from one table considered twice (self join). Some

SELECT commands containing a 'WHERE NOT EXISTS' clause (See Chapter 7) can be considered as performing an operation similar to the complement operation - select all the rows from one table where there is no corresponding row in the second table.

These similarities are illustrated in some of the following examples. Despite the similarities mentioned, there are situations in which UNION, INTERSECT and MINUS are necessary and cannot be replaced by alternative code, particularly when two or more tables are involved in the query.

UNION, INTERSECT and MINUS are additional SQL commands which can make the formulation of some queries more straightforward than any equivalent joins or subqueries. Some of the examples will show alternatives to these commands and attempts will be made to find examples where there *is* no alternative.

It has already been mentioned that SQL often allows the programmer several different ways to formulate a query. In some circles this is called 'redundancy', the notion being that it should be possible, by eliminating this redundancy from a query language such as SQL, to end up with a more compact or 'orthogonal' language. Another view is that in order to provide an ideal HCI (human-computer interface) one should make it as much like spoken language as possible (and of course spoken language contains much redundancy) so that queries are easier to formulate and easier to understand. The former approach looks at the problem from a technical programmer-oriented viewpoint, while the second indicates a wish to make database querying more accessible to non-programmers.

There is currently no proof available that a non-redundant language is necessarily either 'compact' or easily understandable. On the other hand one could take the view that the imprecision of spoken language (there are various examples of this imprecision in the example queries in this text) will remain a barrier to unambiguous query formulation and that a language like SQL represents a reasonable (or at least 'popular') compromise between these different ideals.

6.2 UNION

The general format of a query using UNION is:

```
SELECT statement
UNION
SELECT statement
... ;
```

In its simplest form, a UNION of two or more tables simply *appends* the rows from one table to those of another to produce a set of rows for output. That is, it adds rows from the second table to the rows from the first table. The individual tables remain unchanged; the appending just occurs in the output from the query.

There are other issues to consider, such as attempting to find the UNION of tables which have a different number of columns, differently-named columns, differently-typed columns, identical columns in a different order, or duplicated rows. Various WHERE conditions, joins and subqueries can also be 'mixed in'.

Query 6.1 'Produce a list of students who play either violin or piano'.

The list is to be prepared from the separate class lists for violin and piano classes. Suppose the class lists are currently as follows:

```
VIOLIN                          PIANO
------                          -----


STUD_NO  NAME    AGE            STUD_NO  NAME    AGE
-------  ----    ---            -------  ----    ---
      1  Fred    10                   2  Jane    12
      2  Sally   11                   4  David   10
      4  David   10                   5  Zena    11
```

In practice the tables would probably be different in a shared database:

STUDENT(STUD_NO,NAME),
SUBJECT(SUBJ_NO, SUBJ_NAME)
CLASS(STUD_NO, SUBJ_NO)

which would eliminate the type of redundancy inherent in the separate tables shown. However, for the sake of the example, assume the given structure. The SQL for the query would be:

```
1 SELECT * FROM VIOLIN
2 UNION
3 SELECT * FROM PIANO;
```

with the resulting output:

```
STUD_NO  NAME   AGE
-------  ----   ---
      1  Fred    10
      2  Jane    12
      3  Sally   11
      4  David   10
      5  Zena    11
```

Note that, consistent with the definition of set union, SQL has eliminated the duplicate row (4,'David',10). It has to do this since the output is considered to be a set and by definition, sets contain no duplicates. In effect, the PIANO table has been 'appended' to the bottom of the VIOLIN table although a better description might be 'merged', since the output has clearly been sorted.

This example illustrates the basic operation of UNION. Two or more SELECTs, no matter how complex, are separated by the word UNION.

The two tables VIOLIN and PIANO are said to be 'column homogeneous' since they contain the same column names, types and lengths. These 'attributes' of the columns in the tables can be shown by the SQL command below:

```
1 DESCRIBE VIOLIN;
```

which gives:

NAME	NULL?	TYPE
----	-----	----
STUD_NO		NUMBER(3)
NAME		CHAR(10)
AGE		NUMBER(3)

which is consistent with the CREATE TABLE command used to create the tables before rows were inserted into them (See Chapter 2). Both tables show this same structure.

If required, who is a violinist and who is a pianist can be shown on the report as follows:

```
1 SELECT STUD_NO, NAME, AGE, 'Violin' from VIOLIN
2 UNION
3 SELECT STUD_NO, NAME, AGE, 'Piano' from PIANO;
```

The output is now:

STUD_NO	NAME	AGE	'VIOLIN
-------	----	---	-------
1	Fred	10	Violin
2	Jane	12	Piano
3	Sally	11	Violin
4	David	10	Piano
4	David	10	Violin
5	Zena	11	Piano

Note that David now appears twice because the artificially introduced column showing the instrument means the rows for David are no longer identical. The rather untidy column name for the instrument can be corrected by using a column alias:

```
1 SELECT STUD_NO, NAME, AGE, 'Violin' Instrument
2 FROM VIOLIN
3 UNION
4 SELECT STUD_NO, NAME, AGE, 'Piano' FROM PIANO;
```

The output is now:

```
STUD_NO  NAME     AGE  INSTRUMENT
-------  ----     ---  ----------
      1  Fred      10  Violin
      2  Jane      12  Piano
      3  Sally     11  Violin
      4  David     10  Piano
      4  David     10  Violin
      5  Zena      11  Piano
```

Query 6.2 'List out the ten-year-old violinists and pianists'.

Here a simple WHERE clause is added to select out only the required rows from each table:

```
1  SELECT * FROM VIOLIN
2  WHERE AGE  = 10
3  UNION
4  SELECT * FROM PIANO
5  WHERE AGE  = 10 ;
```

The output is:

```
STUD_NO  NAME     AGE
-------  ----     ---
      1  Fred      10
      4  David     10
```

The duplicate David row has again been removed as expected.

Query 6.3 'Produce a list of students who play either violin or
          cello'.

```
1  DESCRIBE VIOLIN;
```

```
NAME                NULL?    TYPE
----                -----    ----
STUD_NO                      NUMBER(3)
NAME                         CHAR(10)
AGE                          NUMBER(3)


1   DESCRIBE CELLO;


NAME                NULL?    TYPE
----                -----    ----
STUD_NO                      NUMBER(3)
AGE                          NUMBER(4)
NAME                         CHAR(8)
```

The format of the CELLO table is different from that of the VIOLIN table; the number of columns and their names are identical to those of the VIOLIN table but they are in a different order and have different length attributes. The data in CELLO is:

```
CELLO
-----


STUD_NO  AGE  NAME
-------  ---  ----
      4   10  David
      6   11  Josey
```

The SQL query is:

    1 SELECT * FROM VIOLIN
    2 UNION
    3 SELECT STUD_NO, NAME, AGE
    4 FROM CELLO;

and the output is:

```
STUD_NO  NAME        AGE

-------  ----        ---

      1  Fred         10

      3  Sally        11

      4  David        10

      6  Josey        11
```

Notice that the differences in format mentioned above have not caused any problems for SQL. It was simply necessary in line 3 to state the correct order of the columns in the CELLO table so that they would match those in VIOLIN.

Query 6.4 'Produce a list of students who play either violin or
         flute'.

```
1  DESCRIBE FLUTE;

NAME          NULL?  TYPE

----          -----  ----

STUD                 NUMBER(3)

CNAME                CHAR(10)

AGE                  CHAR(3)
```

The first two columns in FLUTE have different names from those in VIOLIN. The AGE column has a different data type. The data in FLUTE is:

```
FLUTE

-----


STUD  CNAME      AGE

----  -----      ---

   7  Ashfak      12
```

If the following query is attempted:

```
1  SELECT STUD_NO,  NAME, AGE FROM VIOLIN
2  UNION
3  SELECT STUD, CNAME, AGE FROM FLUTE;
```

then an error of the following type results:

'expression must have same data type as corresponding
expression'

which refers of course to the AGE column. No objection is made to the difference in column *names*. This can be remedied by using a character-to-number function to convert FLUTE.AGE to numeric:

```
1  SELECT SELECT STUD_NO,  NAME, AGE FROM  VIOLIN
2  UNION
3  SELECT STUD, CNAME, TO_NUMBER(AGE)  FROM
   FLUTE ;
```

The resulting output is then:

```
STUD_NO  NAME       AGE
-------  ----       ---

      1  Fred        10
      3  Sally       11
      4  David       10
      7  Ashfak      12
```

which is correct.

It is also possible to apply the UNION operator to tables where a different number of columns is required from each table. This can be achieved with a combination of projection and padding. The following example illustrates this process:

Query 6.5 'Produce a list of invoices and payments with the
            following column layout:

```
INV_NO  DATE  INV_AMT  PMT_NO  PMT_AMT
------  ----  -------  ------  ------- ,
```

The two tables required are :

INVOICE

INV_NO	C_NO	INV_DATE	AMOUNT
940	1	5-DEC-90	26.2
1002	4	12-JAN-91	149.23
1003	1	12-JAN-91	16.26
1004	2	14-JAN-91	200
1005	3	20-JAN-91	510
1006	5	21-JAN-91	250.1
1017	6	22-JAN-91	412.21

and:

PAYMENT

INV_NO	PMT_NO	PMT_DATE	AMOUNT
940	2	12-DEC-90	13
1005	1	14-JAN-91	510
1017	1	30-JAN-91	100
940	3	19-JAN-91	10

Here are two tables which are clearly not column homogeneous as they stand. Referring to the required output report format, certain observations can be made. Firstly INV_NO is a common column in the two tables. If the query were to be attempted using a more conventional join procedure, as per Chapter 4, INV_NO would constitute the basis of the join criteria, with a WHERE clause of the form:

WHERE INVOICE.INV_NO = PAYMENT.PMT_NO

However, the following SQL query *will associate invoices and their relevant payments by sorting the output on INV_NO.* The SQL query used is:

```
1  SELECT INV_NO,  INV_DATE  DDATE, AMOUNT
2  INV_AMT,
3  0 PAYMENT, 0 PMT_AMT
4  FROM INVOICE
5  UNION
6  SELECT INV_NO,  PMT_DATE  DDATE, 0 INV_AMT,
7  PMT_NO  PAYMENT, AMOUNT PMT_AMT
8  FROM PAYMENT
9  ORDER BY 1 ;
```

The sort occurs due to the ORDER BY clause in line 8. '1' means that the sort is in ascending order of the *first* column INV_NO. The ORDER BY clause in a query using a UNION operator relates to the *whole* query so that there is no need to repeat the ORDER BY clause in each SELECT statement and there is no need for brackets. The query interpreter will often perform a sort-merge operation where two or more tables are involved (for speed and to detect duplicates) and since INV_NO is the 'most significant' (leftmost) column, the ORDER BY is not always necessary, depending on the database DBMS in use. The resulting output is:

INV_NO	DDATE	INV_AMT	PAYMENT	PMT_AMT
940	05-DEC-90	26.2	0	0
940	12-DEC-90	0	2	13
940	19-JAN-91	0	3	10
1002	12-JAN-91	149.23	0	0
1003	12-JAN-91	16.26	0	0
1004	14-JAN-91	200	0	0
1005	14-JAN-91	0	1	510
1005	20-JAN-91	510	0	0

1006	21-JAN-91	250.1	0	0
1017	22-JAN-91	412.21	0	0
1017	30-JAN-91	0	1	100

Data from two tables appear under the same five report columns. For example the second output column, the transaction date, contains data from INVOICE.INV_DATE and PAYMENT.PMT_DATE. This is possible since they both have the same format, that is they are both DATE columns. Under the third column INV_AMT, the value for an invoice is taken from the INV.AMOUNT column and the value for a payment is set to zero since there is no invoice amount column in the PAYMENT table.

This process of 'padding' is necessary to make the projections (subsets of columns) of the two tables column homogeneous, that is, to make them 'match up'. Corresponding columns must be of the same type so that a numeric column in the first table has the corresponding position in the second table 'padded' with some numeric value, here zero. A similar situation exists with respect to payment number. This column exists in PAYMENT but not in INVOICE, which consequently requires a 'padding' zero in this position in the SELECT line.

There is also the question of what column title will appear in the output. In the two tables INVOICE and PAYMENT, both the invoice amount and the payment amount columns are called AMOUNT. The form of the column aliases used in this SQL query is such as to remove any ambiguity or dependence on query interpreter defaults. All corresponding columns are explicitly given the same alias names. Finally, note that the output date column is called DDATE rather than date because DATE may be a reserved word and might 'confuse' the query interpreter, resulting in an error condition.

In summary, this query demonstrates that it is possible and sometimes meaningful to perform a UNION on tables with considerably different columns. It also demonstrates a way of associating rows from different tables using ORDER BY with UNION.

We now consider the *intersection* of the VIOLIN and PIANO sets of rows.

6.3 INTERSECT   < --- (ORACLE SQL*PLUS Only)

Query 6.6 'List details of all students who play both violin
        and piano'.

Remembering the data for violinists and pianists are in two different
tables VIOLIN and PIANO and that these tables have the same format,
the query is simply:

    1 SELECT * FROM VIOLIN
    2 INTERSECT
    3 SELECT * FROM PIANO ;

The set of students selected in line 1 is intersected with the set of
students in line 3 and only those students in both sets appear at the
output:

```
STUD_NO  NAME     AGE
-------  ----     ---
      4  David     10
```

As with UNION, the set of columns selected in both SELECTs must be
of the same number and type.

Query 6.7 'List details of students who play violin, piano
        and cello'.

    1 SELECT * FROM VIOLIN
    2 INTERSECT
    3 SELECT * FROM PIANO
    4 INTERSECT
    5 SELECT STUD_NO, NAME, AGE FROM CELLO;

The output is identical since David plays all three instruments. In line 5,
the columns from CELLO had simply to be placed in the correct order
to make them match the first two tables.

Query 6.8 'List the product numbers of all products which have current deliveries'.

By inspecting the PRODUCT and DELIVERY tables and reading about their 'meanings', hopefully in a data dictionary, it can be seen that a simple INTERSECT on PROD_NO will suffice:

```
1  SELECT PROD_NO  FROM PRODUCT
2  INTERSECT
3  SELECT PROD_NO  FROM DELIVERY;
```

The query simply intersects the set of product numbers from the two tables, with the resulting output:

```
PROD_NO
-------
      1
      2
      3
      4
```

The same result could of course have been achieved using a join such as:

```
1  SELECT DISTINCT A.PROD_NO
2  FROM PRODUCT A, DELIVERY B
3  WHERE A.PROD_NO  =B.PROD_NO;
```

It has already been remarked that the join operation has a 'feel' of intersection about it since only rows that 'match' by the join criteria will be output. Intersection is a very simple case of this, the join criterion being simple equality. However INTERSECT is not directly equivalent to an equijoin because it imposes the column homogeneity constraint.

Query 6.9 'List students who play the piano or both violin and cello'.

```
1  SELECT * FROM PIANO
2  UNION
3  (SELECT * FROM VIOLIN
4    INTERSECT
5    SELECT STUD_NO,  NAME, AGE
6    FROM CELLO) ;
```

The output is:

```
STUD_NO  NAME     AGE

-------  ----     ---

      2  Jane      12

      4  David     10

      5  Zena      11
```

The parentheses are necessary to make it clear that the intersection occurs before the union in this query. The query would in general have different results if the union occurred first. (See Ref. [4]). The reason can be found by considering the fact that for three sets A, B and C,

A + (B.C) is not equivalent to (A + B).C

It would have been considerably more difficult to program this query using joins or subqueries, which illustrates the utility of these set-oriented commands. A join or subquery version of this query is left as an exercise for the interested and patient reader.

6.4 MINUS   <--- (ORACLE SQL*PLUS Only)

The MINUS operator delivers to the output data from all rows of the table(s) in the first query which do *not* have 'corresponding' rows in the second table. The tables, or at least the subset of columns projected for output, must be column homogeneous, as with UNION and INTERSECT. The MINUS operation is analogous to the 'complement' operation of set theory.

Query 6.10 'List students who play violin but not piano'.

```
1 SELECT * FROM VIOLIN
2 MINUS
3 SELECT * FROM PIANO;
```

The output is:

```
STUD_NO  NAME     AGE
-------  ----     ---
      1  Fred      10
      3  Sally     11
```

This query outputs rows for all students who are in the first set (violinists) but not in the second set (pianists). The SQL query is equivalent to the following subquery version:

```
1 SELECT *
2 FROM VIOLIN
3 WHERE STUD_NO  NOT IN
4   (SELECT STUD_NO  FROM PIANO) ;
```

All rows from table VIOLIN which do not have a corresponding STUD_NO in PIANO are delivered to the output. Another formulation uses the outer join:

```
1 SELECT A.*
2 FROM VIOLIN A, PIANO B
3 WHERE A.STUD_NO  =  B.STUD_NO  (+)
4 AND B.STUD_NO  IS NULL ;
```

There is a fourth version of this query using NOT EXISTS - see Chapter 7. Care must be taken with parentheses when more than one logical (AND, OR and NOT) or set (INTERSECT, UNION, MINUS) operation are involved in a query, as previously mentioned. The parentheses ensure that the operations are applied in the required sequence, just as with arithmetic operations. As an example, consider:

Query 6.11 'List the students who play violin but neither piano
            nor cello'.

Calling the sets V, P and C, it is apparent that what is required is:

V.not P.not C

The operation of MINUS on sets A and B, i.e. A MINUS B, is such that:

A MINUS B is equivalent to A.not B

so that the expression for the query can be written:

(V MINUS P) MINUS C but not:

V MINUS (P MINUS C)

which has a different meaning. The difference can be seen by drawing a
Venn diagram or by manipulating the expression using the rules of logic.
Using De Morgan's law for example,

(V MINUS P) MINUS C can be rewritten as V.not P.not C ; whereas

V MINUS (P MINUS C) cannot; one equivalent is V.(Not B +C)

The SQL queries for each of these parenthesis placements are given
below. Note the different output.

    1 (SELECT * FROM VIOLIN
    2 MINUS
    3 SELECT * FROM PIANO)
    4 MINUS
    5 SELECT STUD_NO, NAME, AGE FROM CELLO ;   gives:

```
STUD_NO  NAME     AGE
-------  ----     ---
      1  Fred      10
      3  Sally     11        whereas:
```

1 SELECT * FROM VIOLIN
2 MINUS
3 (SELECT * FROM PIANO
4 MINUS
5 SELECT STUD_NO, NAME, AGE FROM CELLO) ;   gives:

```
STUD_NO  NAME     AGE
-------  ----     ---
      1  Fred      10
      3  Sally     11
      4  David     10
```

An English interpretation of this query might be:

'List all violinists excluding those who also play piano but
not cello'

which is not particularly clear; one is tempted to start placing parentheses
in such English sentences as an aid to clarity, even though there are many
people who will see no problem at all.

6.5 EXERCISES

1. Rewrite Query 6.9 using a join or subquery.

2. Write an SQL statement to answer the query 'Who plays cello
   and either piano or flute but not both'.

Chapter 7

EXISTS and NOT EXISTS

7.1 INTRODUCTION

EXISTS and NOT EXISTS are used in SQL SELECT statements to test, as their names suggest, for the existence or non-existence of rows in a database table. The general structure of a query containing an EXISTS is shown in Fig 7.1 below:

```
SELECT ...
FROM   ...
WHERE  ...
AND    ...
...
AND EXISTS
(SELECT *
 FROM ...
 WHERE ...
 ...)
```

Fig. 7.1 Positioning of EXISTS in an SQL Query

A NOT EXISTS takes a corresponding position. Data from a row in the outer query is delivered to the output provided the WHERE selection criteria are all true, including the EXISTS or NOT EXISTS condition. Each row of the table in the outer query is tested. The EXISTS condition becomes true if the subquery can locate a row in its table(s) which satisfies the subquery's WHERE conditions and the NOT EXISTS condition becomes true if such a row cannot be located.

EXISTS and NOT EXISTS are often replaceable by IN and NOT IN, but there are several situations in which they are not:

1. IN and NOT IN require some value to be passed from the outer query to the subquery for comparison; EXISTS and NOT EXISTS do not.

2. IN and NOT IN usually allow only one value at a time to be passed to the subquery for comparison (there is an exception in the case of ORACLE SQL*PLUS which allows the value of more than one column to be passed); in the case of EXISTS and NOT EXISTS, the values are passed directly into the WHERE conditions of the subquery and so the number of columns whose values are compared is not limited.

3. Where doubly-nested subqueries are involved, EXISTS and NOT EXISTS allow values to be passed from the outer query to the second subquery, whereas IN and NOT IN do not.

Examples illustrating these differences appear in the following text.

7.2 EXAMPLES

Consider the following small three-table database concerning the purchases of products that customers have made:

CUST		PURCHASE		PROD	
----		--------		----	
CNO	NAME	CNO	PRNO	PRNO	DESCR
---	----	---	----	----	-----
1	Alan	1	a	a	Apple
2	Bill	1	b	b	Ball
3	Charles	2	a		

The tables show who has purchased what; for example the first rows of each table show that Alan has purchased an apple.

Query 7.1 'List all customers who have purchased any product'.

```
1 SELECT *
2 FROM CUST
3 WHERE EXISTS
4 (SELECT *
5  FROM PURCHASE
6  WHERE CUST.CNO = PURCHASE.CNO);
```

The output is:

```
CNO  NAME
---  ----
  1  Alan
  2  Bill
```

Rows from CUST are selected in lines 1 to 3 only where there exists a row in PURCHASE with a matching CNO. Each row in the outer query is tested in turn to see if there is a corresponding row generated by the subquery, that is, that there is a matching customer number in the PURCHASE table. This simple example shows how EXISTS works in general and what it is intended for. Note that it will only ever be necessary to include a '*' in the subquery SELECT (rather than column names) since it is the existence or non-existence of a matching *row* that is being tested for. The same result could of course have been obtained using IN:

```
1 SELECT *
2 FROM CUST
3 WHERE CNO IN
4 (SELECT CNO
5  FROM PURCHASE);
```

In the EXISTS version the value passing is via the WHERE clause of the subquery whereas in the IN version, the value is passed via IN and the SELECT clause in the subquery. There is also a join version of the query yielding the same results:

    1 SELECT DISTINCT CUST.*
    2 FROM CUST, PURCHASE
    3 WHERE CUST.CNO = PURCHASE.CNO;

The DISTINCT is necessary because Alan has made two purchases and would otherwise be output twice. It is not necessary in the EXISTS or IN versions because EXISTence and set membership take no account of the number of occurrences. This need for DISTINCT is an example of the slightly more machine or language oriented nature, noted elsewhere, of the join method as compared to the subquery methods.

Query 7.2 'If there are any current purchases, produce a list of
           customers'.

    1 SELECT *
    2 FROM CUST
    3 WHERE EXISTS
    4 (SELECT *
    5   FROM PURCHASE);

This is a perfectly feasible if somewhat contrived example to show that unlike IN, EXISTS does not *require* a value to be passed to the subquery, even via the WHERE clause, although in most queries a value or values will be passed. Thus, this query could not be programmed in either IN or 'join' format. The output is:

```
CNO  NAME
---  ----
  1  Alan
  2  Bill
  3  Charles
```

Notice that each row appears only once. This points up a characteristic of EXISTS (shared by other subquery forms), that each row in the outer query table is tested only once.

Query 7.3 'List details of all customers who have not purchased
any product'.

Any trace of ambiguity in the English version of this query could be
removed by adopting the descriptive style of the *Predicate Calculus* and
re-wording it:

'List details of all customers for whom there does not exist a
purchase'.

See Reference [5] for more discussion on the utility of Predicate Calculus
in formulating precise (although sometimes stilted) English queries. SQL
EXISTS is closely analogous to the existential quantifier of the Predicate
Calculus. As will be seen in a later example, there is not a direct SQL
equivalent of the universal quantifier 'for all'; this has to be *simulated*
using a double NOT EXISTS. A *Set Theory* oriented form of the query
would be:

'List details of all customers whose customer number is not a member
of the set of customer numbers in the PURCHASE table'.

A *numerical* alternative is:

'List details of all customers for whom the number of purchases is
zero'.

The query can also be performed using a join (an outer join), but the
English equivalent of the join version is not very 'natural':

'Perform an outer join on the CUST and PURCHASE tables on
CNO with the (+) sign against the PURCHASE.CNO and select
out only the rows with a null PURCHASE.CNO'.

(This rather mechanical join formulation seems to go against the idea of

SQL's reputation of being a declarative rather than procedural language.) Each of these English formulations, biased towards a different approach, has its own SQL equivalent.

These differing vessions are now shown:

NOT EXISTS

```
1 SELECT *
2 FROM CUST
3 WHERE NOT EXISTS
4 (SELECT *
5   FROM PURCHASE
6   WHERE CUST.CNO = PURCHASE.CNO);
```

NOT IN

```
1 SELECT *
2 FROM CUST
3 WHERE CNO NOT IN        (or '!= ALL')
4 (SELECT CNO
5   FROM PURCHASE);
```

COUNT

```
1 SELECT *
2 FROM CUST
3 WHERE 0 =
4 (SELECT COUNT(*)
5   FROM PURCHASE
6   WHERE CUST.CNO = PURCHASE.CNO);
```

The OUTER JOIN version is shown on the next page.

OUTER JOIN

```
1  SELECT A.*
2  FROM CUST A, PURCHASE B
3  WHERE A.CNO =B.CNO (+)
4  AND B.CNO IS NULL;          (ORACLE SQL*PLUS only)
```

In each case the result will be:

```
CNO  NAME
---  ----
  3  Charles
```

because he is the only customer who has not purchased a single product.

Query 7.4 'List all customers who have purchased a ball'.

Here all three tables must be accessed. PROD is needed to convert the product description 'Ball' into a product number for searching the PURCHASE table.

```
 1  SELECT *
 2  FROM CUST
 3  WHERE EXISTS
 4  (SELECT *
 5   FROM PURCHASE
 6   WHERE CUST.CNO = PURCHASE.CNO
 7   AND PRNO =
 8   (SELECT PRNO
 9    FROM PROD
10    WHERE DESCR = 'Ball'));
```

The second subquery in lines 8 to 10 merely 'decodes' Ball into its correct product number.

The output from the query is shown on the next page.

```
CNO  NAME
---  ----
  1  Alan
```

There are equivalent, and similar-looking queries using IN, and two join versions are given below:

```
1  SELECT *
2  FROM CUST
3  WHERE EXISTS
4  (SELECT *
5   FROM PURCHASE A, PROD B
6   WHERE A.CNO = CUST.CNO
7   AND   A.PRNO = B.PRNO
8   AND   B.DESCR = 'Ball');
```

This version joins PURCHASE to PROD to obtain the PRNO for 'Ball' instead of using a subquery.

```
1  SELECT A.*
2  FROM CUST A, PURCHASE B, PROD C
3  WHERE A.CNO = B.CNO
4  AND   B.PRNO = C.PRNO
5  AND   C.DESCR = 'Ball';
```

This is an 'all join' version.

Query 7.5 'List customers who have purchased all products'.

As can be seen by inspecting the data, Alan is the only such customer. The way this can be seen (and this is of course only practicable with small amounts of data) is:

1. Inspect the PROD table and keep in mind the set of product numbers (a and b).

2. Inspect the PURCHASE table to see which customer number has purchased all product numbers a and b (1).

3. Inspect the CUST table to find the names corresponding to those customer numbers (Alan).

There *is* an 'all' operator in SQL (See Section 5.3) but its operation is limited to arithmetical and string comparisons; it cannot easily be made to perform in the way that is required by this query. In fact what is required is a double NOT EXISTS or a double NOT IN. ANY and ALL are only applicable by virtue of the equivalences:

IN   is equivalent to   = ANY

NOT IN is equivalent to   != ALL

In its NOT EXISTS form the query can be written in English as:

'List customers for whom there does not exist a product which they have not purchased'

or

'List customers for whom there does not exist a product for which there does not exist a purchase by that customer'.

This NOT EXISTS format can easily be translated into SQL as:

```
1   SELECT *
2   FROM CUST
3   WHERE NOT EXISTS
4    (SELECT *
5     FROM PROD
6     WHERE NOT EXISTS
7      (SELECT *
8       FROM PURCHASE
9       WHERE CUST.CNO  =  PURCHASE.CNO
10       AND  PROD.PRNO  =  PURCHASE.PRNO)) ;
```

Thè query can be read as 'Select all columns from CUST rows where there does not exist (lines 1 to 3) any row from PROD where there does not exist (lines 4 to 6) a PURCHASE row for that customer and product (lines 7 to 10)'. In general, when the English version of the query contains the word 'all', there is a strong possibility that the double NOT EXISTS form will be required. The output is:

```
CNO  NAME
---  ----
  1  Alan
```

Now consider the feasibility of using NOT IN instead. If the first two lines are written:

```
1  SELECT *
2  FROM CUST ...
```

then the third line (the WHERE clause) will have to utilize CNO since that is the only column which appears in any other table, so the code so far is:

```
1  SELECT *
2  FROM CUST
3  WHERE CNO NOT IN ...
```

Now the only other table that CNO appears in is PURCHASE, which indicates the continuation of the query as:

```
1  SELECT *
2  FROM CUST
3  WHERE CNO NOT IN
4  (SELECT CNO
5   FROM PURCHASE ...
```

However, this is leading in the wrong direction since CNO must appear in PURCHASE if the customer is to have purchased all products. Clearly the use of NOT IN in this way is inappropriate.

Another approach is to consider obtaining every combination of customer number and product number in the outer query by using a join, and then to test that for a given customer, every such combination exists in PURCHASE. If this is the case then that customer has purchased all products. This approach leads to the code beginning:

```
1  SELECT A.*
2  FROM CUST A, PROD C
3  WHERE (A.CNO, PRNO) ...   <--- (ORACLE SQL*PLUS only)
```

the next step, whether an IN or NOT IN is used, leads to problems, since if an IN is used, customers who had made *any* purchase would be output, and a NOT IN delivers *non-purchases*, in other words potential purchases which have not actually occurred. Neither of these is what is required.

Using the idea of non-purchases, if a customer number is NOT IN the set of non-purchases, then that customer's details should be output; since he or she has not made any of the non-purchases, he or she must have made *all* purchases. This leads to the code:

```
1  SELECT *
2  FROM CUST
3  WHERE CNO NOT IN
4   (SELECT A.CNO
5    FROM CUST A, PROD C
6    WHERE (A.CNO, PRNO) NOT IN   <--- (SQL*PLUS only)
7    (SELECT *
8     FROM PURCHASE)) ;
```

Lines 4 to 5 produce a 'cartesian product join' (See Section 4.2.4) since there are no join criteria between CUST and PROD; *every* combination is tested against PURCHASE, and CNO is extracted from these 'potential purchases' which do not in fact appear in PURCHASE.

It is always useful and informative to translate your SQL queries back into spoken language. The English version of the 'double NOT IN' version reads:

'List details of all customers whose customer numbers do not appear in the list of potential but not actual purchases'.

This may appear obscure, but remember there is in general no such ready English interpretation of most purely procedural 3GL programs written in, say, C or COBOL. The processing performed by this and the equivalent SQL commands would also require a far greater number of lines of 3GL code.

Another SQL form of the query which follows from the same English statement of the query is:

```
1  SELECT *
2  FROM CUST A
3  WHERE NOT EXISTS
4   (SELECT CNO, PRNO
5    FROM CUST B, PROD
6    WHERE A.CNO = B.CNO
7    MINUS
8    SELECT *
9    FROM PURCHASE) ;
```

Lines 4 to 6 deliver the set of 'potential' purchases. The set of 'actual' purchases are subtracted ('minus-ed') in lines 7 to 9 so that the output from the whole subquery from line 4 to line 9 is 'the set of potential purchases which are not actual purchases'. Now it only remains in lines 1 to 3 to select out those customers for whom this set is empty.

A Venn diagram showing the various sets involved in this query is shown in Fig 7.2

Yet another approach to this problem is to list out the customers for whom the number of distinct purchases is equal to the number of products. (In this simplistic example database it has been assumed that no customer purchases a product more than once; this does not affect any of the above). The SQL query is shown overleaf below Fig. 7.2..

Lines 1 to 3 perform an equijoin of the CUST and PURCHASE tables on CNO. Lines 4 and 5 obtain the count of the joined rows for each customer (i.e. the number of purchases for each customer), and lines 5 to

7 ensure that only rows with a count equal to the count of products are output.

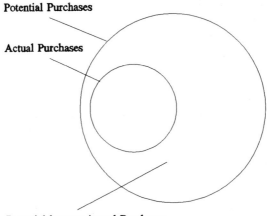

Fig. 7.2 Venn Diagram for Query 7.5

```
1  SELECT A.*
2  FROM CUST A, PURCHASE B
3  WHERE A.CNO =  B.CNO
4  GROUP BY A.CNO, NAME
5  HAVING COUNT(*) =
6  (SELECT COUNT(*)
7   FROM PROD);
```

Query 7.6 'List details of customers who have not purchased all
products'.

As with the above query, there are many variants. The EXISTS / NOT EXISTS version only is given here and appears overleaf. The output is:

```
CNO  NAME
---  ----
  2  Bill
  3  Charles
```

```
 1 SELECT *
 2 FROM CUST
 3 WHERE EXISTS
 4 (SELECT *
 5  FROM PROD
 6  WHERE NOT EXISTS
 7  (SELECT *
 8   FROM PURCHASE
 9   WHERE CUST.CNO = PURCHASE.CNO
10    AND PROD.PRNO = PURCHASE.PRNO)) ;
```

The query is interpreted into English as:

'List customers for whom there exists a product they have not purchased'.

This is very similar in principle to the previous query. Note that customers who have purchased no products are included in the output. If line 3 is a NOT EXISTS and line 6 is an EXISTS, all that results is a rather lengthy version of query 7.3.

In Chapter 4, the following query (Query 4.11) appeared, and was implemented there using an outer join:

Query 7.7 'List out all departments with no employees'.

The tables involved are:

DEPARTMENT

DEPT_NO	DEPT_NAME
1	Sales
2	R & D
3	Billing

EMPLOYEE4

EMP_NO	NAME	DEPT_NO
1	Alan	3
2	Bill	1
3	Corin	3
4	Dennis	1

It can now be seen that an alternative version of the query is as follows:

```
1  SELECT *
2  FROM DEPARTMENT A
3  WHERE NOT EXISTS
4   (SELECT *
5    FROM EMPLOYEE4 B
6    WHERE A.DEPT_NO  =  B.DEPT_NO) ;
```

with the same output:

```
DEPT_NO  DEPT_NAME
-------  ---------
      2  R and D
```

7.3 SIMULATING AN OUTER JOIN

We now have at our disposal the tools necessary (namely UNION from Chapter 6 and NOT EXISTS from this chapter) to simulate the outer join command in SQLs that do not have it.

Query 7.8 'List details of products with any deliveries they may have had'.

```
1  SELECT P.PROD_NO,  DESCR, C_NO,  QTY
2  FROM PRODUCT P, DELIVERY XX
3  WHERE P.PROD_NO  = XX.PROD_NO
4  UNION
5  SELECT P.PROD_NO,  DESCR, 0, 0
6  FROM PRODUCT P
7  WHERE NOT EXISTS
8   (SELECT *
9    FROM DELIVERY XX
10    WHERE P.PROD_NO  = XX.PROD_NO) ;
```

Lines 1 to 4 perform a join, matching up products with deliveries. Lines 4 to 10 append product rows with *no* matching deliveries.

This code will work in ORACLE, INGRES and dBASE IV. Note that in dBASE IV aliases are 'remembered'; if you try to use xx in some other query at a later date you will get an 'alias already exists' message.

7.4 EXERCISES

1. Write an SQL query to list out details of all CUSTOMERs who have INVOICEs with no PAYMENTs.

2. Write an SQL query to list out all customers who are the *only* customer we have in a city.

3. Write an SQL query that does not use the outer join (+) operator, to perform the processing of Query 4.12.

Chapter 8

VIEWs

8.1 INTRODUCTION

The idea of a view in database practice, and in fact the genesis of the term itself, indicates the subjectivist notion of a user being able to 'see' parts of the database in a way that is oriented towards his or her own interests, needs or perspectives. Using SQL, a database 'view' can be set up which will encompass data derived from selected columns and rows from one or more database tables.

There are several situations in which an SQL VIEW can be used to advantage. Both the end user and the database applications programmer often inherit a situation in which the database schema has already been designed and will not be altered radically in design throughout the lifetime of the database. Those early decisions concerning the tables and the attributes that constitute the database consequently have a powerful and continuing effect on the subsequent data processing activities in the organization, and even on the mental picture that the organization has of itself. SQL VIEWs can allow 'new' views of the existing 'base tables' (i.e. the tables as originally defined and physically stored on the database and represented in the schema) to evolve without changing the structure of the underlying base tables and without duplicating any data.

No data is actually stored in a view. The 'virtual table' that a view represents is reconstituted by the DBMS each time a query or program 'calls' it, that is each time a query or program names it. This is transparent to the user and the process; it is 'as if' the virtual table actually existed. No (or very little) additional storage overhead is required since the data in the view is derived ultimately and exclusively from data in the base tables. When data values in the base tables are updated, the views which 'encompass' those tables immediately reflect the new values. In many cases the reverse is also true; a view can be updated and the base tables (and any other views deriving from those base tables) are updated. What really happens of course is that the relevant base tables are updated and the views built upon those base tables simply 'reflect' the changes. It is even possible to create a new view in terms of existing views. There are some restrictions upon updating and querying of base tables via views. Examples illustrating these restrictions are shown below.

Another motivation for views historically was to restrict the access to the database that different classes of end user would have to those tables, rows and columns that related to the type of processing they were required and allowed to perform, and no more. This would bestow enhanced security on the database as a whole, both from the aspect of protecting the secrecy of certain data 'facts' which might require confidentiality among different classes of user within an organization, and as a way of protecting certain data values in a database against unsolicited modification, including changes, insertions and deletions. If collections of views were suitably protected by passwords and those passwords were distributed selectively to the different classes of user, the database could effectively be partitioned into several overlapping 'subschema' reflecting the data needs and privileges of these users.

Using the built-in facilities of SQL, data can be partitioned both vertically and horizontally, that is , in terms of both columns and rows, using views. If the Database Administrator (DBA) grants suitable privileges to a user, he or she can be restricted to accessing table data via a certain SQL VIEW and thus to a certain subset of the data. For example a particular category of user in the Payroll section (defined by the allocation of account codes and passwords) might be allowed to read the name, staff number and age of everyone on the payroll, to read in addition his or her own salary value but nobody else's, and to change but not read certain other data items such as the monthly pay rate.

Apart from giving users a simpler view and restricting access to defined areas, SQL VIEWs can also help the database SQL programmer to break down a complex query into several smaller steps, each VIEW presenting the programmer with a 'view' of the database closer to the way he or she would like to see it in order to make subsequent SELECT statements easier. The alternative method, of creating and dropping temporary tables, is discussed in Chapter 9.

SQL VIEWs are commonly used to:

  - restrict rows

  - restrict columns

  - restrict rows and columns

  - calculate summary data

  - group data

  - join tables

  - contain subqueries.

In using a view, the database user is 'insulated' from the necessity of knowing how the view was created. In fact to him or her it seems like a 'virtual table'.

8.2 CREATING A VIEW

Suppose we want to create a VIEW called LONCUS, which just shows the London rows of the CUS table. The restriction is on the *rows* of the CUS table only; all columns are to be visible in the view. The SQL CREATE VIEW command to do this is:

```
1  CREATE VIEW LONCUS AS
2  SELECT *
3  FROM CUS
4  WHERE CITY  ='London';
```

8.3 VIEWS AND SINGLE-TABLE QUERIES

LONCUS can now be treated as a new table in its own right. Suppose that the base table CUS contains:

C_NO	TITLE	SNAME	INITS	STREET	CITY	POSTC	CRED_LIM	BALANCE
1	Mr	Sallaway	G.R.	12 Fax Rd	London	WC1	1000	42.56
2	Miss	Lauri	P.	5 Dux St	London	N1	500	200
3	Mr	Jackson	R.	2 Lux Ave	Leeds	LE1 2AB	500	510
4	Mr	Dziduch	M.	31 Low St	Dover	DO2 9CD	100	149.23
5	Ms	Woods	S.Q.	17 Nax Rd	London	E18 4WW	1000	250.1
6	Mrs	Williams	C.	41 Cax St	Dover	DO2 8WD		412.21

Then the query:

Query 8.1 'List the contents of the view LONCUS'

can be simply implemented as:

```
1  SELECT *
2  FROM LONCUS ;
```

which will output just the London rows:

C_NO	TITLE	SNAME	INITS	STREET	CITY	POSTC	CRED_LIM	BALANCE
1	Mr	Sallaway	G.R.	12 Fax Rd	London	WC1	1000	42.56
2	Miss	Lauri	P.	5 Dux St	London	N1	500	200
5	Ms	Woods	S.Q.	17 Nax Rd	London	E18 4WW	1000	250.1

Similarly, a view SHORTCUS can be set up which lets all the rows through but restricts the columns:

```
1  CREATE VIEW SHORTCUS AS
2    SELECT C_NO, CRED_LIM, BALANCE
3    FROM CUS;
```

The query:

Query 8.2 'List the contents of view SHORTCUS'

can be implemented as:

```
1  SELECT *
2  FROM SHORTCUS;
```

with the result:

```
C_NO   CRED_LIM   BALANCE
----   --------   -------
  1       1000      42.56
  2        500        200
  3        500        510
  4        100     149.23
  5       1000      250.1
  6                 412.21
```

It is allowable to give new names to the columns in the view, so for example:

```
1  CREATE VIEW SHORTCUS (ACCOUNT, LIMIT, BALANCE)
2  AS
3  SELECT C_NO, CRED_LIM, BALANCE
4  FROM CUS ;
```

creates the same view but with the column names changed to ACCOUNT, LIMIT and BALANCE. These are column aliases for the original column names.

The query:

Query 8.3 'List credit details of London customers'

can be achieved in various ways. Suppose that 'credit details' means the three columns of view SHORTCUS. Clearly there is no way of using SHORTCUS itself to answer Query 8.3 since data about CITY is absent. We could use the LONCUS view:

```
1  SELECT C_NO, CRED_LIM, BALANCE
2  FROM LONCUS;
```

which performs the required relational algebraic project operation to give the required *columns* and utilizes the relational algebraic select intrinsic to the LONCUS view to select the required subset of *rows*. The output is thus:

```
C_NO    CRED_LIM    BALANCE
----    --------    -------
   1        1000      42.56
   2         500        200
   5        1000      250.1
```

It is also possible to create a view LONSHORT (try to keep table and view names more self-explanatory than this) which delivers just these three columns for London customers. This effects a relational algebraic select and project in one view:

```
1  CREATE VIEW LONSHORT AS
2    SELECT C_NO, CRED_LIM, BALANCE
3    FROM CUS
4    WHERE CITY ='London';
```

The query output is identical.

8.4 DEFINING ONE VIEW IN TERMS OF ANOTHER

The view LONSHORT could have been defined in terms of view LONCUS instead of table CUS. Line 4 would then be unnecessary since

the relational algebraic select it represents has already been performed in
LONCUS:

    1 CREATE VIEW LONSHORT1 AS   < ---- Defining one view
    2 SELECT C_NO, CRED_LIM, BALANCE   in terms of
    3 FROM LONCUS;   another

The query:

    1 SELECT *
    2 FROM LONSHORT1;

has the same result. For this query to work, both views LONCUS and
LONSHORT1 must be in place on the database. If for example the view
LONCUS is dropped:

    1 DROP VIEW LONCUS;

and an attempt is made to use the view LONSHORT1 by repeating this
query, then an error of the following type will occur:

    'Table or view does not exist'

This might appear puzzling since LONSHORT1 itself was never dropped.
But a view on which it was based was dropped, and that caused the error.

8.5 CHECKING VIEW DEFINITIONS

A record should be kept in the data dictionary of which views exist and
how they are derived. In ORACLE for example, a record of the text used
to create each view is kept in the ORACLE data dictionary. The data
dictionary can be queried by the DBA and selected users, depending on
their *privileges* (See Chapter 12).

   The following query looks at the part of the data dictionary concerned
with views:

Query 8.4 'What VIEWs are there on the database starting with "LON" ?'.

```
1  SELECT *
2  FROM VIEWS
3  WHERE VIEWNAME LIKE 'LON%';
```

This gives:

```
VIEWNAME        VIEWTEXT        <---- ORACLE allows you to see
--------        --------                a summary of the views


LONCUS          SELECT *
                FROM CUS
                WHERE CITY = 'London'


LONSHORT        SELECT C_NO, CRED_LIM, BALANCE
                FROM CUS
                WHERE CITY = 'London'


LONSHORT1       SELECT C_NO, CRED_LIM, BALANCE
                FROM LONCUS
```

which is a very useful way of checking how a view was derived. It can be seen clearly here that if the LONCUS view is dropped then LONSHORT1 will also be unavailable, with the result that any reference to LONCUS or LONSHORT1 will give the error shown above. However, even after LONCUS is dropped, the definition of LONSHORT1 is still contained in the data dictionary item VIEWS, so that:

```
1  SELECT *
2  FROM VIEWS
3  WHERE VIEWNAME LIKE 'LON%';
```

gives:

```
VIEWNAME        VIEWTEXT

--------        --------


LONSHORT        SELECT C_NO, CRED_LIM, BALANCE
                FROM CUS
                WHERE CITY = 'London'

LONSHORT1       SELECT C_NO, CRED_LIM, BALANCE  <-- View is
                FROM LONCUS                         still
                                                    there
```

If LONCUS is ever reinstated, all the views built on it will work again.

8.6 SUMMARY VIEWS

One common and very useful purpose to which VIEWs can be put is in the construction of summary data. For example we may want to create a view containing summary financial data on our customer accounts.

```
1  CREATE VIEW SUMMARY1 AS
2  SELECT CITY, SUM(CRED_LIM)  MAX_RISK,
3    SUM(BALANCE) DEBT
4  FROM CUS
5  GROUP BY CITY ;
```

Query 8.5 'List the summary financial data on customer accounts'.

```
1  SELECT *
2  FROM SUMMARY1;
```

In line 2 of the CREATE VIEW command an alternative way of specifying column aliases (rather than having them in the CREATE VIEW line) is shown. Notice that here we have a GROUP BY in a view, the totals being grouped by city. The column aliases are in fact mandatory here, since the aggregate functions SUM(CRED_LIM) and SUM(BALANCE) are not valid column names. The output from Query 8.5 is:

CITY	MAX_RISK	DEBT
Dover	100	561.44
Leeds	500	510
London	2500	492.66

which is a very useful summary report. The means of obtaining the summary (such as the details of the GROUP BY) need not be remembered by end users since the logic is encapsulated in the view; all that is required in fact is to remember the VIEW name. In this way the end user can be insulated from the more involved aspects of the database queries, which can be left to the programmer to develop and test. The VIEW is always up-to-date because whenever the view is used, its built-in SELECT command is rerun.

8.7 VIEWS OF JOINED TABLES

One of the major uses for views is to give the database user the impression that the database contains tables that are in precisely the format that he or she requires for the application in hand. This makes thinking about the problem and the formulation of SQL queries simpler. Quite often, as we have seen in previous chapters, a query will require more than one database table to be accessed to produce the desired output. In many such cases, associated queries would be easier to write and reports easier to generate if the relevant data appeared to be all in one table.

In Chapter 2 the processes of Entity Analysis and Normalization tended to split data into separate tables, each table corresponding to a 'real world' object type. The major object in doing this was to eliminate data redundancy and the associated insertion, deletion and update anomalies.

In creating views of joined tables, we are apparently reversing this process and 'denormalizing'. However, remembering that views do not actually store any data, no data duplication will result, and we will obtain the advantage of having a single table which contains all relevant data items.

One common requirement in accounting systems, in particular the sales ledger subsystem, is to provide customers with a monthly statement of account. A typical statement is shown in Fig. 8.1. The data required in the statement can be broken down into:

1. Customer Account data

2. Invoice data

3. Payment data

Assuming this data is contained in the tables CUS, INVOICE and PAYMENT, it is possible to create a view, based on a join of corresponding rows in the tables, which will make the writing of a report program to print statements considerably simpler. The details of the required join have already been covered in Chapter 4, Query 4.12. The necessary view can thus be created by the following CREATE VIEW command:

```
1  CREATE VIEW STATEMENT AS
2  SELECT A.C_NO, SNAME, B.INV_NO, B.AMOUNT
3    INV_AMOUNT, PMT_NO, PMT_DATE, C.AMOUNT
4    PMT_AMOUNT
5  FROM CUS A, INVOICE B, PAYMENT C
6  WHERE A.C_NO = B.C_NO
7  AND  B.INV_NO = C.INV_NO (+);
```

Note the use of column aliases in lines 3 and 4 to prevent the attempt being made to create a view with two identically-named columns 'AMOUNT'.

INGRES has a special feature called 'joindefs' which facilitates the generation and storage of such multi-table views.

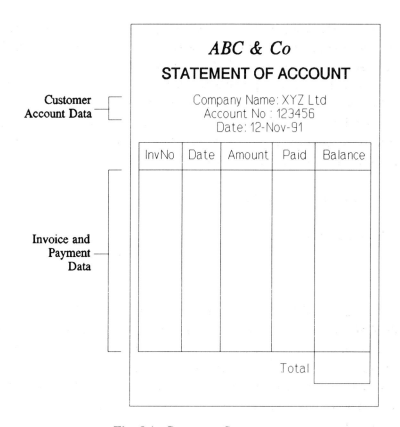

Fig. 8.1 Customer Statement

8.8 JOINING VIEWS

It is possible to join a view to a table or another view. For example we
may wish to join CUS to SUMMARY1 on CITY:

Query 8.6 'Produce a report that shows me each customer's debt
          as against the corresponding city debt'.

```
1 SELECT C_NO,  SNAME, A.CITY, BALANCE
2   DEBT, ROUND(BALANCE / DEBT * 100, 2) PROPORTION
3 FROM CUS A, SUMMARY1 B
4 WHERE A.CITY  =  B.CITY ;
```

The output from this query is:

C_NO	SNAME	CITY	DEBT	PROPORTION
4	Dziduch	Dover	149.23	26.58
6	Williams	Dover	412.21	73.42
3	Jackson	Leeds	510	100
1	Sallaway	London	42.56	8.64
5	Woods	London	250.1	50.77
2	Lauri	London	200	40.6

In line 3 it can be seen that the *table* CUS has been joined to the *view* SUMMARY1. Similarly, one view can be joined to another. The report column 'PROPORTION' is a calculated column showing the proportion of the total city debt each customer's balance represents. The ROUND function rounds PROPORTION to 2 decimal places.

It is possible that the introduction of a view will result in duplicate rows. Take for example the DELIVERY table:

```
DELIVERY
--------

C_NO  PROD_NO  QTY  DEL_DATE
----  -------  ---  --------
   3        2    2  3-NOV-90
   3        1    3  3-NOV-90
   1        4    6  7-NOV-90
   5        3    4  12-NOV-90
   3        3    1  12-NOV-90
```

If we define a view CUS_DELS containing just C_NO and DEL_DATE:

```
1  CREATE VIEW CUS_DELS  AS
2    SELECT C_NO, DEL_DATE
3    FROM DELIVERY;
```

then the first two rows become duplicates i.e. they are the same. This is not in theory allowed on a relational database where every table represents a relation which is a set of tuples and a set is by definition not allowed to contain duplicates. Whether or not a view (not defined in the mathematical theory of relations) is allowed to contain duplicates is open to debate. Clearly in practical DBMSs they *are* allowed to:

```
1  SELECT *
2  FROM CUS_DELS;
```

gives:

```
C_NO   DEL_DATE
----   ---------
   3   03-NOV-90
   3   03-NOV-90
   1   07-NOV-90
   5   12-NOV-90
   3   12-NOV-90
```

The first two rows are identical. In relational database theory (as distinct from the mathematical theory of relations - the former is an extension of the latter) one guarantee of no two rows being identical is the notion of the primary key. Every relation should have one. A primary key 'identifies' a row in the sense that no two rows are allowed to contain the same value of the primary key column or columns. In many practical tables it will be only this value (or some other candidate key) which is guaranteed to distinguish rows from each other. Clearly then, if a view definition omits all or part of the primary key then there is the potential for duplicate rows to occur.

Because in relational database theory the idea of a duplicate row is confused with the idea of duplication of data, measures are often taken to remove such duplication. It could be argued on the other hand that two occurrences of a phenomenon is basically different from one occurrence of the phenomenon and duplicate rows should be allowed, just as duplicate values are allowed in statistical data. The whole question turns on the notion of 'identity'. Do, for example, two 'identical' objects have the same 'identity'? Why is it sometimes necessary to *invent* a primary key (i.e. an identifying attribute)?

These are interesting questions to speculate on and need not be dismissed as 'merely' philosophical. It is true that philosophers have failed to give a satisfactory (clear, generally accepted and useful) answer through many centuries of speculation on the notion of identity. Perhaps it is now up to computer science to help to provide this answer, in a similar way to its contribution of fresh ideas and computer-derived terminology to some of the questions of cognition. 'Mundane' questions asked by data analysts are often surprisingly similar to 'profound' questions asked by philosophers. It may be that attempts to improve database technology will lead to improvements in our understanding of other aspects of the world by demonstrating in practice the unviability of some philosophical notions that had previously held sway, and positing better alternatives. Entity Relationship Modelling and the new terminology and practice of Object-Oriented Analysis can both be viewed in this light. This is one of the things that makes ours such an interesting subject.

8.9 UPDATING VIEWS

All updates to a base table should be immediately reflected in all views that encompass that base table. For example if the balance of a certain customer in the CUS table is increased by £100 then the view LONCUS based on CUS should show this:

```
1  UPDATE CUS
2  SET BALANCE  =  BALANCE + 100
3  WHERE C_NO  =  5 ;
```

will update the base table CUS, and

```
1  SELECT C_NO,  BALANCE
2  FROM LONCUS
3  WHERE C_NO  =  5 ;
```

will produce the output:

```
C_NO     CRED_LIM     BALANCE
----     --------     -------
  5         1000        350.1
```

which shows that the balance of C_NO 5 has been increased by £100.

Similarly, if the *view* is updated, then the base table will reflect the change:

```
1  UPDATE LONCUS
2  SET BALANCE = BALANCE + 100
3  WHERE C_NO = 5 ;
```

```
1  SELECT  C_NO, BALANCE
2  FROM CUS
3  WHERE C_NO = 5 ;
```

The query will show the increased balance in the base table CUS.

There are several restrictions on the updating of views:

1. DELETES

   (a) The view must be based on *one* table only.

   (b) The view must not contain a GROUP BY or DISTINCT.

2. UPDATES

   as above plus

   (c) The view must contain no calculated column expressions.

3. INSERTS

as above plus

(d) All columns in the base table which were defined
as NOT NULL by the CREATE TABLE command should be
in the view.

All of these restrictions make sense. If an attempt was made to delete
from a join view, then the number of rows deleted in each of the joined
tables may be unexpected. If a row from a view containing a GROUP BY
were deleted, then should all the rows in the base table that contributed
to the summary data be deleted? This is also the situation with
DISTINCT; more than one base table row may have 'contributed' to a
view row. These problems, or closely-related ones, could occur if it was
legal to perform updates and inserts on a view.

If an UPDATE were attempted on a calculated column in a view, then
what should happen to the values of the columns in the view and the base
tables from which the calculated column is derived? If an attempt were
made to INSERT a row into a view containing a projection of a base
table and some of the columns in the base table which were NOT NULL
were not included in the view, then the values in the base table that were
left out *would* end up with null values.

Note that it *is* possible to delete a whole row from a base table via a
view defined as a projection of that base table.

8.10 VIEWS AS PROGRAMMERS' STEPPING STONES

Some queries are made much easier to write by breaking them up into
separate parts and using a view as a 'stepping stone' between the
individual queries. Consider the following query:

Query 8.7 'Which party won the election?'

Assume a table with the following structure and data:

```
CANDIDATE
---------
```

CAND_NO	NAME	CONS_NO	PARTY	NO_OF_VOTES
1	Fred	1	Labour	100
2	Jim	1	Cons	120
3	Peter	1	Liberal	50
4	John	2	Labour	150
5	Mike	2	SLD	50
6	Jane	2	Cons	100
7	Mary	2	Green	150
8	Keith	1	Ind	150
9	Sue	1	SDP	160

Note that the winning party is the one which obtains the most won constituencies, not necessarily the most votes overall across the country. This query is quite difficult to implement 'in one go'. It can with advantage be broken down into the following steps:

Query 8.7.1 'Get the winning party in each constituency'.

Since the output from this query will be useful in the next step, the output will be 'saved' in a view:

```
1  CREATE VIEW CONS_WINNERS  AS
2  SELECT CONS_NO,  PARTY
3  FROM CANDIDATE A
4  WHERE NO_OF_VOTES   =
5   (SELECT MAX(NO_OF_VOTES)
6    FROM CANDIDATE B
7    WHERE A.CONS_NO  =  B.CONS_NO) ;
```

Note the use of a correlated subquery. Winning candidates are selected by inspecting all other candidates in the same constituency and checking that none has a higher number of votes.

The view CONS_WINNERS which results will contain in this instance:

CONS_NO	PARTY
1	SDP
2	Labour
2	Green

Note that here two parties have both 'won' in constituency 2. The next step is to tot up the number of won constituencies that each party obtained.

Query 8.7.2 'Get the number of constituencies won by each party'.

This can be achieved by creating another view:

```
1  CREATE VIEW WON_CONSTITS
2  (PARTY, NO_OF_CONSTITS)   AS
3  SELECT PARTY, COUNT(*)
4  FROM CONS_WINNERS
5  GROUP BY PARTY ;
```

which will in this case produce the output in view WON_CONSTITS:

PARTY	NO_OF_CONSTITS
SDP	1
Labour	1
Green	1

Note that here we have three joint winners, an unprecedented event which should nevertheless be accommodated in the query design. The next step is to list out the party (parties) with the highest number of won constituencies. This takes us back to the original Query 8.7:

```
1 SELECT PARTY
2 FROM WON_CONSTITS
3 WHERE NO_OF_CONSTITS  =
4  (SELECT MAX(NO_OF_CONSTITS)
5   FROM WON_CONSTITS)  ;
```

which in a normal situation would yield the one winning party. A similar but more enlightening query would be:

Query 8.8 'List each party and the number of constituencies won, best first'.

For this query the view WON_CONSTITS would also be used. The SQL command is simply:

```
1 SELECT *
2 FROM WON_CONSTITS
3 ORDER BY NO_OF_CONSTITS  DESC ;
```

Note that the ORDER BY has to be performed by the query itself, since *it is not possible to define an* ORDER BY *condition in a view.*

The use of views in step-by-step formulation of queries should be the exception rather than the rule. It is wise to look around for a suitable *existing* view to base your query upon. If your query is going to be stored and re-used, make sure that the continued existence of the view (or views) is assured. Casual creation of new views can result in their uncontrollable proliferation and in some installations the DBA will reserve such privileges for himself or herself. The creation of a view can be justified by:

1. The continued need for a query which needs such a view as a 'stepping stone'.

2. A convenience. Several tables are frequently used together in queries or reports.

3. A security device. Access to data items in the database can be precisely specified.

This last item is now discussed.

8.11 SECURITY AND VIEWS

Suppose we have on the database a table EMPLOYEE with the following structure:

E_NO	NAME	JOB	SALARY	DEPT
1	Alan	Manager	2000	1
3	Carol	Accountant	1700	1
2	Brian	Clerk	1200	1
4	Dianne	Manager	2300	2
5	Lena	Clerk	1500	2

It may be required to allow all employees to be able to 'see' all data except salaries. This can be achieved by the DBA by the following two steps:

```
1  CREATE VIEW EMP1 AS
2  SELECT E_NO,  NAME, JOB, DEPT
3  FROM EMPLOYEE ;
```

```
1  GRANT SELECT     <---- Granting privileges
2  ON EMP1                on a view.
3  TO PUBLIC ;
```

This means that, assuming PUBLIC has no privileges (See Chapter 12) over EMPLOYEE, then their only window into EMPLOYEE is via the view EMP1 which does not contain the SALARY column of the EMPLOYEE base table.

Another security requirement may be to allow only managers to 'see' salaries, and then only of their own departments. The following view definition assumes that every manager has an account code equal to his or her name and that that name is 'unique' i.e. nobody else in the organization has that name. The view can be modified to remove these constraints. The code employed is:

```
1  CREATE VIEW EMP2 AS
2  SELECT *
3  FROM EMPLOYEE
4  WHERE DEPT =
5   (SELECT DEPT
6    FROM EMPLOYEE
7    WHERE NAME = USER     <--- System Variable
8    AND JOB = 'MANAGER') ;
```

```
1  GRANT SELECT
2  ON EMP2
3  TO PUBLIC ;
```

The subquery in lines 5 to 8 delivers the department number provided the user is the manager of the department. The outer query delivers all columns (including the salary) of all rows in that department. The actual security inherent in this example turns on the knowledge of the password of the departmental manager.

8.12 EXERCISES

1. Create a view which shows for each INVOICE, the invoice details and all PAYMENT details, even for those invoices which have received *no* payments.

2. Create a view which shows the name and age (just once) of every musician in the VIOLIN, PIANO, CELLO and FLUTE tables.

Chapter 9

SQL Case Studies

9.1 INTRODUCTION

In this chapter we are going to consider several 'real life' case studies in which SQL queries are involved in interesting and sometimes quite challenging ways. Previous chapters have used various smaller examples to illustrate particular SQL programming points. The aim here is not only to discover some more features of SQL but also to get a feel for one or two of the difficulties the programmer may come across in the larger type of example. As with any other programming language, getting the right algorithm or problem-solving method, independent of the language used, is the real challenge and real interest.

This process of finding the right algorithm (and data structures) is often considered to be an important part of Systems Analysis although it is probably true to say that the current tools and techniques of Systems Analysis will not solve the problem for you; you still have to do the most important and interesting part, the problem-solving part, yourself.

It is worthwhile spending some time, once you have identified the crux of the problem, in thinking, experimenting, diagram drawing and discussing the problem with interested colleagues. The fundamental 'divide and conquer' idea of analysis - breaking larger problems down into smaller, more manageable chunks - *is* often useful; we shall give more examples showing how SQL VIEWs can be used as an aid here.

Remember that larger problems can usually be decomposed in more than one way and this again is up to the individual; established Systems Analysis methodologies do not usually give you a definitive answer here. A good idea to have in mind when you 'analyse' (break down or decompose) a problem is to aim to minimize the 'linkages' between the separate parts you have created.

In this way, the separate parts can be considered in a greater degree of isolation from each other, which helps the analyst to focus in on a *part* of the problem. It also makes it possible to have separate people working on separate parts of the original large problem.

The usual situation for 'larger' problems, and most database type problems are large in some way - large quantities of data and/or large numbers of related entity types - is that the data structures are generally 'fixed' in the Data Analysis phase, as discussed in Chapter 2. The idea is that to obtain 'program - data independence', the Entity Modelling (Entity Analysis) phase should be performed without too much thought for particular programs that will have to run against the data. In this way all programs will be equally advantaged (or disadvantaged) in their processing.

Entity Modelling and Normalization and in general the 'database approach' were a great leap forward over the *ad hoc* design methods that preceded them. However, some of the case studies which follow illustrate the rather close dependency there can be between data structure and SQL statement design. In any case, a representative query set can be very useful as a check on the emerging database schema design, as discussed in Chapter 2.

There is another class of case study below, which is characterized by the idea 'Easy to Say but Hard to Do'. The Workshop Groups problem was motivated entirely by an interesting, important and apparently quite tricky query, which could however be expressed in the straightforward English form 'Who is in a second-term workshop group with somebody he or she was in a group with in the first term?' - a quite reasonable request which turns out to be fairly demanding when an SQL solution is sought.

Another case study in this class is the Recruitment example, one of whose queries is 'Who qualifies for a course for which he has applied'. This English version is even easier to understand, but getting the right SQL is fairly demanding, even with a well-designed database and a classroom full of intelligent final year computing students! The obstacles to getting the right SQL might include the set-oriented nature of SQL; most of the aforementioned students wanted to solve this problem using a more procedural 'get this and then check that' approach.

It is perhaps worth commenting here that Embedded SQL reverts to record-at-a-time processing (See Chapter 11) and that many programmers hold the view that therein lies its strength. My own opinion is that a lot more can be done with *interactive* SQL than is generally recognized, once the programmer has obtained some experience in using it and begun to understand its power. It is really quite difficult to find examples where interactive SQL *cannot* be pressed into getting the solution. (See the last two case studies). Also in this category of 'Easy to Say but Hard to Do' problems is the query 'Who won the election?' in the Candidate case study. This problem was mentioned briefly in Chapter 8.

The Motor Manufacturer problem illustrates an interesting aspect of ORACLE SQL*PLUS - the CONNECT BY feature - without which the simple parts explosion listing required for vehicle assembly would probably not be possible in SQL. Here we have a class of problem which involves a tree data structure of indeterminate depth which requires a recursive process (or a stack of indeterminate height) to scan. A similar problem is to print out an organization chart showing a company's management hierarchy. Again, representing a family tree of variable 'depth' would require CONNECT BY. Not only unenhanced SQL but even many popular procedural programming languages would find these processes cumbersome.

Finally, for the sake of, well, just wanting to know, there are two examples of problems which probably are *not* suitable for SQL, even though they contain lots of similarly-structured 'records' and in that sense *are* 'database' type problems. For some reason, they are both connected with food. The Dieting case study and the Recipes case study both have a flavour of searching for combinations and optimization about them and suggestions are given about more suitable approaches. The discussion around them attempts to give a feeling for the frontiers of SQL 'territory'. In any case they can be viewed as a challenge to your SQL programming prowess!

9.2 CASE STUDIES

9.2.1 Case Study 1 - The Workshop Groups Problem

At the Polytechnic of Peace and Light, final year students in both the PGD and BSc courses take part in two assessed workshop projects, one in the first term and one in the second. Each project requires two presentations and the second presentation of each project is accompanied by supporting documentation. Workshop lectures and activities are combined for the two courses. The bulk of the work leading up to the presentations is performed by workshop groups, which consist of a combination of students from both courses. Normally there are three members to a group but occasionally groups of two or four members are allowed. The groups each specify their project title and contents in the first presentation of each term and show what they have produced in the form of working systems in the second presentation.

There are conventions relating to group composition. Firstly there should be a maximum of two BSc students in any group. Groups with no BSc members are allowed. Secondly, groups are completely reconstituted in the second term, so that nobody should be in a group with someone he or she was in a group with in the first term.

Assessment occurs during the workshop presentations and is carried out by three or four members of academic staff who each assign marks to groups on a number of agreed criteria, each of which has an agreed relative weighting. The criteria and their weightings may vary from one presentation to another, although the number of criteria is always three. The marks from each staff member are combined at an academic workshop group meeting after each presentation, to produce a single workshop mark for that group in the range zero to three hundred, even for groups of two or four members. This mark is then divided among the workshop group members in a way decided by the group itself and the figure for each group member is recorded because it will contribute to his or her final award classification.

The work of the individual group leading up to final presentations is as follows. After deciding on a workshop project title and sgreeing this and the general content of the project with staff members, the work is divided into a number of stages and allocated to group members according to their interests and abilities. The completion of some of the stages is often a prerequisite for subsequent stages and group meetings are regularly called to record progress and co-ordinate group activities. The requirements of the group for computing and other resources necessary for producing and presenting an adequate project must be agreed shortly

after the first presentation in each term so that rooms and resources can
be allocated in good time. A timetable for presentations, which normally
last for twenty minutes, is published two weeks before the due date.

Database Design

An entity model for this case study is shown in Fig. 9.1.

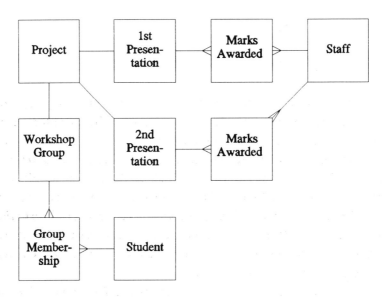

Fig. 9.1 Entity Model For Workshop Groups Database

An aspect of this case study that leads to interesting questions relating
to SQL programming is one of the group composition rules. It says that
in the second term, no person should be in a workshop group with
someone he or she was in a group with in the first term.

In order to investigate this query in isolation a database table GROUPS
has been created and contains the following sample data.

There would of course be other tables representing the other entity
types of interest in the database but the query which motivated this case
study primarily concerns this table GROUPS.

TERM	GROUP_NO	MEMBER
1	1	1
1	1	2
1	1	3
1	2	4
1	2	5
1	2	6
2	10	3
2	10	2
2	1	5
2	1	7

The first column shows the term number: 1 for the first term groups and 2 for the second term groups. Notice that group numbering in the second term starts again at 1; there is a group number 1 in the first term and a group number 1 in the second term. The identifier for a *group* is consequently a composite of TERM and GROUP_NO. The identifier for a *row* in the table (the 'primary key') is a composite of all three column names: TERM, GROUP_NO and MEMBER. The identifier for a *student* is the value of MEMBER; students retain their workshop MEMBER number throughout the year. For interest, the entity model for this part of the database is shown in Fig. 9.2.

Note that there are three 'primary' entity types, TERM, GROUP and MEMBER, and an association between all three, the unfortunately-named GROUPS. Some people would call GROUPS a 'linker' or an 'associative entity type'.

I prefer to just consider it a plain entity type and search around for a proper name for what it really represents; this, I feel, forces me to look again at the 'real world situation' to identify the thing (entity type or class) I am trying to model and give it a name.

To me, entity modelling is not a *creative* process; it is a process of correctly describing what you see. A better name for the entity type would have been MEMBERSHIP, or perhaps GROUP_MEMBERSHIP because a single membership is the thing that involves one term, one group and one student.

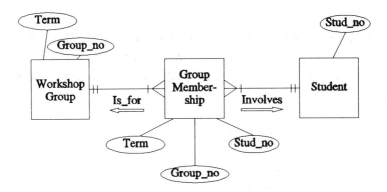

Fig. 9.2 Entity Model for Part of Workshop Groups Database

The query we are interested in is:

Query 9.1 'Who is in a second-term group with someone they were
in a first-term group with?'

Problem Analysis

If you look closely at the table you will be able to see that students 2 and
3 were together in a group in term 1 and together in a group in term 2
(term 1 group 1 and term 2 group 10). Imagine you had a hundred
students in term 1 and the same hundred students in term 2. There would
be two hundred rows in the GROUPS table and a manual search
('eyeball') through a printed version of the table to pick up people who
were together twice would be very lengthy; unless, that is, you think about
the problem a little bit; you can say you are doing systems analysis if you
like!

The algorithm you would choose for this manual search would depend
on you. In discussing this with people I have discovered that there are lots
of algorithms that come forward, and several different assumptions that
could be made, for example whether the table was sorted in one of a
variety of different ways.

First Thoughts

First of all let us look at the problem using a fairly naive 'blind search', *without* sorting. Imagine there are four 'copies' of the table. Copies A and B are for the first term, and copies C and D are for the second term.

```
FOR EACH member in Copy A
    FOR EACH member in Copy B
        FOR EACH member in Copy C
            FOR EACH member in Copy D
                APPLY the 'same group' tests
                IF in same group twice OUTPUT warning ENDIF
            NEXT D
        NEXT C
    NEXT B
NEXT A
```

So initially the first row of each copy will be fetched and the tests applied. Then the next D will be fetched and tested, then the next D and so on until the end of the D rows. Next, the second C row is fetched and the first D re-fetched and the tests applied again going right through D again for each C row. And so on ...

There are a hundred rows in each copy. Clearly, each row in A will be fetched once, so there are 100 A fetches. Each row in B will be fetched 100 times, so there are 10,000 B fetches. Each row in C will be fetched 10,000 times and so there are 1,000,000 C fetches. And each row in D will be fetched 1,000,000 times so there will be 100,000,000 D fetches. For each of these D fetches, the 'same group' test will be applied. The number of fetch-and-tests can be enumerated as follows:

```
D table fetches        100,000,000
C table fetches          1,000,000
B table fetches             10,000
A table fetches                100
-----------------------------------
Total    fetches       101,010,100
```

If the number of students is increased to 200, the number of fetches is 1,608,040,200 which is over one thousand six hundred million fetches! So the algorithm rapidly degrades in performance with increased data. The word 'fetch', the way I have used it, simply means being able to locate and inspect a row from the database table GROUPS. How long this takes on average depends on a number of practical factors, such as whether all the rows are memory-resident or if disk accesses are required during the search, the buffer size etc. Assuming an average fetch time of one millisecond (0.001 sec) for example, then the total time to complete this query for 200 students is over four hundred hours!

Second Thoughts

Let's consider a 'best case' for our search in which the MEMBER numbers are allocated sequentially in term 1. The term 1 data would then have a 'sorted' appearance similar to the term 1 part of the test data in the GROUPS table above. All the term 1 rows are first, the GROUP_NOs gradually go up and the MEMBER number is in strict ascending order as shown.

In term 2 we have a choice of the ideal sequence of rows. Suppose they are in MEMBER number sequence again. Then the GROUP_NO will be unsorted. If they are in GROUP_NO sequence the MEMBER number will be unsorted.

The point about sorted data is that our eyes are very good at finding an item in a sorted list; that is the major reason for learning the alphabet and one of the reasons for learning to count. We are also good at looking for simple patterns, for example 'Are any of these three or four numbers identical?'. Single-processor computers on the other hand make a bit of a song and dance about such things. Try writing a program for this or the problem 'Put these three numbers in order'and you will see what I mean. The program looks fairly involved for such a simple problem. Then do a trace or a 'dry run' of your program code to see how it executes; again fairly tortuous for problems we humans can do almost instantly (using methods we cannot explain, incidentally).

To simplify our algorithm further we can now imagine that we have two sheets of paper, the left-hand sheet containing the first term data and the right-hand sheet the second term data. The left-hand sheet is sorted on GROUP_NO and MEMBER and the right-hand sheet sorted on just MEMBER.

Now to check for people being in a group with each other twice we could take a pair of members from the same group in term 1 and check that this pair had different groups in term 2. We would then take the next pair in that term 1 group and check that they also had different groups in term 2. In a group of three there are three distinct pairs; in a workshop group of four members there are six distinct pairs but since this does not occur very often and might be counterbalanced by the occasional group of two, we shall ignore it.

So for each first term group there are three pairs to check. For each of these pairs we just have to find the same pair on the second page and check that the group numbers are different. Since there are approximately a hundred same-group pairs in the first term and a hundred pairs to check with in the second term data, it looks like we have about 100 * 100 = 10000 comparisons to do. That would take only a few hours to do manually, assuming one or two seconds for each step of 'get a first-term pair, search for the pair in second term and check they are in different groups'. The interactive SQL version of the code that eventually emerged from this 'compare the pairs' approach is:

```
1  SELECT DISTINCT A.TERM,A.GROUP_NO,A.MEMBER,
2  B.MEMBER, C.TERM,C.GROUP_NO,C.MEMBER,D.MEMBER
3  FROM GROUPS A,GROUPS B,GROUPS C,GROUPS D
4  WHERE A.TERM = 1
5  AND   B.TERM = 1
6  AND   C.TERM = 2
7  AND   D.TERM = 2
8  AND A.GROUP_NO  = B.GROUP_NO
9  AND C.GROUP_NO  = D.GROUP_NO
10  AND A.MEMBER < B.MEMBER
11  AND C.MEMBER < D.MEMBER
12  AND A.MEMBER = C.MEMBER
13  AND B.MEMBER = D.MEMBER
```

Giving:

TERM	GROUP_NO	MEMBER	MEMBER	TERM	GROUP_NO	MEMBER	MEMBER
1	1	2	3	2	10	2	3

which is correct. Members 2 and 3 *were* together in both terms.

The efficiency questions relating to this form of the SQL query will be considered later; let us first consider the logical aspects of the query. This is a four way self-join. Line 3 shows the table GROUPS being mentioned four times with aliases A, B, C, and D.

The idea is that we will compare first term pairs with second term pairs. If we find matching pairs we will output them. Lines 4 to 7 specify that the first pair is from term 1 and the second pair is from term 2. Lines 8 and 9 ensure that the members of a pair are both from the same workshop group.

The operation of lines 10 and 11 is fairly subtle. Why a less-than ('<')? In joining tables, every row is considered against every other row and a join occurs if the criteria are met. In a self-join, one of the rows a given row would be considered against would be itself. To prevent this type of join occurring I first of all tried a not-equals ('!=') here. That worked, but I would still be joining, say, member 2 to member 3 and later member 3 to member 2. Clearly if 2 is in the same group as 3 then 3 is in the same group as 2 - it does not need to be restated. The less-than sign prevents this type of duplicate output.

Lines 12 and 13 check for the two pairs of members being identical. You might ask 'What if A =D and B =D?'. Well since A < B and C < D, if the pairs are identical then the firsts will match and the seconds will match.

Now we consider the speed question. Even though the SQL query is logically correct, it might be thought that it will tend to execute slowly, and use lots of space. If four copies of the table *really were* joined then a million rows would result. If the rows were not in any particular order, the performance could be expected to be similar to the 'First Thoughts' figures.

In practice, the DBMS query interpreter intervenes to optimize the query to the best of its ability. Firstly, the matching criteria in SQL lines 4 to 13 will be applied *before* the rows are joined. And the speed of queries with a low hit-rate (proportion of rows retrieved) may be improved by making use of indexes on GROUP_NO and MEMBER. The decisions the query interpreter and optimizer make are quite decisive in this query. In practice, it has been found that the ORACLE query optimizer for example performs a 'sort-merge' on the four 'copies' of the GROUPS table and the process takes approximately 30 seconds.

This might be a suitable point to repeat our injunction concerning the need for being careful and conscientious about test data, since errors in the query might not be apparent when inspecting output from large 'real' tables. Note that even after satisfying himself that the query is working, the programmer does not know that there is not a better (faster, simpler or less memory-intensive) form of the query. He does not even know, despite 'rigorous' test data that one day a piece of data may come along that is not handled properly. In short, he cannot be certain that his program is correct. In this respect programming is no different to many other fields of human endeavour.

Also note that having a DBMS, knowing SQL, and knowing various systems analysis techniques, have not given us a single solution algorithm. That is why I have tried to outline as far as I can remember, the reasoning that went into deriving this algorithm. The truth is, we do not know how we think. You could summarize the above points by saying that 'in general' (usually), a programmer does not know how he or she wrote the program, does not know if it works, and does not know if there is a better way to write it.

Query 9.2 'Which workshop groups have more than two degree
        students or contain other than three group members?'

The format of the STUDENT table is shown below. The method used to derive the answer to this query was to consider each half of the problem separately. 'Which groups have more than two degree students?' can be done first and will deliver a set of workshop groups. 'Which groups contain two or four members?' can be done second and will deliver another set of groups.

```
STUD_NO   NAME      COURSE
-------   ----      ------
      1   Art       BSc
      2   Buck      BSc
      3   Charlie   BSc
      4   Dizzy     PGD
      5   Errol     PGD
      6   Fats      BSc
      7   Gerald    PGD
```

Of course there may be some groups that have more than two degree students and other than three members. We can prevent those groups being printed twice by taking the UNION of these two sets.

Incidentally, you might have considered using an OR in the WHERE clause of a single SELECT in this sort of fashion:

SELECT ...
FROM GROUPS, STUDENT
WHERE {number of degree studs > 2}   <Condition1>
OR   {number of members != 3}   <Condition2>

The problem with this is that the numbers of students in workshop groups cannot be found until after a GROUP BY has occurred, which means using a HAVING after grouping. Let's proceed then on the assumption that a UNION is necessary and write the SQL for <Condition1>first.

Query 9.2.1 'Which workshop groups have more than two degree students?'

```
1 SELECT TERM, GROUP_NO,  COURSE, COUNT(*)
2 FROM GROUPS, STUDENT
3 WHERE MEMBER =  STUD_NO
4 AND COURSE =  'BSc'
5 GROUP BY TERM, GROUP_NO,  COURSE
6 HAVING COUNT(*) >  2 ;
```

This produces the correct output:

```
TERM   GROUP_NO   COURSE   COUNT(*)
----   --------   ------   --------
   1          1   BSc             3
```

In Line 2, a join had to be performed between GROUPS and STUDENT so we could see what course everyone was on. Line 3 shows the join criterion which is on student number (which is called MEMBER in one table and STUD_NO in the other - probably not a good design decision). Line 4 selects out rows where the course is BSc. But is it really necessary to include COURSE in the GROUP BY clause? Remembering that WHERE is executed before GROUP BY (See Chapter 3), so the only students who will be counted will be BScs anyway.

If you attempt to run the above query without COURSE in the GROUP BY clause, SQL will object because every item on the SELECT line other than aggregate functions must be in the GROUP BY clause. That is one of the rules for using GROUP BY discussed in Chapter 3. You can see the logic of this rule. If line 4 did not exist then there would be more than one value for COURSE in a group, so SQL would not know which one to print. However line 4 ensures that there is only one value possible for COURSE namely 'BSc'. Unfortunately SQL is not 'clever' enough to see this, but this is only a minor point which can be remedied by removing COURSE from the SELECT line and giving the COUNT(*) a column alias 'BSc_ Count' if required to improve the appearance of the output:

```
1  SELECT TERM, GROUP_NO,  COUNT(*) BSc_Count
2  FROM GROUPS, STUDENT
3  WHERE MEMBER =   STUD_NO
4  AND COURSE =  'BSc'
5  GROUP BY TERM, GROUP_NO
6  HAVING COUNT(*) >  2;
```

which results in the output:

```
TERM    GROUP_NO    BSC_COUNT
----    --------    ---------
 1         1            3
```

We now move on to the second part of Query 9.2.

Query 9.2.2 'Which workshop groups contain other than three group members?'

1 SELECT TERM, GROUP_NO, COUNT(*)
2 FROM GROUPS, STUDENT
3 WHERE MEMBER = STUD_NO
4 GROUP BY TERM, GROUP_NO
5 HAVING COUNT(*) != 3;

This produces the correct output:

```
TERM    GROUP_NO    COUNT(*)
----    --------    --------
 2         10           2
```

because group 10 in term 2 only had two members. Finally we consider how to form the UNION of the two results to answer the original query 9.2. In order for a UNION to work, the two 'projections' must be 'column homogeneous'; in other words the columns mentioned in the SELECT line of each table must be compatible. (See Chapter 6 for a more detailed discussion). If the required columns are TERM, GROUP_NO, COURSE and COUNT(*) then the composite query will be as shown below.

Note the ' ' in line 8 to ensure compatibility between the columns of the two halves of the query. Note that COURSE could not have been placed in the SELECT in line 8 because there could be different values for COURSE in groups of other than three members. This is reflected in the fact that the GROUP BY in line 11 is on TERM, GROUP_NO and so COURSE must not appear in the SELECT line (SQL Rule) and if it did it could have more than one value for the single output line for this workshop group.

```
 1  SELECT TERM, GROUP_NO, COURSE, COUNT(*)
 2  FROM GROUPS, STUDENT
 3  WHERE MEMBER = STUD_NO
 4  AND COURSE = 'BSc'
 5  GROUP BY TERM, GROUP_NO, COURSE
 6  HAVING COUNT(*) > 2
 7  UNION
 8  SELECT TERM, GROUP_NO, ' ', COUNT(*)
 9  FROM GROUPS, STUDENT
10  WHERE MEMBER = STUD_NO
11  GROUP BY TERM, GROUP_NO
12  HAVING COUNT(*) != 3 ;
```

The resulting output is:

TERM	GROUP_NO	COURSE	COUNT(*)
1	1	BSc	3
2	10		2

There is still the temptation to try to combine the two halves of the query and remove the UNION. Considering the fact that COURSE could in practice be removed from the output report without a great loss of information leads to the idea that both halves of the query could have COURSE removed from the SELECT line and the GROUP BY line. The problem then, as mentioned above, is with the combination of WHERE conditions and HAVING conditions on the groups. It appears likely therefore that the above is the best SQL obtainable for this query.

Query 9.3 'Produce a listing showing the composition of each
        workshop group on a single line. Groups may have two
        or three members'.

This query illustrates a limitation of the outer join provided by the (+) operator in ORACLE SQL*PLUS. While this is an extremely useful feature in many situations and reduces the length of some queries considerably, this query needed to use an alternative approach.

In Chapter 4 Query 4.9 a query involving a three-way self-join of the GROUPS table was discussed. The GROUPS table in use for that example was as follows:

```
GROUPS
------

TERM    GROUP_NO    MEMBER
----    --------    ------

  1         1          1
  1         1          2
  1         1          3
  1         2          4
  1         2          5
  1         2          6
  2        10          3
  2        10          2
  2        10          9
  2         1          5
  2         1          7
  2         1          8
```

The aim was to produce a report where the members for each group were shown on one line per group and the output was (correctly) as follows:

```
TERM    GROUP_NO    MEMBER    MEMBER    MEMBER
----    --------    ------    ------    ------

  1         1          1         2         3
  1         2          4         5         6
  2         1          5         7         8
  2        10          2         3         9
```

The three-way self-join worked because every group had three group members. Consider the same query where it is possible that some groups may legally have two OR three members. Suppose the GROUPS table contains the following data:

GROUPS
- - - - - -

TERM	GROUP_NO	MEMBER
1	1	1
1	1	2
1	1	3
1	2	4
1	2	5
1	2	6
2	10	3
2	10	2
2	1	5
2	1	7

Notice that groups 10 and 1 in term 2 only have two members whereas the rest of the groups have three members. A three-way self inner join (as in Query 4.9) would not work because it would omit all data for the two-member groups. All attempts by the present author to use the outer join in ORACLE SQL*PLUS using the (+) operator in several different query configurations have also failed, all resulting in the production of spurious two-member output rows from the groups that have three members.

The SQL Query shown below is suggested as a solution.

The query produces the correct output as follows:

TERM	GROUP_NO	MEMBER	MEMBER	MEMBER
1	1	1	2	3
1	2	4	5	6
2	1	5	7	0
2	10	2	3	0

There are several points worthy of attention in this query. Lines 1 to 5 are identical with those of Query 4.9 and deal with workshop groups in which there are three members. Lines 7 to 16 deal with groups with only two members. The output from the SELECTs dealing with these two cases is appended using the UNION operator and if there were groups allowed with a number of members greater or less than two and three, using this style of solution would require a SELECT for each case.

Line 7 ends in a 'dummy' column with the constant value zero. This is necessary because SQL will only allow the UNION of 'column homogeneous' sets of rows, that is the rows must have the same number of columns and corresponding columns must be of the same type. Zero was used because the third MEMBER column is numeric.

```
 1   SELECT A.TERM, A.GROUP_NO, A.MEMBER, B.MEMBER, C.MEMBER
 2   FROM GROUPS A, GROUPS B, GROUPS C
 3   WHERE A.TERM = B.TERM AND B.TERM = C.TERM
 4   AND A.GROUP_NO = B.GROUP_NO AND B.GROUP_NO = C.GROUP_NO
 5   AND A.MEMBER <  B.MEMBER AND B.MEMBER <  C.MEMBER
 6   UNION
 7   SELECT A.TERM, A.GROUP_NO, A.MEMBER, B.MEMBER, 0
 8   FROM GROUPS A, GROUPS B
 9   WHERE A.TERM =  B.TERM
10   AND    A.GROUP_NO =  B.GROUP_NO
11   AND    A.MEMBER <  B.MEMBER
12   AND NOT EXISTS
13   (SELECT *
14     FROM GROUPS C
15     WHERE B.TERM =  C.TERM AND B.GROUP_NO =  C.GROUP_NO
16     AND    C.MEMBER != A.MEMBER AND C.MEMBER != B.MEMBER) ;
```

The second SELECT with its subquery SELECT * FROM GROUPS WHERE NOT EXISTS can be described in ordinary English as: 'All the matching GROUPS - JOIN - GROUPS rows where there does not exist a third member in the same group'.

In lines 5 and 11 the '<' signs ensure that permutations of three and two member numbers respectively do not appear at the output. In lines 7 to 16 table alias names A and B are re-used (they had also been used in lines 1 to 5). There is no connection between the table alias names on either side of a UNION operator. SQL treats the SELECTs on each side of the UNION operator as separate queries and merely appends the results of the second to the results of the first.

Summary

This case study has covered

- Speed considerations in multiple self-joins

- Use of UNION with GROUP BY

9.2.2 Case Study 2 - The Motor Manufacturer

A large motor manufacturer produces about twenty different models of motor car. Several different sites are involved; production of each model is designated to a particular site although certain of the larger sites produce more than one model.

Each car utilizes several hundreds of component parts; a given type of part may be used on more than one model of car and there are many thousands of different parts in use across the company.

Provision of parts to the production sites is organised centrally. Most parts are purchased from outside suppliers; there are about 200 such suppliers and it is company policy to have a main supplier and at least one alternative supplier for each part.

Some component parts are made up from other, smaller, components; in this case it is usual to stock both the assembled part as well as the collection of smaller components.

Certain models can be customised by purchasers ordering special factory-fitted options (e.g. sunroofs, 'go-faster' wheels etc.) from a menu of such options. Certain special options are applicable to more than one model of car. The company is considering the installation of an integrated database, managed by a proprietary Database Management System, in order to facilitate both manufacturing and financial management.

Database Design

There are various entity models that can be offered for this case study and which one is produced depends on some of the assumptions made to fill in where the specification is not complete or is unclear on the definitions or 'meaning' of each of the entity types and relationships in the model. These should all be made clear in a data dictionary. When the model is being produced using a CASE (Computer Aided Software Engineering) tool, you are encouraged to store these definitions which will then be of great use for all other subsequent users (systems analysts, database programmers, even end users). Typical test data is shown below and an entity model is shown overleaf in Fig. 9.3.

PART1		FITTING1	
PART_NO	DESCR	PART_NO	PARENT
1000	Dreambaby	1000	
2000	Mustang	2000	
100	Chassis	100	1000
200	Body	200	1000
300	Interior	300	1000
10	Frame	10	100
20	Transmission	20	100
30	Engine	30	100
1	Block	1	30
2	Ignition	2	30
110	Chassis	110	2000
210	Body	210	2000
310	Interior	310	2000
11	Frame	11	110
21	Transmission	21	110
		30	110

From the SQL point of view, one of the most interesting aspects of this case study concerns the entity types PART and FITTING on the entity model. A 'fitting' relates to just two parts, a major part and a minor part. The idea is that the process of constructing a car involves taking a minor part, for example a bracket and 'fitting' it to a major part for example a panel. The panel may later take the role of a minor part in another fitting when it is fitted to, say, a chassis which in this fitting is a major part but will be a minor part in a subsequent fitting. A MODEL is said to be a particular type of part in this entity diagram: a completed vehicle. How accurately this reflects the actual practice of motor car assembly will determine how useful the database based on this entity diagram will be.

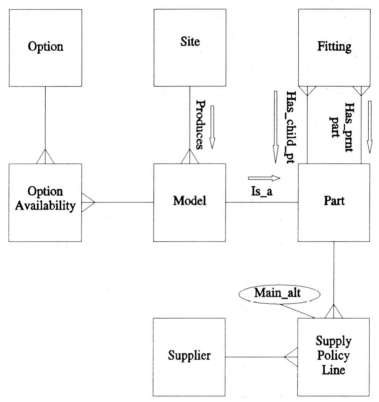

Fig. 9.3 Entity Model for Motor Manufacturer Database

The query of interest which motivates the inclusion of this case study concerns just the PART and FITTING entity types. The PART1 and FITTING1 tables shown above were created to test the feasibility of this part of the design.

PART1 is simply a list of parts, including two obvious *models*, the

Dreambaby and the Mustang. The FITTING1 table indicates the relationship of parts.

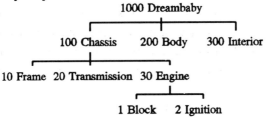

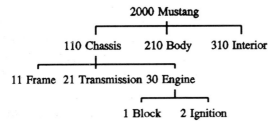

Fig. 9.4 Tree Diagram of Parts Explosion for two Car Models

The column PARENT shows the 'major part' and the column PART_NO shows the 'minor part'. This hierarchical relationship of part to part can be illustrated as a tree diagram. See Fig. 9.4.

There are in effect two tree diagrams; one for each model. However, notice that part 30 is used in construction of both parts 100 and 110. In general, many parts will be 'minor' parts of more than one 'major' part, for example a 6BA bolt may be used in many positions around the car. Also, some parts will in practice occur at several different 'levels' in the tree.

If every part were represented once only on the diagram, it would no longer be a 'tree' diagram but a 'network' diagram. In general these are hard to draw without lines crossing so the tree convention has grown up. One consequence of this is that some 'nodes' (parts in this example) will have to be shown more than once. (An example of a 'true' tree diagram is an Organization Chart showing who manages whom in a company where everyone except the top manager has only one manager. The top manager is said to be at the 'root' of the tree).

One instance of a report that would be useful in the Motor

Manufacturer database which has a tree structure is a Parts Explosion Report. This shows the hierarchical relationship of part to part and gives an indication of how the car models can be constructed, what parts are needed to make a given part and what parts are made from a given part. The last might be useful to determine which parts cannot be made if a given part goes out of stock. We shall concentrate on the following query:

Query 9.4 'Produce a Parts Explosion diagram for the Dreambaby model'.

We cannot, using SQL, produce the tree diagram in exactly the form shown in Fig. 9.4. It might be possible but the drawing of lines showing the relationship of parts, and the limitations regarding the width of screens and stationery would present programming difficulies. However some method of indicating the hierarchy is necessary.

It is true that the table FITTING1 does contain sufficient information to show the hierarchy, but you do not want to have to pick your way through such a linear-looking table to *infer* the relationship of parts. To demonstrate that tuple *order* would not be sufficient to show the relationship of parts (even if it could be guaranteed on a relational database which it generally cannot), consider the very simple case where part 1 contains part 2 contains part 3. If you represented the data as

```
PART
- - - -
   1
   2
   3
```

then it is unclear whether part 1 contains parts 2 and 3 or part 1 contains part 2 contains part 3 or whether they are all at the same 'level'. It is this notion of level that gives the clue, and ORACLE SQL*PLUS has the facility of inferring level in its CONNECT BY extension to SQL. It puts the current value of level into a variable called LEVEL which is accessible to the SQL programmer.

The method we shall use to show the relationship between a major part

and a minor part is indentation. Minor parts will be indented a few places
to the right under their 'owning' major part, the number of indentation
places being proportional to the value of LEVEL. In the simple case
shown above, the output can then be made to appear in the form

PART

- - - -

   1

     2

       3

which conveys hierarchical information more clearly than FITTING1 does,
and achieves it with just one column.

This format is suitable for Query 9.7, except that we want to have the
name of the part included in the query too. This means that FITTING1
and PART1 will have to be joined.

I could not get CONNECT BY to work with a join, even when the join
was disguised by using a view. So I had to create a temporary database
table and drop it again later. Here I am creating the temporary table:

```
1  CREATE TABLE TEMP1 AS
2  SELECT FITTING1.PART_NO,  DESCR, PARENT
3  FROM FITTING1, PART1
4  WHERE FITTING1.PART_NO  =  PART1.PART_NO;
```

The join is necessary so that the part description DESCR can be tacked
on to make the output more informative. Shown below is the actual query
with the results. Note the (rather primitive, I admit) attempt at showing
the structural relationship of the parts by just indenting the PART_NO.

Incidentally, none of this would have been possible in INGRES SQL,
which doesn't have CONNECT BY. I think you might also have difficulty
in INGRES '4GL' because the tree scan inherent in CONNECT BY and
necessary to produce a Parts Explosion is by nature recursive.

Several popular 3GLs also prohibit recursion so imbedding an SQL
SELECT in one of these would also not yield the desired result. This
illustrates the utility of having such a facility in SQL. Imagine having to

perform stack processing in COBOL where an iterative method is used!

```
1 SELECT LPAD('.', 2*LEVEL)||PART_NO PARTS_EXPLOSION
2    DESCR, PARENT
3 FROM TEMP1
4 CONNECT BY PRIOR PART_NO  =  PARENT
5 START WITH PART_NO  =  1000;
```

Alternatively, if you didn't know that the Dreambaby corresponded to part 1000, you could replace line 5 with

```
5 START WITH DESCR = 'Dreambaby'
```

It is not really necessary to have the right-hand column PARENT shown in the report since the left-hand column shows the major-minor part relationship. In line 1, the variable LEVEL can be seen in one of the arguments of the LPAD function. Here, the LPAD function is being used to print a number of dots '.': in fact the number of dots to print is to be two times the value of LEVEL. In this way the PART_NO value can be indented a variable number of places.

The '||' is a concatenation operator so that the expression LPAD('.', 2*LEVEL)||PART_NO can be considered a single output 'column'. PARTS_EXPLOSION is an alias for this output column to make the output column heading more meaningful. The output that results is:

```
PARTS_EXPLOSION          DESCR          PARENT
---------------          -----          ------

..1000                   Dreambaby
....100                  Chassis        1000
......10                 Frame          100
......20                 Transmission   100
......30                 Engine         100
........1                Block          30
........2                Ignition       30
....200                  Body           1000
....300                  Interior       1000
```

To ensure that there is enough space for all the indentation (you will not necessarily know in advance how many levels there are), the run of this query should be preceded by the command

COLUMN PARTS_EXPLOSION FORMAT A21

This defines the 'virtual column' PARTS_EXPLOSION as alphabetic of width 21 for the duration of the run. Line 4 is the CONNECT BY line. The clause

PRIOR PART_NO = PARENT

establishes which is the higher-level column. It can be read as 'the prior of PART_NO is PARENT'.

  PRIOR is used in this way to denote the fact that if you are proceeding from the root of the tree downwards to lower levels, then you will reach the part number in the PARENT column before you reach the part number in the PART_NO column.

  Finally in line 5 the clause START WITH PART_NO = 1000 gives a condition 'PART_NO = 1000' to determine the row to start from. It is not necessary to start from the root of the tree. In this example, a production engineer might just want to produce a parts explosion for a sub-assembly such as the engine. This line would then read

START WITH PART_NO = 30

  The temporary table TEMP1 should now be dropped to avoid cluttering up the database with unnecessary data.

DROP TABLE TEMP1 ;

The CONNECT BY feature can also be used in the other direction, from a lower level through to the root (or roots). For example here we might wish to answer the query 'Which assemblies will be affected if this component goes out of stock?'. In all, CONNECT BY is a very useful command.

Summary

In this case study we have covered

- How tree-structured data can be represented as a relation and thus as an SQL table.

- How to think of a network such as that representing the relatedness of parts in an assembly environment as a tree-structured 'parts explosion'.

- How scanning or 'walking' a tree of unknown depth is a recursive process.

- The fact that some DBMSs and even some common 3GLs cannot perform recursion.

- How to use the CONNECT BY feature of ORACLE SQL*PLUS to do a recursive tree walk and hence complete a Parts Explosion report.

9.2.3 Case Study 3 - Student Recruitment

A Polytechnic uses the following procedures for student recruitment. Applications are received throughout the year, right up to a month before courses begin in the first week of October. Applicants can apply for a single course on a Polytechnic application form but may submit several forms, one for each course. Applicants are accepted on a maximum of ONE of the courses for which they have applied and are sent an acceptance or rejection letter as appropriate. These letters are sent out bi-monthly at the end of odd-numbered months. Applicants can either accept or reject places offered on courses and the number of offers made must reflect maximum course size criteria.

The Polytechnic wants the best-qualified applicants it can get, but since it favours a simple recruitment policy, applicants are made offers on a first-come first-served policy for those who meet the qualification criteria for each course. A fixed number of offers, 150 per cent of the number of places nominally available, is made. At the end of each month the number of places still vacant is recalculated and when this is zero no further applicants are accepted.

In order to be qualified for a place on a course an applicant must have all the qualifications required at the stated level or better. There are usually a number of ways to qualify for a course. For example, to qualify for entry to Course A, an applicant requires, in the words of the recruiting officer for that course, "An 'A' Level Maths at 'C' or above, an 'A' Level Physics at 'B' or above and at least 'O' Level English at grade 2 or better, with any pass grade in a foreign language". Another course has several routes. See Fig. 9.5.

Some courses have three or more routes. Entrance requirements are sometimes even in the form 'Any three of the following six quals', and there are other variations as well. The aim is to computerise the admissions system and to use a database.

The initial objective is to test the feasibility of such a system with particular reference to a consideration of the practicability of implementing a non-interview policy, at least for most applicants, based on matching the set of qualifications an applicant has with one of the sets of qualifications a course requires. The practibility of the approach should be demonstrated using a prototype database and program fragments.

Such *matching* type problems occur with considerable frequency and are often suitable for a database approach. Dating agencies and computerised car sales are other examples with an emphasis on matching. In matching problems, one is matching the desired attributes of a set of required objects with the actual attributes of a set of available objects. The matching process is made more difficult if inexact matching is allowed, in which case some notion of 'distance' between the two sets of attributes is often employed.

Database Design

An entity model for the ACQ (Applicant-Course-Qualification) problem is shown in Fig 9.6. Some of the attributes of particular interest are shown on the model to aid in 'reading' it.

```
Qual                            Level

----                            -----


'A' Level Maths                 'C' or better
'O' Level English                3  or better
HNC or HND Electronics          2 credits


OR


'A' Level Physics               'D' or above
'O' Level English                2  or better
HND Electronics                 1 distinction and rest credits
```

Fig. 9.5 Sample of a Qualification Set

A certain amount of analysis had already occurred before the model took the form of Fig. 9.6. For example the notion of 'grade rank', an attempt to deal with the diversity of qualification grades, has had a certain impact on the shape of the model. This is discussed further below. Other solutions are possible, and some of them may result in different entity models.

The tables that resulted from this model, and some accompanying test data, follow. Primary keys have double-underlining and foreign keys have single underlining.

In the APPLICATION table the columns POLY_A_R and APP_A_R show the status of an application. A_R stands for Accept-Reject. For example if the Polytechnic had made an offer but the applicant had not yet accepted or rejected it, the first column would be 'A' and the second 'null'. 'A' means 'accept', 'R' means 'reject' and null means 'neither of these'. The applicant might reject the offer or the Polytechnic might reject the application. These flags are meant to make it unnecessary to test each applicant all over again every time a list of successful applications or similar is required.

For the relational zealot, this is not strictly necessary, since other parts of the database contain enough information to indicate acceptance or rejection. However, by suffering this limited redundancy in the flags you

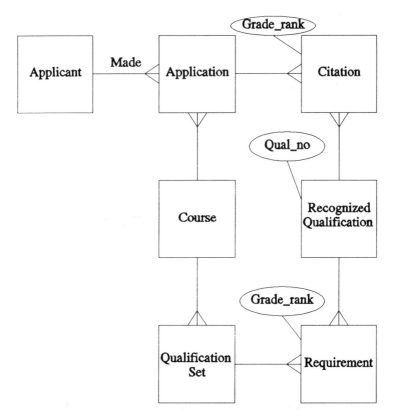

Fig. 9.6 Entity Model for Student Recruitment Database

gain speed and some simplification of frequently-used queries and programs, but of course you then have to live with some potential for inconsistency on the database.

Say, for example, the grade rank of some qualification was 'eased' such that an already-rejected application could now satisfy the requirements. If the update had been done on a 'look and change' basis the need to re-evaluate applications may be overlooked.

This type of redundancy also often occurs in database tables containing counts and totals. They can be very useful to get quick answers without counting or totalling each time but the approach may lead to inconsistency.

APPLICANT

APP_NO	NAME
1	Alan
2	Brenda
3	Corin

APPLICATION

APP_NO	COURSE_NO	POLY_A_R	APP_A_R
1	1	null	null
1	2	null	null
2	1	null	null
3	2	null	null

COURSE

COURSE_NO	NAME	MAX_C_SIZE	NO_OF_ACCEPTS
1	Notional Concepts	50	20
2	Welding Therapy	30	10

QUAL_SET

COURSE_NO	QUALSET_NO	NO_OF_OPT_QUALS
1	1	0
1	2	0
2	3	0

REQUIREMENT
- - - - - - - - - - -

QUALSET_NO	QUAL_NO	GRADE_RANK	MAIN_OPT
1	1	3	m
1	2	2	m
2	1	2	m
2	2	3	m
3	2	1	m

APPLICATION_QUAL
- - - - - - - - - - - - - - - -

APP_NO	COURSE_NO	QUAL_NO	GRADE_RANK
1	1	1	2
1	1	2	1
2	1	1	4
3	1	2	1

The usual compromise is to have limited redundancy and specify update programs with suitable validation to ensure database integrity. A data dictionary may be of help here if it contains answers to questions like:

'If this is a calculated field, what other database fields
are used in the calculation?'

A 'qualification set' is a set of qualifications and associated grades (minimum ranks) required by ONE course. It was decided to define it this way to simplify the terminology and the database design. In the QUAL_SET and REQUIREMENT tables, the column QUAL_SET.NO_OF_OPT_QUALS shows the number of optional qualifications a qualification set has and REQUIREMENT.MAIN_OPT shows whether a qualification cited in a qualification set is a 'main' or an 'optional' qual for that qualification set. This was done to allow a course recruiting officer to specify requirements in this way:

'We want this, this and this, and any three out of this list, OR these two and any five of them'

which it was felt would give him or her a good deal of flexibility in specifying his or her 'shopping list' of qualification requirements. Note the key concept of 'grade rank', which is a number from 1 to N denoting the 'goodness' of each qualification grade obtained and required. It was designed to overcome the problem that for some qualifications a grade of 'A' is better than 'B', for some others a '1' is better than a '2', for others a 'Distinction' better than a 'Credit' etc. When a new recognized qualification comes along, all its possible grades can be ranked, with the best having the number 1, second best 2 etc. This data could be stored on a table GRADE_RANK

```
GRADE_RANK(qual_no, grade_name, grade_rank)
```

In this way a unified system is obtained. The grade rank can then be obtained and stored in the APPLICATION_QUAL table on entry of an application using the RECOGNIZED_QUAL and GRADE_RANK tables. Some sort of menu system would be used to display on demand to the user these grade rank numbers for each grade. The user would then select one. There is limited redundancy here. It would be possible for the user to type the grade description in for an obtained qualification (e.g. 'Upper Second' or '2.1') and the data entry program would try and match this against a row in the GRADE RANK table. Due to potential spelling problems and different ways of saying the same thing, it was decided to leave this small pattern match problem to the human user. People are good at that anyway and it simplifies our design. When doing frequently-used and important processes like matching applicants' quals with needed quals it is probably faster to just have to access APPLICANT_QUAL than have to infer the grade rank each time using a join or subqueries to navigate from APPLICANT_QUAL through RECOGNIZED_QUAL to GRADE_RANK.

There is no problem of some quals having a different 'weighting' from one course to another; the person specifying the requirements is at liberty to specify any grade rank he or she thinks appropriate and this value will appear in REQUIREMENT.GRADE_RANK. This would not be the case in a 'points' system where the points for a given qualification grade would have to be stored on the database for each course. The specification mentions 'a design for a suitable system' - rather a tall order in this context. In answer to this, you might include extensive diagramming and code listings to describe the procedures used. I shall not include much of this since to me things like data entry screens, while essential, are pretty routine and will not constitute part of my 'prototype'. When I do prototypes I like to achieve one or both of the following:

1. A means of illustrating to my client or user what the system will look and feel like.

2. Experimental fragments of code to convince me that key parts of the software system are feasible and will run efficiently.

By looking at the entity model and at the table definitions, it is possible to imagine all sorts of queries that could be answered by the database simply by navigating through the database from one entity type (table) to another, usually via the relationships explicitly indicated by foreign keys. I find it useful to build up a list of such queries even before completing the entity model, and have them extended by my user. The user will often understand queries, in their English form of course, better than he or she will understand entities and tables. Some of the queries in the list I have made will be altered by the user and some new ones will probably be added. That list of queries will form an important resource in designing the system, and the discussion necessary in formulating them will help in defining key terms.

At the same time, it is advisable to be working on the entity model and building that up. It will give you an alternative way of speaking and thinking about the problem in terms of entities, attributes, identifiers (keys) and relationships. The list of queries, although probably incomplete, will serve as an acid test of the schema; if it cannot 'do' any of the key queries then it will need to be altered until it can.

Work on simple data entry processes and screen design is in my view not much use at this stage. We know this work is always possible and many 4GL environments give quite a large amount of help in automating this process. Many of these 'screen painters' actually require the relevant database tables to be already in place, although there are on the market some older types of '4GL' that start the whole design process by inviting the analyst to design screens and 'automatically' generating tables from them. While this may lead to short-term time savings, in the long run it can result in a fairly unstructured set of files that cannot be related and many of which contain identical data.

The key for me in this exercise is 'the practibility of implementing the non-interview policy'. It was this that initially inspired the formulation of the case study and its inclusion in this book. My list of queries would have to include things like:

1. 'How many places are left on the B.Sc. Womens' Studies course?'

2. 'What percentage of applicants are home-based?'

3. 'Which applicants qualify for the courses for which they have applied?'

and many others...

Since 3. seems the hardest, and it is important, and it navigates a lot of entity types, it is the one I shall implement.

Query 9.5 'Which applicants qualify for the courses for which
            they have applied?'

I would expect the output from this query to look as shown on the next page. Note that an applicant may qualify for more than one of the courses for which he has applied. It will often be the case that the applicant may qualify for a course for which he or she has not applied. That indicates an interesting but probably not frequently-used query which the database is capable of answering. There are many, many more.

```
Applicant      Course
---------      ------
Fred           Notional Concepts
Fred           Vision Formation
Sally          Welding Therapy
Sindy          Relativity qua Relativity
June           Bedridden but Proud
Sally          Denotational Semantics - a Feminist Perspective
Nigel          The Metaphysics of Overt and Copious Over-
               consumption
June           Howling Therapy for the Over-Forties
Fred           Graveyard Landscaping Therapy for the Under-
               fives
Gary           Learning to Teach Education
Gary           Hexactinellid Spiculation
June           Structured Grieving - A Relational Approach
    etc.
```

Looking at the entity model it appears that the chosen query will have to:

1. Start from APPLICANT to get his/her name.

2. Go via APPLICATION to find a COURSE for which he/she has applied.

3. Get a QUAL_SET for the course being applied for.

4. Consider the set of main REQUIREMENTs for the qual set.

5. Check that there does not exist a main requirement that the applicant does not have by comparing REQUIREMENTs with APPLICANT_QUALs.

6. Check that for this same qual set the number of alternative requirements the applicant has is greater than or equal to the number required and that each of these is acceptable.

If either of the two conditions in 6. is not met then reject the course for that applicant. A very basic attempt which ignores alternative requirements and just considers main requirements is as follows:

```
1   SELECT DISTINCT A.NAME APPLICANT_NAME, C.NAME COURSE_NAME
2   FROM APPLICANT A, APPLICATION B, COURSE C, QUAL_SET D
3   WHERE A.APP_NO = B.APP_NO
4   AND B.COURSE_NO = C.COURSE_NO
5   AND C.COURSE_NO = D.COURSE_NO
6   AND POLY_A_R IS NULL
7   AND APP_A_R  IS NULL
8   AND NOT EXISTS
9    (SELECT *
10    FROM REQUIREMENT E, APPLICATION_QUAL F
11    WHERE A.APP_NO = F.APP_NO
12    AND D.QUALSET_NO = E.QUALSET_NO
13    AND E.QUAL_NO = F.QUAL_NO (+)
14    AND F.GRADE_RANK > E.GRADE_RANK
15    OR  F.QUAL_NO IS NULL);
```

Lines 9 to 15 indicate situations in which an applicant obtains a numerically higher (worse) grade rank than that required by one of the needed quals on a particular qual_set for one of his/her applied_for courses or he/she does not even have the qualification. If such a situation does not exist and there are no outstanding optional quals and the course is not full (neither of these latter two conditions is tested in this prototype query), then the applicant can be made an offer.

Summary

This case study has described the implementation of a query which navigates six tables. The query chosen is merely a prototype and requires further extensions. Generating a list of desirable extensions and their implementation is left as an exercise for the reader.

9.2.4 Case Study 4 - The Candidate Problem

For this case study we are going to start with a database already in place and concentrate on some relevant queries. The database contains details of General Election candidates, their constituencies, electors and polling stations. An entity model for this database is shown in Fig. 9.7.

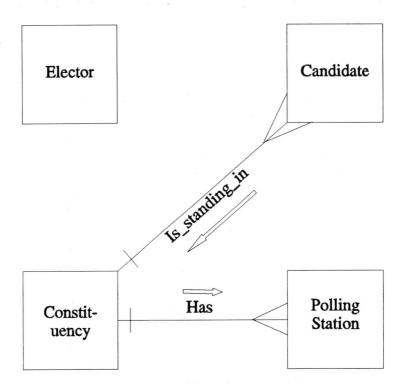

Fig. 9.7 Entity Model for Candidate Database

Note that there is no relationship linking the entity type 'Elector' to any of the other entity types. This is not common but can legitimately occur on an entity-relationship diagram. The reason for it in this example is that a secret ballot system is in use so that who voted for whom (otherwise shown as a 'voted_for' relationship between elector and candidate) is not recorded. The alternatives are either to show the relationship on the diagram and in later documentation indicate the reason for not implementing the relationship, or not to show the relationship on the diagram and give the reason at that stage. In a rigorous structured analysis and design method such as SSADM, there is ample opportunity in the various prescribed stages and steps to document this design decision. The only table used in the queries is CANDIDATE, which is shown below.

CANDIDATE

CAND_NO	NAME	CONS_NO	PARTY	NO_OF_VOTES
1	Fred	1	Labour	100
2	Jim	1	Cons	120
3	Peter	1	Liberal	50
4	John	2	Labour	150
5	Mike	2	SLD	50
6	Jane	2	Cons	100
9	Sue	1	SDP	160
7	Mary	2	Green	150
8	Ulrike	1	Indep	150
10	U Li	3	Red Guards	150
21	Rosa	3	Simbianese	30
29	Patty	3	Simbianese	12
41	Astrid	3	Liberal	3
50	Gordon	3	Labour	160
52	Ben	1	Green	70

There are four queries we shall consider here:

1. 'Which is the constituency with the greatest number of candidates?'

2. 'Which is the winning party in each constituency?'

3. 'Which is the party with the greatest number of winning candidates?'

4. 'What is the percentage of the vote won by each party?'

The first of these is now considered.

Query 9.6 'List the constituency with the greatest number of
         candidates'.

Occasionally, different versions of SQL may perform slightly differently
and one such case is shown here. It has even been known for an upgrade
from one version given vendor's software to display slightly different
results from the next upgrade version. It is interesting to note these cases
when they occur and to discuss them with other users and document
them. Non-trivial software packages have always evolved, so for
experienced programmers this is nothing new. In the case of the products
mentioned in this book, help-lines are available from each vendor which
will give confirmation of version changes and any such 'features'. It is
worthwhile to use this facility because the vendors can only continue to
maintain their high standards of help if users report on their experiences.

Version 1:

```
1 SELECT CONS_NO, COUNT(*)   <---- Works in ORACLE
2 FROM CANDIDATE                    but not in INGRES
3 GROUP BY CONS_NO
4 HAVING COUNT(*) =
5 (SELECT MAX(COUNT(*))
6   FROM CANDIDATE
7   GROUP BY CONS_NO) ;
```

Which produces the correct result in ORACLE SQL*PLUS:

```
CONS_NO   COUNT(*)  <----- Constituency with most
-------   --------         candidates
      1          6
```

Lines 5 to 7 find the maximum count of rows when the rows are grouped
together by constituency number. Lines 1 to 4 list out the constituency

number and the count of candidates having that maximum count of rows. This version of the query (Version 1) does not work in INGRES; it produces a syntax error. If the query is altered slightly to use a '> =ALL' instead of an '= max' the query becomes:

Version 2:

```
1 SELECT CONS_NO, COUNT(*)  <---- Works in INGRES
2 FROM CANDIDATE                    but not in ORACLE
3 GROUP BY CONS_NO
4 HAVING COUNT(*) > =ALL
5 (SELECT COUNT(*)
6   FROM CANDIDATE
7   GROUP BY CONS_NO)  ;
```

The surprise result from ORACLE SQL*PLUS is then:

CONS_NO	COUNT(*)
1	6
2	4
3	5

If just lines 5 to 7 (i.e. just the subquery) are typed in, giving:

```
1 SELECT COUNT(*)
2 FROM CANDIDATE
3 GROUP BY CONS_NO;
```

then the result, as expected is:

COUNT(*)
6
4
5

If the SQL*PLUS subquery is replaced by these explicit values like this:

```
1  SELECT CONS_NO, COUNT(*)
2  FROM CANDIDATE
3  GROUP BY CONS_NO
4  HAVING COUNT(*) > = ALL
5   (6,4,5);
```

then the correct result is again output:

```
CONS_NO    COUNT(*)
-------    --------
      1          6
```

Clearly this is a bug - the only one I have ever found in ORACLE!

Version 2 works correctly in INGRES, giving:

```
CONS_NO    COL2
-------    ----
      1       6
```

The results can be summarized:

```
                  +--------------------+--------------------+
                  |     Version 1      |      Version2      |
+-----------------+--------------------+--------------------+
| ORACLE SQL*PLUS |         ok         |  Incorrect Output  |
| INGRES SQL      |    Syntax Error    |         ok         |
+-----------------+--------------------+--------------------+
```

These results are so rare that the software version you are using will probably work correctly for all the queries in this book. It is one of the responsibilities of the database programmer to look out for these occurrences however, and to report them so that they can be remedied.

Query 9.7 'List the winning party in each constituency'.

The correct results are:

```
CONS_NO    PARTY
-------    -----
      1    SDP
      2    Labour
      2    Green
      3    Labour
```

produced by:

```
1 SELECT CONS_NO,  PARTY
2 FROM CANDIDATE C1
3 WHERE NO_OF_VOTES   =
4  (SELECT MAX(NO_OF_VOTES)
5   FROM CANDIDATE C2
6   WHERE C2.CONS_NO  =  C1.CONS_NO)
7 ORDER BY CONS_NO  ;
```

This is a correlated subquery, meaning that for every outer query row, all the rows in the inner query have to be inspected. For every candidate, that candidate will only be output if he or she has the same number of votes as the maximum number of votes for that constituency. Getting this maximum requires a scan, in the subquery, of every row in the table. The existence of a correlated subquery is indicated by an alias (here C1) that appears in the subquery and refers to a table in the outer query. There are two winners in constituency 2 since both the Labour and Green candidates obtained 150 votes, which was the highest score.

Query 9.8 'Which party had the greatest number of winning candidates?'

OR

'Which party won the election?'

This query comes in our category of 'Easy to Say But Hard to Do'. This is described in Chapter 8 in the context of views, but several other issues emerge in the following. It is easiest to break it down into a number of steps:

1. Get winning party in each constituency as in Query 9.10.

2. Get the count of rows in this for each party.
   (Group by Party)

3. Select the resulting row with the highest count.

These three steps are represented in Fig. 9.8 below.

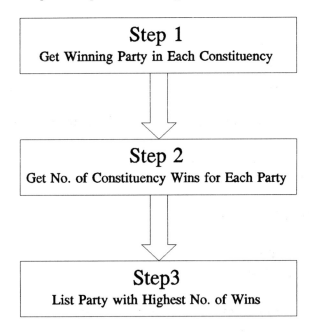

Fig. 9.8 The Step-by-Step Approach to Query 9.11

Step 1: Create a table containing the winning party in each
constituency:

```
1  CREATE TABLE TEMP1 AS
2  SELECT CONS_NO, PARTY
3  FROM CANDIDATE C1
4  WHERE NO_OF_VOTES  =
5  (SELECT MAX(NO_OF_VOTES)
6    FROM CANDIDATE C2
7    WHERE C2.CONS_NO  = C1.CONS_NO);
```

```
1  SELECT *
2  FROM TEMP1;
```

```
CONS_NO  PARTY       <-------- Winning parties
-------  -----

      2  Labour
      1  SDP
      2  Green
      3  Labour
```

Step 2: Create a table showing the count of wins for each party:

```
1  CREATE TABLE TEMP2 AS
2  SELECT PARTY, COUNT(*) NO_OF_WINS
3  FROM TEMP1
4  GROUP BY PARTY;
```

```
1  SELECT *
2  FROM TEMP2;
```

```
PARTY    NO_OF_WINS   <----- No of wins for each party
-----    ----------

Green         1
Labour        2
SDP           1
```

Step 3: List the party with the highest number of wins.

```
1 SELECT PARTY, NO_OF_WINS
2 FROM TEMP2
3 WHERE NO_OF_WINS   =
4  (SELECT MAX(NO_OF_WINS)
5   FROM TEMP2);
```

```
PARTY      NO_OF_WINS    <----- Winning party
-----      ----------
Labour         2
```

The temporary tables should now be deleted.

> DROP TABLE TEMP1;

> DROP TABLE TEMP2;

Variations

There are, as usual, several different SQL variations that can be made. It would be interesting to be able to eliminate the need for the temporary tables.

Variation 1: Eliminating temporary table TEMP2

One way of getting rid of TEMP2 above is to implement Step 2 as follows, using HAVING.

```
1 SELECT PARTY, COUNT(*)
2 FROM TEMP1
3 GROUP BY PARTY
4 HAVING COUNT(*) =
5  (SELECT MAX(COUNT(*))
6   FROM TEMP1
7   GROUP BY PARTY) ;
```

This gives the correct output. Notice that the subquery is a virtual repeat of the main query, with a consequent increase in execution time. This is of course necessary because we wish to ensure that the count of successful candidates by party is the maximum count. It is a pity that one cannot simply write:

```
1  SELECT PARTY, MAX(COUNT(*))
2  FROM TEMP1
3  GROUP BY PARTY;
```

This results in the ORACLE error: 'not a single group set function'.

This is due to the agreed syntax of SQL. One can often find such examples where a different syntax would be desirable in a particular case.

Variation 2: Managing without *any* temporary tables

It *is* possible to manage without using any temporary tables, but the SQL looks rather ungainly and since it is not so easy to follow, may be more susceptible to error when changes are made.

```
 1  SELECT PARTY, COUNT(*)
 2  FROM CANDIDATE C1
 3  WHERE NO_OF_VOTES   =
 4   (SELECT MAX(NO_OF_VOTES)
 5    FROM CANDIDATE C2
 6    WHERE C2.CONS_NO  = C1.CONS_NO)
 7  GROUP BY PARTY
 8  HAVING COUNT(*) =
 9   (SELECT MAX(COUNT(*))
10    FROM CANDIDATE C3
11    WHERE NO_OF_VOTES   =
12     (SELECT MAX(NO_OF_VOTES)
13      FROM CANDIDATE C4
14      WHERE C4.CONS_NO  =  C3.CONS_NO)
15      GROUP BY PARTY)  ;
```

This gives the correct result:

```
PARTY           COUNT(*)
-----           --------
Labour              2
```

Again in this query, lines 8 to 15 are a virtual repeat of lines 1 to 7 and are there to ensure that only the party with the maximum number of winning candidates is output. If it were possible to have the top line as

```
1  SELECT PARTY, MAX(COUNT(*))
```

then lines 8 to 15 would not be needed. There are probably many other SQL queries which will achieve the desired output. It is possible for example to use VIEWs instead of temporary tables to break the problem down into smaller parts, as here. For example Step 1 could have been implemented using a view VIEW1 (assuming a suitable view did not already exist) rather than the temporary table TEMP1:

```
1  CREATE VIEW VIEW1 AS      <----- Using a VIEW instead of
2  SELECT CONS_NO,  PARTY               a temporary table
3  FROM CANDIDATE C1
4  WHERE NO_OF_VOTES   =
5  (SELECT MAX(NO_OF_VOTES)
6    FROM  CANDIDATE C2
7    WHERE C2.CONS_NO  =  C1.CONS_NO);
```

```
1  SELECT *
2  FROM VIEW1;
```

```
CONS_NO  PARTY    <---- Same result
-------  -----
      2  Labour
      1  SDP
      2  Green
      3  Labour
```

Similarly, Step 2 and Step 3 can be rewritten replacing TEMP tables with VIEWs. The VIEWs still ought to be dropped at the end of the query run unless they are already in existence for other reasons. Hovever, since they do not use up very much disk space, it is not as crucial to drop a VIEW after use as a temporary table. In my opinion the method of using temporary tables is the most advantageous solution in this example because:

1. It is simpler to understand than the 'monster' query above which uses no temporary tables or views.

2. It is modular, so each step can be checked separately.

3. Temporary tables do not in general suffer from the variety of restrictions that VIEWs have.

4. Temporary tables can offer faster query processing than VIEWs.

This last point is worth expanding on. Suppose you had a query which was frequently used, and it involved the use of columns from several tables. If the query uses a view to 'do' the join then the join is done each time the query is executed. If the join is a lengthy process the query becomes virtually useless in interactive mode.

If instead the join is done once, say at the start-of-day processing, and the result placed in a temporary table and the queries access the temporary table rather than a view, then the queries using the table will be much faster because no joining is required each time the query is run. There are of course some disadvantages. Any updates must of course be done to the 'base' tables; there is no point updating the temporary table since it will be over-written next morning. These updates will not show on the temporary table so the day's processing is being performed using progressively out-of-date data. Whether this is important or not depends on the application. There are many applications where it will not be and yesterday's data is up-to-date enough. Using a view on the other hand, any updates to base tables will immediately 'show through' onto the view so it is always up-to-date.

Query 9.9 'List the percentage of the total vote obtained by
          each party.'

Using the modular approach, and looking at the CANDIDATE table, it
again seems sensible to break the problem down into the three steps:

Step 1. Get the overall total number of votes T.

Step 2. Get the total number of votes for each party.

Step 3. Divide each result in step 2 by T and display.

Step 1 can easily be achieved by:

    1 SELECT SUM(NO_OF_VOTES)
    2 FROM CANDIDATE;

which gives:

    SUM(NO_OF_VOTES)

               1455

which we can write on a piece of paper to remember it. Steps 2 and 3 can
be done together by:

    1 SELECT PARTY, ROUND(SUM(NO_OF_VOTES)/14.55,   2)
    2 FROM CANDIDATE
    3 GROUP BY PARTY
    4 ORDER BY 2 DESC ;

which gives the required output:

PARTY	SUM(NO_OF_VOTES)/14.55
Labour	28.18
Cons	15.12
Green	15.12
SDP	11
Indep	10.31
Red Guards	10.31
Liberal	3.64
SLD	3.44
Simbianese	2.89

In Line 1 the ROUND function rounds the result of the division to two places of decimals. This is an ORACLE version; check your manual for your SQL's version. Line 4 sorts the result by the second column and the DESC option puts the party with the highest vote share first. Had we wished to produce this result without having to write down the total number of votes and then plug that value into the GROUP BY query, it would have been necessary to store that result somewhere first.

One way to do this is by using a temporary table containing the value.

```
1  CREATE TABLE TEMP2 AS
2  SELECT SUM(NO_OF_VOTES)   T
3  FROM CANDIDATE;
```

```
1  SELECT *
2  FROM TEMP2;
```

gives:

```
   T
 ----
 1455
```

This value contained in this single row in table TEMP2 can now be used in the main query instead of the written-down value 1455 by joining it in the query to every row of CANDIDATE.

```
1  SELECT PARTY, ROUND(SUM(NO_OF_VOTES)/T*100,2)
2  FROM CANDIDATE, TEMP2
3  GROUP BY PARTY,T
4  ORDER BY 2 DESC ;
```

which gives the same correct results. Incidentally, SQL does not have assignment statements, so the SQL code shown below is not possible.

In SQL, the '=' is a relational operator used in equality tests only. Remember SQL is supposed to be declarative which in this context means the query describes what you want rather than the steps required to obtain what you want. This is contrasted with procedural where you have to say *how* to get the required output.

```
1  SELECT PARTY,                 < ----- Misconceived Query
2  ROUND(SUM(NO_OF_VOTES)/T*100,2)
3  FROM CANDIDATE
4  WHERE T =
5   (SELECT SUM(NO_OF_VOTES)
6    FROM CANDIDATE)
7  GROUP BY PARTY
8  ORDER BY 2 DESC ;
```

In practice of course there are the following observations to be made about using SQL:

- For anything other than trivial queries you *do* have
  to think about how you are going to get the output.

- You may have to break the problem down into steps, as
  we have done in some of our queries.

- Some queries would run much faster using a procedural
  approach.

- The act of declaring what you want *is* a procedure.

Against this, SQL commands allow you to perform a great deal of processing in just a few lines of code, which are usually much more concise and easier to understand than the many lines of the equivalent procedural C or COBOL program. In this way the SQL could be thought of as a mini-spec of the query requirement in a language which is widely understood and large parts of which are standardised. And it is always possible to make SQL procedural by using it in its embedded form. The mini-spec aspect of it then largely disappears of course.

As a final comment, the SQL query interpreter need not execute the command in precisely the way indicated by the query itself. An intelligent query interpreter should be able to find a way to produce efficient procedural code from your SQL mini-spec. For example, in the Workshop Groups example the SQL query proposed a four-way self-join of a hundred-row table. We proposed a much more efficient procedural approach. Building more intelligence into the query interpreter should some day allow it to automatically perform the transformation from the four-way join to the efficient procedure.

9.3 NOT SUITABLE FOR SQL?

SQL is of course not the ideal language for solving *every* problem that would normally be solved on a computer. SQL is not the best tool for many complex engineering, scientific or financial calculations for example. It is certainly not suitable for entertainment software. Its most suitable domain is the type of computer application usually described as *data processing*. One of the features most characteristic of data processing problems is the appearance in the problem of large numbers of similarly-structured *records* which are searched in relatively simple patterns. The following two problem outlines have this feature but are still, on the whole, probably not suitable for a purely SQL solution.

Since knowing which software approach to use is probably one of the most important decisions the analyst-programmer has to make, it is worthwhile looking at these two examples to attempt to identify what features they contain which make them unsuitable for SQL. Looked at positively, this gives us more information about what SQL *is* good for: a better description of SQL's proper domain.

9.3.1 Case Study 5 - The Recipes Problem

In our cupboard we have a number of ingredients. We also own a recipe book 'Healthy Eating For One' which contains the recipes for various meals that we could make. The question is, given our current quantities of ingredients and our recipe book, which meals could we make?

The problem certainly contains data that could easily be represented as records. The essential elements of the data can be represented in two tables:

```
RECIPE_LINE(RECIPE_NO,INGRED_NO,QTY_REQD)
INGREDIENT_OWNED(INGRED_NO,QTY_OWNED)
```

Query 9.10 'Which meals can I make?'

Let's simplify the problem as much as possible; assume that you would always want to make a meal of the size shown in the recipe.

The problem then becomes similar to the Student Recruitment problem of Case Study 4 where there are a number of Required Qualifications (Required Ingredients) for a Course (Recipe) and a number of Available Qualifications (Ingredients Owned).

Clearly a similar (even simpler) type of solution is possible here. Difficulties arise when the problem is posed in a slightly different way:

Query 9.11 'How much of each meal can I make?'

In this case, the quantity you can make is the quotient :

```
Quantity Available
------------------
Quantity Required
```

for the ingredient required that you have *least* of. Is this an SQL problem?

9.3.2 Case Study 6 - The Dieting Problem

In this problem we have two sets of record-structured data. The first is a collection of data listing the quantities of a given set of nutrients for each of a large number of common foods. The second is the quantity of each nutrient you require per day to stay healthy. This varies according to your gender, age, lifestyle and height. Each food has a cost per unit weight. You wish to find a combination of foods which will provide at least your minimum nutrient requirements and cost the minimum amount.

To simplify the problem as much as possible while still retaining its essence, assume the data structures are as follows:

```
FOOD(FOOD_NO, IRON_QTY, VIT_C_QTY, CAL_QTY, PRICE_PER_100_GRAMS)
WHAT_YOU_NEED(IRON_QTY, VIT_C_QTY, CAL_QTY)
```

In practice there is unlikely to be a single food that can fulfill all requirements, let alone at the minimum price. An algorithm has to be found which 'tries' different quantities of each food and varies the quantities in such a way as to converge towards lower overall cost while still staying within the dietary requirements.

This is of course a Linear Programming problem and would most readily be solved using an algorithm known as the Simplex Method. The difficulty with using SQL in this problem is that it has no 'true' iteration; no sense of getting 'closer' to a goal. It would probably be possible to program this in SQL using, say, a pre-defined table of different combinations of stepped quantities of each ingredient, doing some rather large *joins* to investigate different combinations and selecting the least cost. Execution time would rise directly with the number of predefined combinations and inversely with step size. At best, the answer obtained would be an approximation.

9.4 EXERCISES

1. Write the SQL for Case Study 5.

2. Attempt to write SQL for Case Study 6. (Good Luck!)

Chapter 10

INSERT, DELETE and UPDATE

10.1 THE INSERT COMMAND

The INSERT command is used for adding new rows into an SQL table or view. The syntax of the INSERT command can take two forms:

```
INSERT INTO table-or-view-name
[ (column-name, ... ) ]
VALUES (value, ... ) ;
```
and
```
INSERT INTO table-or-view-name
[ (column-name, ... ) ]
query ;
```

The first form of the INSERT command inserts just *one* row, whereas in the second form the number of rows inserted depends on the query.

The purpose of the optional list of column names is to specify which columns are to receive values if all of them are not going to. The values in the VALUES clause of the first form or the values delivered by the query in the second form should match up with the columns for which they are intended.

If no column list is included, then *all* columns will be updated. Any columns in the table (or the relevant columns in the base tables of the view) not mentioned in the list will receive a value of NULL (they must not have been declared NOT NULL in the CREATE TABLE).

Example 1

1 INSERT INTO INVOICE
2 INV_NO, C_NO, INV_DATE, AMOUNT
3 VALUES (1018, NULL, '25-jan-91', 100) ;

This command inserts the required values into the respective columns of the INVOICE table. Note that the C_NO is not presently known. It is not defined as NOT NULL so it is legal to insert the value NULL as shown. The same effect could have been obtained with:

```
1  INSERT INTO INVOICE
2  INV_NO, INV_DATE, AMOUNT
3  VALUES ( 1018, '25-jan-91', 100) ;
```

Example 2

```
1  CREATE TABLE STRING_PLAYERS
2   (STUD_NO  NUMBER(3),
3   NAME    CHAR(10),
4   AGE    NUMBER(3) ) ;
```

```
1  INSERT INTO STRING_PLAYERS
2  SELECT * FROM VIOLIN
3  UNION
4  SELECT STUD_NO, NAME, AGE FROM CELLO ;
```

In this example rows are inserted into the STRING_PLAYERS table from the two tables VIOLIN and CELLO. The same effect could have been obtained with:

```
1  CREATE TABLE STRING_PLAYERS  AS
2  SELECT * FROM VIOLIN
3  UNION
4  SELECT STUD_NO, NAME, AGE FROM CELLO ;
```

The query in the second form may be of any complexity; any of the SELECTs from previous chapters could appear here.

The first form of INSERT is not often used interactively, except for adding small quantities of data to a test database perhaps. Even then, it is usually easier to add rows using a forms-based interface such as

SQL*FORMS (ORACLE) or QBF (INGRES) or the base dBASE IV command APPEND. The first form of INSERT is more likely to be found embedded in a 3GL host program where a database row is to be composed from data input from, say, an input screen or a non-database transaction file after extensive validation processing.

10.2 THE DELETE COMMAND

The syntax is:

```
DELETE FROM table-or-view
[WHERE condition] ;
```

The restrictions on deleting from a view discussed in Chapter 8 apply. The WHERE condition specifies which rows will be deleted. If it is omitted, *all* rows will be deleted.

Example 1

```
1  DELETE FROM CUS
2  WHERE CRED_LIM  IS NULL ;
```

Example 2

```
1  DELETE FROM INVOICE A
2  WHERE AMOUNT  < =
3   (SELECT SUM(AMOUNT)
4    FROM PAYMENT B
5    WHERE B.INV_NO  =A.INV_NO)  ;
```

Example 2 contains a correlated subquery (lines 3 to 5). For each invoice in the INVOICE table, the sum of all the payment amounts for that invoice is calculated. If the sum is not less than INVOICE.AMOUNT then the INVOICE row is deemed 'paid' and is removed. This process is sometimes called 'ageing' in accounts systems. It is performed after the month's statements have been sent out to customers.

10.3 THE UPDATE COMMAND

The basic form of the UPDATE command contained in ORACLE, INGRES, dBASE IV, and both the ISO 9075 and ANSI-86 standards is:

```
UPDATE table-or-view
SET column = expr, column = expr, ...
[ WHERE condition ] ;
```

subject to the restrictions on the update of views (see Chapter 8). The WHERE condition may contain a query involving other tables. ORACLE SQL*PLUS also allows a second form:

UPDATE table-or-view
SET (column, column, ...) =(subquery)
[WHERE condition] ;

Here it is possible for the new values of the columns to be derived from a subquery involving the same or a different table.

As we have found in previous sections, SQL*PLUS quite often has extra features compared to the other DBMSs and standards definitions. In most cases it is possible to find examples where the code would be considerably more difficult without the ORACLE extansion.

Example 1

```
1  UPDATE PRODUCT
2  SET PRICE =PRICE * 0.9
3  WHERE QIS > 2 * REORDQ ;
```

This is a simple example using the first format of the command. Here we are reducing the price of all products whose quantity-in-stock is more than double the reorder quantity.

Example 2

```
1  UPDATE PRODUCT
2  SET PRICE =PRICE * 0.9
3  WHERE QIS > 2 * REORDQ
4  OR NOT EXISTS
5   (SELECT *
6    FROM DELIVERY
7    WHERE  PRODUCT.PROD_NO  =  DELIVERY.PROD_NO
8    AND DEL_DATE > '1-jan-90' ) ;
```

In this example, which is still within the first format, the condition contains a query. In lines 5 to 8 we are adding an additional way for the price of a product to qualify for a ten per-cent price reduction: if none have been sold since the beginning of 1990.

Example 3

Suppose we have two SQL tables:

PRODUCT				SALE	
-------				----	
p_no	descr	qis		p_no	qty
----	-----	---		----	---
1	aaa	10		1	3
2	bbb	10		3	2
3	ccc	10			

We wish to decrement the column product.qis to reflect the sales of these products shown in sale.qty for matching p_no. We wish here to derive the new values in one table from those in another. There is no facility for this in the first UPDATE format.

The following ORACLE - recommended code will do this:

```
1  UPDATE PRODUCT P
2  SET P.QIS =
3  (SELECT P.QIS - S.QTY
4    FROM SALE S
5    WHERE S.P_NO  =  P.P_NO)
6  WHERE P.P_NO  IN
7  (SELECT S.P_NO
8    FROM SALES) ;
```

The outer WHERE ensures that only matching P_NO's are processed i.e. the only product rows that are updated are those that have a corresponding sale row.

10.4 COMMIT AND ROLLBACK

If at any stage of a session (either interactive or during the execution of an embedded SQL program) it becomes apparent that one or more of the previous INSERTs, DELETEs or UPDATEs was in error, then the execution of a ROLLBACK command will make the database revert to the state it was in before the sequence of modifications began, or the state it was in at the time of the last COMMIT.

COMMIT commits (writes) any changes onto the database. If you update a table and then query it without COMMITting, the change will appear to have occurred. However, if any error occurs, then a ROLLBACK will also occur. It is therefore wise to COMMIT as soon as you are satisfied with any changes that you have made. COMMIT automatically occurs when you quit from SQL. After changes have been committed, they cannot be rolled back.

10.5 VIEWS

There are various restrictions pertaining to the update of base tables via a view. The most restricting is that INSERTs, DELETEs and UPDATEs can only be applied to views defined on a *single base table*.

Chapter 11

Embedded SQL

11.1 INTRODUCTION

Up to this point the discussion has been centered exclusively on interactive SQL. SQL commands were typed in and executed immediately, or perhaps retrieved from a stored file and run. For example:

```
SQL> GET QUERY1          <---- Retrieve the command you
                               want.


SQL> RUN                 <---- Execute it.
```

QUERY1 is a useful query which had been previously saved. There is a facility for saving commands like this in most versions of SQL. Before the query is run it must be interpreted, that is, translated into machine code (the internal language of the computer) and executed. This is done every time the query is run. The SQL command is complete in itself and performs all of the processing for the query without any supporting code. It can be considered as a very small, very powerful interpreted program.

There is an alternative way of using SQL commands. They can be embedded into a program written in one of the widely-used high level languages (3GLs - Third Generation Languages) such as C, COBOL, FORTRAN, ADA or Pascal or even into a 2GL (Assembler Language) program. Examples of SQL commands embedded in C are given here. In embedded (also spelt 'imbedded') SQL, SQL commands are inserted at various places in a 3GL 'host' program.

The 3GL program acts as a 'host' to the SQL commands in that it provides them with an environment in which they can access the database. In fact with many DBMSs the only way a 3GL program can access the database is by using embedded SQL commands; there is no more direct way that a 3GL program can communicate with the DBMS software. SQL is not the only database language that can be embedded but it is quickly becoming the dominant one, being provided as an essential part of most commercial DBMSs.

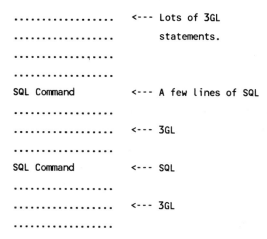

Fig. 11.1 Host 3GL program with Embedded SQL

There are several situations in which embedded SQL is used in preference to interactive SQL. The first reason for using it is not really a valid reason at all. Conventional 3GL programmers, particularly those who have used a particular language for several years, may have invested considerable time and intellectual effort learning all of its detailed facilities and smart ways to cope with a whole range of data processing situations in that language. They may feel that there is no need for new languages since they can write everything in their favourite 3GL. There is this natural (elitist?) tendency to enthuse in something difficult that you have mastered and others have not and this is understandable. There is also the tendency to resist change and to be comfortable with the familiar. For such programmers nothing much can be done in interactive SQL, it's too slow, it allows users too much freedom and so on. They will use SQL but only in its embedded form, thinking of an embedded SQL SELECT command as nothing more than a different form of READ statement; wherever you would have put a READ, put a SELECT or FETCH instead to access a database record. In this way, the minimum amount of re-education is required on the part of the programmer and he or she can still claim to be *au fait* with SQL. It is possible to proceed this way but such programmers ought to consider the advantages of the appropriate use of interactive SQL or some other 4GL facility of the DBMS to get the query, report or update completed more quickly.

A second reason for using embedded SQL is speed. It takes time for the query interpreter to translate the text of an interactive SQL command into executable machine code. That is one delay. The second delay can in many cases prove more problematic. It concerns the fact that the query optimizer may make bad decisions when generating a query execution plan. For example it might join two large tables before joining a third smaller one, or it might join two large tables before applying a low hit-rate WHERE criterion to one of the joined tables, or it might not use an index that would have improved the execution speed of the query by reducing access time. With embedded SQL, particularly in its 'deliver one row' form (see below) a programmer is able to obtain sufficient control to define the sequence and type of database access himself. By a suitable choice of algorithm the speed can be improved by several orders of magnitude, as we saw in the Workshop Groups case study of Chapter 9, where instead of an expensive multiple self-join, the required processing was performed using an efficient single-pass routine.

The question is, how much program logic do you do yourself, and how much do you allow the SQL translator and optimizer to generate for you? This question must be answered by the informed analyst/programmer taking into account all the relevant factors, not the least of which is the nature of the problem itself, and where possible (schedules and Standards permitting) basing the decision on practical experiments using a test database.

We have seen in previous chapters that interactive SQL is capable of quite sophisticated queries involving fairly complex logic. It is not always clear initially when you have a complex query to perform, which approach is going to be more advantageous, and as already stated there is a distinct tendency, particularly among experienced 3GL programmers, to reject the interactive SQL option. Perhaps this book will go some way towards correcting this tendency.

On the other hand some problems are undeniably more suitable for a procedural, step-by-step algorithmic approach. The 3GL host program can provide complex sets of conditions under which different embedded queries, updates or reports will be executed, all 'under the same roof', that is, all within the same host program. The program can engage in a dialogue with the user to decide which actions are appropriate. In general, the use of a 3GL host can improve the look and feel of the human-computer interface. The user can be presented with formatted screens of data, pull-down menus etc. This and the security aspects which follow are important considerations when the program is to be used by non-technical operational staff who require the program to be largely self-explanatory in use or those who want to use the database to deal regularly with a fairly small number of related queries or updates. The type of activity that occurs at the local Electricity or Gas Board showroom when you want to query your account or change address is an example of the latter.

An improvement in security (risks related to accidental or deliberate rule-braking) over that obtainable using interactive SQL can be achieved by incorporating additional checks on user id, and the allocation of a restricted set of processes, tables, rows, columns and views to identified user groups.

One aspect of security is database integrity, which is the correctness, completeness and internal consistency of the database. Integrity can be enhanced in the embedded situation by a whole range of checks. Some of the integrity checks that can be performed are:

- Simple single-field validation (see below).
- Consistency between different fields on an input screen.
- Consistency between an input field and one or more
  database fields.

The usual single-field checks that can be applied are:

- Length.
- Type (e.g. numeric, alpha, money).
- Range.
- Check Digits.

Cross-field consistency checks can include for example the test that SEX = 'F' if MATERNITY_BENEFIT = 'Y'. It may also be required to check that a customer ACCOUNT record shows sufficient credit for an ORDER record to be accepted onto the database.

Embedded SQL can also give the programmer more control over database error handling.

Another familiar data processing situation is batch processing, where the database is required to be updated by a whole batch (collection) of input transactions (changes or movements). The usual procedure here is to take each transaction record, validate it, and have it update one or more records on the database.

Various contingencies can arise during this process; a transaction record may not find a corresponding database record for example. Different transactions will have to be treated differently and the procedures for doing this are usually best implemented using a procedural embedded SQL approach.

There are several stages involved in developing an embedded SQL program and these are shown in Fig. 11.2. Note the additional stage involving the pre-processor (precompiler). This will be either 'bundled' with the DBMS software when you purchase it, or available as an optional extra.

There will need to be a separate pre-processor for each host language you are going to use. Its purpose is to 'expand' the macro-like SQL statements (they are macros from the point of view of the lower-level 3GL host) into the host language.

In most cases the resulting 3GL code when listed will not look particularly self-documenting; it is simply a set of calls to DBMS routines which will be linked in by the linker program.

All major DBMSs allow you to write embedded SQL programs and are compatible with many of the more popular 3GL languages and compilers. Not every compiler can be used with the DBMS manufacturer's precompilers however and it is necessary to check this compatibility beforehand.

We now discuss some examples of embedded SQL programs using C and COBOL. Again, there may be minor variations in syntax from one DBMS to another.

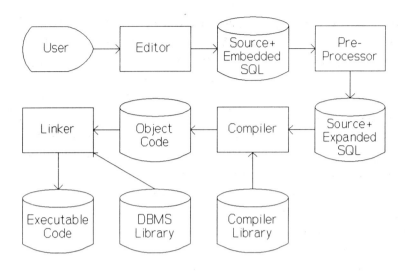

Fig. 11.2 Developing an Embedded SQL Program

11.2 EMBEDDING SQL IN C

C is a popular 3GL which originally was closely associated with the world of minicomputers and the UNIX operating system. Today, mainframes, minis and microcomputers are all able to use this language and use it in conjunction with DOS and other microcomputer operating systems.

In the examples which follow I shall not dwell on the details of C syntax but concentrate more on the embedded SQL commands and their meaning. The line numbers are not part of the program but are included here for purposes of explanation.

Normally of course you would not use an embedded program to do something as simple as create a database table. However this program serves the purpose of demonstrating some of the embedded commands. All of the commands that begin with EXEC SQL are embedded SQL commands and they will be converted to C source code when the precompiler is run.

Lines 1 to 12 are comments. Lines 13 and 14 call in two standard C source libraries which the program requires. At compile time these lines are expanded into C source code. Lines 18 to 20 are used to 'declare' the variables (just 'answer' in this example) that will be used by the program.

Program 11.2.1 Creating a Table

```
01   /* Program listing before pre-compilation          */
02
03   /*******************************************************/
04   /*    Program Name  :  create.sc                    */
05   /*    Date Created  :  August 91                    */
06   /*    Author        :  F.Taty                       */
07   /*    Description   :  This program connects to the */
08   /*                     database "Project", creates a */
09   /*                     table "TEST" and disconnects  */
10   /*                     from the database.            */
11   /*******************************************************/
12
13   #include <stdio.h>              <--- Get Standard C Libraries
14   #include <stdlib.h>
15
16   #define nl printf("\n");
17
18   EXEC SQL BEGIN DECLARE SECTION;  <--- Declare Variables
19       char   answer;
20   EXEC SQL END DECLARE SECTION;
21
22   EXEC SQL INCLUDE SQLCA;          <--- Get the SQLCA
23
24   int main(void)
25   {                                       <--- Database Error
26     EXEC SQL WHENEVER SQLERROR STOP;          Handling
27     EXEC SQL CONNECT "project";        <--- Connect to the DB
28     printf("Connected to database PROJECT.");
29     nl;
30     nl;                                <--- Check user ok
31     printf("Are you sure you want to create table TEST (y/n):");
32     answer= getche();
33     if (answer=='Y'||answer=='y')
```

```
34   {
35     nl;
36     nl;
37     printf("Please wait... Creating table TEST.");
38     EXEC SQL CREATE TABLE TEST        <--- Create the table
39       (sample_no       integer1,
40        description     c20,
41        issue_date      date,
42        cost            money);
43     nl;
44     nl;
45     printf("Table TEST created successfully.");
46   }
47   else
48   {
49     printf("Table not created.");
50   }
51   nl;
52   nl;
53   EXEC SQL DISCONNECT;        <--- Disconnect from the database
54   printf("Disconnect from database TABLE");
55 }
```

There is a special name for variables that are used in both the C code and the SQL commands. They are called *host variables*. Host variables appear in the next program, but here, 'answer' is just a normal variable since it is not used in any SQL commands. It is still declared in the BEGIN DECLARE section however.

In line 22 the SQLCA (SQL Communications Area) is declared. This area is used to pass values between the DBMS and the program and for handling errors. Lines 24 to the end are the declaration of the main C function. Line 26 is used to define what action should be taken if a database error occurs. In this case the action taken is simply to stop. Alternative actions are CONTINUE, STOP, GOTO a label or CALL a C procedure. CONTINUE ignores the error and continues execution after the offending EXEC SQL command. There may be several WHENEVER

SQLERROR commands in the program. The most recently executed
WHENEVER applies.

Line 27 connects the program to the database 'project' and line 53
disconnects it. In lines 28 to 32 the user is asked if he wants to go ahead
and create the table. Line 32 puts the user's response in the variable
'answer'. In lines 34 to 46 a positive response is assumed.

In Lines 38 to 42 the table is actually created with the column names
shown.

The pseudo-code for this program is:

```
Get Source Library Routines

Declare Variables

Define Error Handling

Connect Program to Database

Check user wants to Carry On

IF yes

     Create Table

ELSE

     Suitable Message

ENDIF

Disconnect Program from Database
```

Since the program logic of create.sc is so simple, the pseudo code requires
little further explanation. The next program is a little longer but in
principle still quite simple.

Program 11.2.2 Updating a Table using Cursors

```
001  /* Program listing before pre-compilation          */
002
003  /********************************************************/
004  /*    Program Name   :   empl_su.sc                 */
005  /*    Date Created   :   August 91                  */
006  /*    Author         :   F.Taty                     */
007  /*    Description    :   This program connects to the   */
008  /*                       database 'Project', gets a    */
009  /*                       restaurant code from the user, */
010  /*                       selects all the employees from */
011  /*                       that restaurant using a cursor */
012  /*                       structure, displays the list,  */
013  /*                       gets a percentage salary       */
014  /*                       increase or decrease from the  */
015  /*                       user, updates the employee     */
016  /*                       table, prints another list     */
017  /*                       with the new salaries, and     */
018  /*                       disconnects from the database. */
019  /********************************************************/
020
021  #include <stdio.h>
022  #include <stdlib.h>
023
024  #define nl printf("\n");
025
026  /* Table Declaration */
027
028  EXEC SQL DECLARE employee TABLE
029    (emp_no       vchar(4),
030     last_name    vchar(25),
031     first_name   vchar(25),
032     dob          date,
033     address1     vchar(25),
034     address2     vchar(25),
```

```
035      address3      vchar(25),
036      rest_code     vchar(4),
037      job_code      vchar(4),
038      hour_sal      money);
039
040   /* Host Variable Declaration */
041
042   EXEC SQL BEGIN DECLARE SECTION;
043      char    emp_no[5];
044      char    last_name[26];
045      char    first_name[26];
046      char    dob[26];
047      char    address1[26];
048      char    address2[26];
049      char    address3[26];
050      char    rest_code[5];
051      char    job_code[5];
052      double hour_sal;
053      float  change;
054   EXEC SQL END DECLARE SECTION;
055
056   /* SQL Communications Area */
057
058   EXEC SQL INCLUDE SQLCA;
059
060   /* Main C Function */
061
062   int main(void)
063   {
064     EXEC SQL WHENEVER SQLERROR STOP;
065     EXEC SQL CONNECT "project";
066     printf("Connected to database PROJECT.");
067     nl;
068     nl;
069
070     printf("Enter the restaurant code: ");
```

```
071    gets(rest_code);
072    nl;
073    nl;
074
075  /* Declare a cursor for listing rows of EMPLOYEE table */
076
077    EXEC SQL DECLARE SAL_CURS1 CURSOR FOR
078      SELECT EMP_NO, LAST_NAME, FIRST_NAME, HOUR_SAL
079      FROM EMPLOYEE
080      WHERE REST_CODE=:rest_code;
081
082  /* Open the Cursor */
083
084    EXEC SQL OPEN SAL_CURS1;
085
086  /* End-of-File condition for subsequent FETCH loop */
087    EXEC SQL WHENEVER NOT FOUND GOTO close1;
088    printf("*** OLD SALARIES ***");
089    nl;
090    nl;
091    printf("%-12s %-21s %-21s %-11s","Emp no","Last name",
092         "First name","Salary-hour");
093    nl;
094    printf("%-12s %-21s %-21s %-11s","------","---------",
095         "----------","-----------");
096    nl;
097    for (; ;)
098    {
099      EXEC SQL FETCH SAL_CURS1 INTO :emp_no, :last_name,
100        :first_name, :hour_sal;
101      printf("%-12s %-21s %-21s %-11.2f",emp_no, last_name,
102        first_name, hour_sal);
103      nl;
104    }
105    nl;
106
```

```
107  /* Close Cursor at End-of-File */

108

109    close1:

110    EXEC SQL CLOSE SAL_CURS1;

111    printf("Cursor 1 Closed.");

112    nl;

113    nl;

114

115  /* Get % salary change */

116

117    printf("Enter the salary increase or decrease: ");

118    scanf("%f",&change);

119    nl;

120    nl;

121    printf("Please wait... Updating table.");

122

123  /* Declare a cursor for updating rows of EMPLOYEE table */

124

125    EXEC SQL DECLARE SAL_CURS2 CURSOR FOR

126      SELECT EMP_NO, LAST_NAME, FIRST_NAME, HOUR_SAL

127      FROM EMPLOYEE

128      WHERE REST_CODE=:rest_code

129      FOR UPDATE OF HOUR_SAL;

130

131    EXEC SQL OPEN SAL_CURS2;

132

133  /* End-of-File condition. */

134

135    EXEC SQL WHENEVER NOT FOUND GOTO close2;

136

137  /* Update Loop */

138

139    for(; ;)

140    {

141      EXEC SQL FETCH SAL_CURS2 INTO :emp_no, :last_name,

142        :first_name, :hour_sal;
```

```
143
144     EXEC SQL UPDATE EMPLOYEE
145        SET hour_sal = hour_sal * (100 + :change) / 100
146        WHERE CURRENT OF SAL_CURS2;
147     }
148     nl;
149     nl;
150
151  /* Close the cursor */
152
153     close2:
154     EXEC SQL CLOSE SAL_CURS2;
155     printf("The salaries have been updated.");
156     printf("Cursor 2 is closed.");
157     nl;
158
159  /* New cursor to list the updated table */
160
161     EXEC SQL DECLARE SAL_CURS3 CURSOR FOR
162        SELECT EMP_NO, LAST_NAME, FIRST_NAME, HOUR_SAL
163        FROM EMPLOYEE
164        WHERE REST_CODE=:rest_code;
165
166     EXEC SQL OPEN SAL_CURS3;
167
168  /* End-of-File Condition */
169
170     EXEC SQL WHENEVER NOT FOUND GOTO close3;
171
172     nl;
173     nl;
174     printf("*** NEW SALARIES ***");
175     nl;
176     nl;
177     printf("%-12s %-21s %-21s %-11s", "Emp no", "Last name",
178        "First name", "Salary-hour");
```

```
179    nl;
180    printf("%-12s %-21s %-21s %-11s","------", "----------",
181      "----------", "-----------");
182    nl;
183
184 /* New salaries print loop */
185
186    for(; ;)
187    {
188      EXEC SQL FETCH SAL_CURS3 INTO :emp_no, :last_name,
189        :first_name, :hour_sal;
190      printf("%-12s %-21s %-21s %-11.2f", emp_no, last_name
191        first_name, hour_sal);
192      nl;
193    }
194    nl;
195
196 /* Close the cursor */
197
198    close3:
199    EXEC SQL CLOSE SAL_CURS3;
200    printf("Cursor 3 is closed.");
201    nl;
202    nl;
203
204 /* Disconnect from database */
205
206    EXEC SQL DISCONNECT;
207    printf("Disconnected from database.");
208
209 /* End of function main */
210
211 }
```

The Pseudo-code for this program is as follows:

```
Function                                        Line No
--------                                        -------

Get Source Library Routines                       021

Declare Table                                     028

Declare Host Variables                            042

Define Error Handling                             064

Connect Program to Database                       065

Get Restaurant Code from User                     070

Get Employees in that Restaurant                  077

DOWHILE not end of Employees                      097

  Get Next Employee                               099

  Print Employee Details                          101

ENDWHILE                                          104

Get % Salary Change for these Employees           117

Get Employees in that restaurant                  125

DOWHILE not end of Employees                      139

  Get Next Employee                               141

  Update Salary of current Employee               144

ENDWHILE                                          147

Get Employees in that Restaurant (now updated)    161

DOWHILE not end of Employees                      186

  Get Next Employee                               188

  Print Employee Details                          190

ENDWHILE                                          193

Disconnect Program from Database                  206
```

This program is not intended to demonstrate the most efficient way of implementing the required procedure. The aim is to show the syntax required for embedded SQL in a simple single-table update program.

The program uses *cursors* which provide a means of defining and extracting a subset of data items on the database and also provide a pointer to the current 'record'. This scheme allows a substantial reduction in programming effort, in terms of the number of lines of code you have to write, a standard method of database interface, and the power of SQL commands, combined with the facility for accessing and processing individual records before moving on and processing other records. The terminology is rather imprecise. 'Cursor' is apparently used to mean both a notional pointer and the set of records retrieved or defined by the cursor. This does not in practice matter since most programmers think in terms of 'what you do' rather than 'what it means'.

The operation of cursors can be seen in this program in lines 077 to 104. In line 77, the cursor SAL_CURS1 is defined as the set of rows retrieved by the SQL SELECT command:

```
078     SELECT EMP_NO, LAST_NAME, FIRST_NAME, HOUR_SAL
079     FROM EMPLOYEE
080     WHERE REST_CODE=:rest_code;
```

which is quite similar in appearance to interactive SQL. The WHERE clause involves the value of the host variable 'rest_code' which was declared in line 050. The value of rest_code was obtained from the user in line 071. Whenever host variables appear in SQL commands they are preceded by a colon. Notice that database columns and host variables may have the same name. REST_CODE is a column in table EMPLOYEE and rest_code is a C variable. So the SELECT defines a number of records, notionally stored in memory in a database buffer area with the cursor SAL_CURS1 pointing at the first record. The actual retrieval of rows into the database buffer area occurs when the cursor is 'opened' in line 084.

In line 099 the record in the database buffer area pointed at by SAL_CURS1 is FETCHed (copied) into the host variables :emp_no, :last_name, :first_name, and :hour_sal, all defined in lines 42 to 54, the

DECLARE section:

```
099     EXEC SQL FETCH SAL_CURS1 INTO :emp_no, :last_name,
100        :first_name, :hour_sal;
```

This is the effect of the FETCH:

Database Column		Host Variable
--------		--------
EMP_NO	-------->	:emp_no
LAST_NAME	-------->	:last_name
FIRST_NAME	-------->	:first_name
HOUR_SAL	-------->	:hour_sal

The database data is now available for processing in the host program because the data has been transferred to host variables. The C loop provided by lines 097, 098 and 104 repeatedly FETCHes a record and prints it. Each time the FETCH of line 099 is executed the cursor SAL_CURS1 is incremented. The loop would in fact be an infinite loop, but for the operation of line 087:

```
087     EXEC SQL WHENEVER NOT FOUND GOTO close1;
```

Until any subsequent WHENEVER NOT FOUND command is executed, any FETCH that does not find a record results in control being passed to label 'close1'. This is the mechanism used here for ending the infinite loop and carrying on to subsequent processing - the processing after the label 'close1' in line 109. In line 110 the cursor SAL_CURS1 is closed.

The next section of processing involves altering the salaries of all staff in the restaurant identified by :rest_code. Line 118 gets the percentage change from the user. A new cursor is defined in lines 125 to 129:

```
125     EXEC SQL DECLARE SAL_CURS2 CURSOR FOR
126       SELECT EMP_NO, LAST_NAME, FIRST_NAME, HOUR_SAL
127       FROM EMPLOYEE
128       WHERE REST_CODE = :rest_code
129       FOR UPDATE OF HOUR_SAL ;
```

This defines SAL_CURS2 to embrace the same set of rows from EMPLOYEE as SAL_CURS1 did. However line 129 specifies that the purpose of this cursor is to update the rows. Line 131 opens the cursor and line 135 says what to do at end-of-file for the following update loop. The code within the loop bounded by lines 139 and 147 does the actual update of the HOUR_SAL column in the EMPLOYEE table for the given restaurant code.

In lines 141 to 142, a row from the database table is fetched into the corresponding host variables. Lines 144 to 145 contain the following code:

```
144     EXEC SQL UPDATE EMPLOYEE
145       SET hour_sal = hour_sal * (100 + :change) / 100
146       WHERE CURRENT OF SAL_CURS2 ;
```

This embedded SQL command changes the value of the HOUR_SAL column by the percentage contained in the host variable ':change', whose value was obtained from the user in line 118. The phrase 'WHERE CURRENT OF' in line 146 means 'pointed at by', so line 146 indicates that the EMPLOYEE row to be updated is the 'current' one.

'Currency' is a concept borrowed from CODASYL network databases; it simply indicates the 'current' row as determined by relevant prior processing. In more complex programming examples, there can be several cursors simultaneously open in a database, each cursor marking the 'current' position i.e. the current row, within a table or view. It is possible to have more than one cursor open simultaneously on one table, so that the sort of processing performed in an interactive SQL self-join (or subquery which refers to the same table as the outer query) can be obtained. The idea of currency is the feature that distinguishes embedded SQL usage from interactive SQL usage, where one is meant to be thinking in terms of *sets* of rows rather than individual rows.

In following lines in this program, cursor SAL_CURS2 is closed, SAL_CURS3 is declared and opened, and the specified rows from table EMPLOYEE are listed out again, this time with their new values of salary. This cursor is closed in line 199 and the program is disconnected from the database in line 206, so that the DBMS no longer has to consider this program and its effects on the database tables. If *several* programs were simultaneously accessing the EMPLOYEE table, the DBMS would have to perform the appropriate locks to co-ordinate database updates and reads so that database integrity was maintained.

11.3 EMBEDDING SQL IN COBOL

11.3.1 Listing Specified Rows

The following COBOL program performs processing equivalent to the interactive:

```
SELECT INV_NO,  AMOUNT
FROM INVOICE
WHERE C_NO  = '&1' ;
```

Where '&1' is a parameter whose value is decided at run-time.

```
01  IDENTIFICATION DIVISION.
02  PROGRAM-ID. EX1.
03  ENVIRONMENT DIVISION.
04  CONFIGURATION SECTION.
05  DATA DIVISION.
06  WORKING-STORAGE SECTION.
07      EXEC SQL BEGIN DECLARE SECTION END-EXEC.
08  01  CUSNUM  PIC S99 COMP.
09  01  INVNUM  PIC S9999 COMP.
10  01  INVAMT  PIC 9(5)V99.
11      EXEC SQL END DECLARE SECTION END-EXEC.
12      EXEC SQL INCLUDE SQLCA END-EXEC.
13  01  INVAMT-DISP REDEFINES INVAMT PIC ££££9.99.
```

```
14  PROCEDURE DIVISION.
15  MAIN-PARA.
16     EXEC SQL WHENEVER NOT FOUND CONTINUE END-EXEC.
17     EXEC SQL WHENEVER SQLERROR GOTO ERROR-PARA END-EXEC.
18     DISPLAY "CUSTOMER ACCOUNT NO: ".
19     ACCEPT CUSNUM.
20     EXEC SQL DECLARE C CURSOR FOR
21       SELECT INV_NO, AMOUNT
22       FROM INVOICE WHERE C_NO = :CUSNUM
23     END EXEC.
24     EXEC SQL OPEN C END-EXEC.
25     EXEC SQL FETCH C INTO :INVNUM, :INVAMT END EXEC
26     PERFORM GET-INV-ROW UNTIL SQLCODE NOT = 0.
27     EXEC SQL CLOSE C END-EXEC.
28     STOP RUN.
29  GET-INV-ROW.
30     DISPLAY INVNUM, INVAMT-DISP.
31     EXEC SQL FETCH C INTO :INVNUM, :INVAMT END EXEC.
32  ERROR-PARA.
33     DISPLAY "ERROR, SQLCODE = " SQLCODE.
34     EXEC SQL CLOSE C END-EXEC.
```

In lines 7 to 11 host variables are declared. Note that the match between the SQL column descriptions and the COBOL PICTURE is installation-dependent. Line 12 'pulls in' the data items used for interfacing the database to COBOL, including SQLCODE.

Lines 16 and 17 handle 'exceptions'. NOT FOUND corresponds to an SQLCODE value of 100 (no row found in the FETCH) or a negative value (database error). CONTINUE means 'go to next statement' which is what we want here; when there are no more rows 'in the cursor' (i.e. the set of rows delivered by the OPEN in line 24 and defined in lines 20 to 23) then SQLCODE will take the value 100 and control will drop down to line 27 where the cursor is closed and execution stops. Successful FETCHes result in an SQLCODE of zero.

The program follows a conventional COBOL 'shape' with FETCH retrieving the 'next' row in the set of rows retrieved by the cursor.

11.3.2 Selective Updates

The following program either adds 15 per cent VAT to an invoice amount
or deletes the invoice record if its value is below one pound:

```
GET invoice record
DOWHILE not EOF
        if invoice amount >=  1
                increase invoice amount by 15 %
        else
                delete invoice record
        endif
        GET next invoice record
  ENDWHILE
```

```
001   IDENTIFICATION DIVISION.
002   PROGRAM-ID. EX2.
003   ENVIRONMENT DIVISION.
004   CONFIGURATION SECTION.
005   DATA DIVISION.
006   WORKING-STORAGE SECTION.
007       EXEC SQL BEGIN DECLARE SECTION END-EXEC.
008   01  INVAMT PIC 9(5)V99.
009       EXEC SQL END DECLARE SECTION END-EXEC.
010       EXEC SQL INCLUDE SQLCA END-EXEC.
011   PROCEDURE DIVISION.
012   MAIN-PARA.
013       EXEC SQL WHENEVER NOT FOUND CONTINUE END-EXEC.
014       EXEC SQL WHENEVER SQLERROR GOTO ERROR-PARA END-EXEC.
015       EXEC SQL DECLARE C CURSOR FOR
016         SELECT AMOUNT FROM INVOICE
017          FOR UPDATE OF AMOUNT
018       END-EXEC.
019       EXEC SQL OPEN C END-EXEC.
020       EXEC SQL FETCH C INTO :INVAMT END-EXEC.
021       PERFORM PROCESS-A-ROW UNTIL SQLCODE NOT =  0.
```

```
022    EXEC SQL CLOSE END-EXEC.
023    EXEC SQL COMMIT WORK END-EXEC.
024    STOP RUN.
025  PROCESS-A-ROW.
026    IF AMOUNT NOT <  1
027        EXEC SQL
028           UPDATE INVOICE
029           SET AMOUNT = AMOUNT * 1.15
030           WHERE CURRENT OF C
031        END EXEC
032    ELSE
033        EXEC SQL
034           DELETE FROM INVOICE
035           WHERE CURRENT OF C
036        END EXEC
037        .
038    EXEC SQL FETCH C INTO :INVAMT END-EXEC.
039  ERROR-PARA.
040    DISPLAY "ERROR ", SQLCODE
041    EXEC SQL CLOSE C END-EXEC.
```

Only one host variable INVAMT is needed in this program since it is the only variable used by both the COBOL and SQL. In line 15 all rows from the INVOICE table are retrieved. Which columns are retrieved is not particularly significant; only AMOUNT needs to be inspected here. The main purpose of the program is to step through the rows one-by-one (the 'cursor' points to a row and is incremented for each FETCH) and either delete the row (line 34) or update the value of AMOUNT (line 29). Line 17 also states which columns are to be updated.

11.4 EMBEDDING SQL IN dBASE IV

11.4.1 Retrievals from Joined Tables

This program displays details of outstanding invoices and customer name in descending order of invoice amount for overdrawn customers. Details for each invoice are shown on the screen until the user presses a key.

```
00  * ex1.prs
01  store 0 to ws_inv_no
02  store 0 to ws_amount
03  store space(10) to ws_sname
04  clear
05  declare c1 cursor for
06    select inv_no, amount, sname
07    from cus, invoice
08    where cus.c_no = invoice.c_no
09    and balance >  cred_lim
10    order by amount desc ;
11  open c1 ;
12  do while .t.
13    fetch c1 into ws_inv_no, ws_amount, ws_sname ;
14    if sqlcode >=  100
15       close c1;
16       return
17    endif
18    clear
19    a7,10 say "Invoice No: " + str(ws_inv_no)
20    a9,10 say "Amount: "
21    a9,18 say ws_amount
22    a11,10 say "Customer: " + ws_sname
23    ?
24    ?
25    wait
26  enddo
```

This program demonstrates the directness and simplicity of dBASE code which manages to achieve more in fewer lines and be more readable (in my opinion) than any other procedural language. This stems from the fact that the original dBASE II was *purpose-built* for database work. Combined with SQL it is indeed a very powerful database tool. Contrast this with the other popular host languages. C was a language for writing an operating system, FORTRAN was for scientific and engineering calculations, COBOL was for general DP and PL/I was for *everything*. dBASE took on board the experiences (good and bad) of using these older languages.

Lines 1 to 3 in this program initialize (and simultaneously define the type of) the host variables. Remember, the only variables that will be *host* variables are those accessed by both SQL and dBASE.

Line 4 clears the screen and lines 5 to 10 declare the cursor c. Note the join criteria and the ORDER BY. A lot of the 'work' at table level is being done by SQL. The host dBASE code is for row-by-row processing and 'fancy' I/O.

The open command in line 11 gets the rows into a buffer and the fetch of line 13 places the cursor. There is no need for a 'read ahead' (as in line 20 of the previous COBOL program in section 11.3.2 for example) due to the ability to jump out of the loop using the 'return' statement of line 16.

Lines 14 to 17 test for the end-of-file condition. SQLCODE is zero for a successful fetch, 100 or more for unsuccessful fetch (eof here) and negative for an error.

Lines 19 to 22 are screen-oriented output commands. ' + 'is a string concatenation operator and '?'s' just prints blank lines.

The 'wait' command puts the message 'press any key to continue' on the screen.

The 'dowhile .t.' of line 12 with the 'enddo' of line 26 represent an infinite loop which can only be got out of with the 'return' of line 16. If this is too 'unstructured' for you, you can use instead the looping structure:

```
a 20,10 say "Continue (y/n): " get ans picture "!"
do while ans <>  "N"

      ...

      ...
   a 20,10 say "Continue (y/n): " get ans picture "!"
enddo
```

or similar. The "!" picture converts input to upper case. The order of displaying and getting data within the loop would also have to be reversed.

11.4.2 Updates Dependent on Another Table

In this program the quantity in stock in the PRODUCT table is decremented by the quantity delivered to customers in the DELIVERY table for each product. This can be programmed in interactive SQL but the following program illustrates some new embedded programming points.

```
00  ex2.prs
01  store 0 to ws_prod_no
02  store 0 to ws_del_qty
03  clear
04  declare c2 cursor for
05      select prod_no, qty
06      from delivery;
07  open c2;
08  do while .t.
09      fetch c2 into ws_prod_no, ws_del_qty;
10      if sqlcode >= 100
11          close c2;
12          return
13      endif
14      update product
15      set qis = qis - ws_del_qty
16      where prod_no = ws_prod_no;
17  enddo
```

In lines 1 and 2 the host variables are initialized. In lines 4 to 6 a cursor is declared for the DELIVERY table. The reason for using a cursor for DELIVERY is that sequential access is required across *all* rows. No cursor is declared for PRODUCT since we require random access on it; given a particular DELIVERY.PROD_NO, we want to find the PRODUCT row with the same PROD_NO. A cursor would be no use here since the sequence of PRODUCT rows accessed (and updated) is not top-to-bottom; indeed some rows may be updated more than once.

The speed of this random access of the PRODUCT table would be enhanced by an *index* on PROD_NO if PRODUCT were a large table, since the row would be retrieved quicker and there would be no need to update the index itself (see Chapter 12 for more on indexing).

In line 9 the relevant columns of the rows of DELIVERY are read into the host variables and after a check for end-of-file on DELIVERY (lines 10 to 13), the relevant PRODUCT row is updated in lines 14 to 16. This program assumes that every DELIVERY is for a product that actually exists on the PRODUCT table, otherwise lines 10 to 13 would cause processing to cease as soon as a 'no match' occurred.

11.5 EXERCISES

1. Modify the program ex2 of 11.4.2 to cater for mismatching
   DELIVERY and PRODUCT rows.

2. Looking at the delivered quantities and quantity in stock in
   PRODUCT and DELIVERY, what can you infer?

3. How would you prevent the accidental repeat of the execution of ex2?

4. Compare the appearance of the six programs given and award marks
   for clarity.

Chapter 12

Database Administration

12.1 THE ROLE OF THE DBA

The database administrator (DBA) has several responsibilities. These may be vested in one person, or, as is often the case, a database administration team. The DBA is called upon to give advice on many aspects of the database to different people in the organization, including end users, managers, data analysts, systems analysts and database and systems programmers. Since the DBA has overall responsibility for the security and efficiency of the database, members of the DBA team are as likely to be found in board meetings as steering committees and program specification walk-throughs. It is the contribution that SQL can make to security and efficiency that forms the content of this chapter; in particular the GRANT and CREATE INDEX commands.

12.2 THE GRANT COMMAND

The facilities and syntax associated with GRANT vary from one DBMS and Standard to another. ORACLE is given as a representative example here. The GRANT command is used by the DBA to provide two basic types of security: user security, which is concerned with the three general levels of access privilege that each user can have with respect to the database as a whole; and data security, which grants users privileges with respect to individual tables and views. It is possible for the DBA to pass on the ability to grant privileges to other users, as we shall see. There are consequently two forms of the SQL GRANT command.

12.2.1 The First Form of the GRANT Command

The first form of GRANT command is used by the DBA to enroll and drop users from the DBMS. Every user must have an id and a password. The syntax of the first form of the GRANT command is:

```
GRANT { CONNECT | RESOURCE | DBA } TO <username>
[ IDENTIFIED BY <password> ]
```

This shows that there are three broad classes of database privilege: CONNECT, RESOURCE, and DBA. (Not in the ISO 9075 Standard see below). The DBA grants these privileges to users with the given username and password. There is nothing the DBMS can do to stop several users sharing the same username and password and of course a given user may have several usernames and passwords that he or she uses for different purposes. The allocation of people to usernames and passwords is an organizational problem carried out by the DBA. The (username, password) to person mapping is normally expected to be 1:1.

   CONNECT privilege is the most basic privilege and in granting it to a user, the IDENTIFIED BY clause must be used. The CONNECT privilege permits:

1. Access to the DBMS.

2. The ability to SELECT, INSERT, DELETE and UPDATE other users' tables and views (provided such other users have granted the corresponding privileges to this user - see the *second* form of GRANT).

3. The creation of views and synonyms.

However, the user with only CONNECT privilege cannot create any tables or indexes.

Example 1

```
1 GRANT CONNECT TO SALLY
2 IDENTIFIED BY ARMY ;
```

Having been 'connected' to the system, id SALLY can now access certain tables and views. Assuming JOHN had granted SELECT privilege to his table CUS, SALLY could perform the query:

```
1  SELECT *
2  FROM JOHN.CUS ;
```

Here, the user SALLY, who has only CONNECT privilege, is retrieving data from a table CUS owned by JOHN. SALLY could create a synonym, to give this table another name:

```
1  CREATE SYNONYM CUSTOMER
2  FOR JOHN.CUS ;
```

The query could then be written:

```
1  SELECT *
2  FROM CUSTOMER ;
```

with the same effect.

A user with CONNECT privilege can change his or her own password at any time using GRANT CONNECT:

```
1  GRANT CONNECT TO SALLY
2  IDENTIFIED BY MANDER ;
```

so MANDER is SALLY's new password.

CONNECT privilege is sufficient for the majority of database users such as operational staff, managers etc., who will only want to inspect and update data. *What* they can inspect and update can be precisely defined by the *second* form of the GRANT command. For many application programmers, who will not need to create tables and views, but will just write programs and queries to access existing ones, CONNECT will also be sufficient.

Users with RESOURCE privilege have all the privileges they obtained when they received CONNECT privilege, and in addition they can:

1. CREATE tables and indexes

2. GRANT privileges on those tables and indexes to other
    users, (using the second form of GRANT) and
    REVOKE those privileges.

If there is not a single corporate database, and users will be
experimentally creating and dropping their own tables in a variety of small
applications , then these users will need RESOURCE privilege. Typical
users requiring RESOURCE in addition to CONNECT would be the
development team of database designers in the design phase of the system
life cycle, DBAs when the system has been implemented but still requires
changes and extensions to the design, and students working on a large
number of completely separate projects.

DBA privilege bestows all the powers of CONNECT and RESOURCE,
and in addition it allows the owner of this privilege to:

1. Access any user's data, with the ability to perform
    any SQL operations on it.

2. Use the first form of the GRANT command to grant
    CONNECT, RESOURCE and DBA privileges.

3. Create PUBLIC synonyms.

4. Perform detailed auditing and disk space allocation,
    organization, and backup functions.

A DBA can also remove privileges from a user using REVOKE:

    1 REVOKE CONNECT FROM JOHN ;

Any tables created by JOHN will remain, but he will not now have access
to the database.

In a similar way, DBA, RESOURCE and CONNECT privileges may be
selectively revoked.

12.2.2 The Second Form of the GRANT Command

This form of the GRANT command grants privileges to users with respect to tables or views. The syntax is:

```
GRANT { privilege, ... | ALL } ON table-or-view
TO { user | PUBLIC }  [ WITH GRANT OPTION ] ;
```

The privileges can be any combination of SELECT, INSERT, DELETE, UPDATE, ALTER, and INDEX to a table, and just the first four to a view. ALL grants all of the privileges possessed by the granter. UPDATE may be followed by a list of columns, limiting the grantee to updating just *those* columns in the table or view.

Limiting the ability to *see* certain columns and rows is achieved using the definition of the view and then granting SELECT privilege to the view rather than the base table(s).

PUBLIC grants the specified privilege to all users. The optional WITH GRANT OPTION authorizes the grantee to grant all or part of these privileges in turn to other users.

Example 1

```
1  GRANT ALL
2  ON CUS
3  TO SALLY
4  WITH GRANT OPTION ;
```

This grants all the privileges that the granter has to user SALLY on table CUS. It also allows her to pass any of these privileges on to other users.

Example 2

```
1  GRANT SELECT,
2  UPDATE (NAME, POSTC)
3  ON CUS
4  TO BRIAN ;
```

This allows BRIAN to *see* all columns and rows in table CUS but to only *update* the two columns NAME and POSTC.

Example 3

```
1  CREATE VIEW CUSVIEW1 AS
2  SELECT C_NO,  NAME, POSTC
3  FROM CUS
4  WHERE CITY = 'London' ;

1  GRANT SELECT
2  ON CUSVIEW1
3  TO FRED ;

1  GRANT UPDATE (CRED_LIM)
2  ON CUS
3  TO FRED ;
```

In this sequence, a view CUSVIEW1 is created to limit the rows and columns of CUS that FRED is allowed to see. (He has no SELECT privilege on CUS itself; his 'view' is being limited by the VIEW). He is however allowed to update the value of CRED_LIM on any row, without seeing it.

Should it become necessary to limit the *rows* of CUS in which FRED is allowed to update the CRED_LIM column, say to the London customers only, it would be necessary to revoke the update privilege on CUS and to grant it throught the view CUSVIEW1 instead:

```
1  REVOKE ALL
2  ON CUS
3  FROM FRED ;

1  GRANT UPDATE (CRED_LIM)
2  ON CUSVIEW1
3  TO FRED ;
```

Now FRED can only see C_NO, NAME and POSTC and only update CRED_LIM. Here is an example of FRED updating the credit limit of Mr. Sallaway:

```
1  SELECT *
2  FROM CUSVIEW1
3  WHERE UPPER(NAME) = 'SALLAWAY' ;
```

This checks that there is only one Sallaway. Assuming FRED is now confident he has his man, he can update Sallaway's credit limit (without seeing what it was):

```
1  UPDATE CUSVIEW1
2  SET CRED_LIM  = 2000
3  WHERE UPPER(NAME) = 'SALLAWAY' ;
```

FRED might alternatively use C_NO for Sallaway to reduce typing in line 3:

```
3  WHERE C_NO  =1 ;
```

12.2.3 Listing Your Privileges

There are many system tables of interest in the *data dictionary*. The names of these tables vary from one DBMS to another but they will in general contain tables showing which tables and views exist, who the owners are, what privileges users have, etc. In ORACLE, you can find what your privileges are on other users' tables and views by:

```
1  SELECT GRANTOR, TNAME, A, D, N, I, S, U
2  FROM SYSTABAUTH
3  WHERE GRANTOR != USER
4  AND   GRANTEE  = USER ;
```

USER evaluates to your current login id. GRANTOR is the person who granted you access and you are the grantee. SYSTABAUTH is the data dictionary table that contains this data. TNAME is the name of the table or view, and the letters in line 1 stand for ALTER, DELETE, INDEX, SELECT and UPDATE. If you have the privilege, a G will appear under that column. Line 3 restricts the output to other people's tables.

To find out who has access privileges on your tables and views, type:

```
1  SELECT GRANTEE, TNAME, A, D, N, I, S, U
2  FROM SYSTABAUTH
3  WHERE GRANTOR = USER
4  AND GRANTEE != USER ;
```

12.3 THE CREATE INDEX COMMAND

12.3.1 Introduction

There are two main objectives that indexing seeks to achieve:

1. Increasing the execution speed of queries.

2. Ensuring that given columns have 'unique' values.

An index is an extra table associated with an actual data table such as CUS or INVOICE which, just like the index in a book, is a way of quickly finding a required item of information. In the case of database indexes, the required item will be one or more rows in a table. As in the book index, the index entry contains on its lefthand side the item required, and on the righthand side, one or more locations (ROWIDs) that the item can be found. A ROWID (Row Identifier) is the *address* in the database where that row resides.

With large tables, the use of an index can considerably reduce the time taken to find particular items. In base dBASE IV, the use of an index also gives an apparent change of sequence of the rows, so that if one index is in use a LIST command lists out rows in one order, while choosing another index will cause the rows to be listed in another order. In SQL, including the dBASE IV, ORACLE and INGRES variants and in the standards, the *DBMS itself* decides which indexes if any are to be used in the execution of a query. The listed sequency of rows is determined by the ORDER BY clause as we have seen (Chapter 3).

Indexes are created by the user if he or she has been granted appropriate privileges, otherwise by the DBA. There is a tendency for users to create indexes for a variety of reasons, usually as an experiment to see if the speed of particular queries can be improved. This can lead to an unjustified proliferation of indexes and it might be better where large shared databases are in use, for the DBA to control the creation of indexes. Indexes can in some circumstances actually slow down database updates involving INSERT and DELETE and UPDATE commands. When a new row is inserted for example, not only the base table but also the index (in fact every index related to that base table) must be updated with a new index entry.

At this point it is also worthwhile dispelling a database myth. Some programmers believe that primary keys must be indexed because that is how you retrieve rows - via the primary key. Both beliefs are false. Primary keys *can* be indexed but it is not mandatory. As we have seen, the selection criteria in the WHERE clause may involve any number of columns, key and non-key. In a query like:

    1 SELECT *
    2 FROM CUS
    3 WHERE BALANCE > 100 ;

only the BALANCE column will be inspected; the primary key C_NO will not be considered. Even if there were an index on C_NO, it would not be used in this query.

It is possible to ensure the 'uniqueness' of the primary key (See chapter 2 for a discussion of 'uniqueness' and 'primary key') using SQL indexes. The reason for wanting to ensure this uniqueness is just so we can have a handy, short identifier for each row in the table and for the real-world object that the row models. If (in the roughly ISO 9075 and ANSI 86 SQLs under discussion) no index has been created on what the DBA considers is the primary key in a table, or the UNIQUE option has not been used in such an index, then there is nothing to stop duplicate primary key values emerging. Later versions and standards of SQL address this and other database *integrity* issues. The basic syntax of the CREATE INDEX command is:

CREATE [UNIQUE] INDEX index-name
ON table-name (column-name [ASC | DESC], ...) ;

An index may use more than one index column. You may create different indexes for different combinations of columns in the table, and different indexes with the same columns in a different order. These indexes will be used for different purposes.

Remember that each time you create an additional index you are going to further slow down the updates (in general - there may be some cases where the additional time to update the index is more than compensated for by the reduction in time taken to *find* the row or rows to be updated).

Every index must have a unique system-wide name, which is another reason for allocating index-creating responsibilities to the DBA. The user does not name the index to be utilized in a particular query; that is left to the query interpreter. Naming the index is necessary so that it can subsequently be DROPped (by name) if required.

Note that the index entries may be in ASCending or DESCending order so that when the DBMS decides to use an index, the rows will be processed in that order.

12.3.2 Improving Speed of Access

Example 1

    1 CREATE INDEX INV_C_NO
    2 ON INVOICE (C_NO) ;

This creates an index table called INV_C_NO whose lefthand side contains a list of C_NO s in ascending (ascending is the default) order. This will be useful in a query in which a particular customer's invoices are required, or one in which a JOIN involving, say, CUS and INVOICE on C_NO is required. Whether or not this index *does* improve the speed of access to invoices on customer number is best tested by experiment.

Query 12.1 'Get all the invoices for Sallaway'

1 SELECT INV_NO, INV_DATE, AMOUNT
2 FROM CUS A, INVOICE B
3 WHERE SNAME ='Sallaway'
4 AND A.C_NO =B.C_NO ;

Here, the query interpreter and optimizer in the DBMS will do the relational algebraic *select* (also known as *restrict*) on CUS first to retrieve the C_NO of Sallaway. This value (1) will then be fed into the INV_C_NO index (the optimizer will 'decide' this) to quickly locate all the ROWIDs for INVOICE rows containing that C_NO value. This is faster than sequentially searching the whole INVOICE table for rows with matching C_NOs.

Note that any SQL query will work (provided it is syntactically and semantically correct) and give the same output whether or not there is an index; the only difference will be in execution time of the query. For a small table the execution time of a query might be *increased* because *two* tables then have to be accessed - the index table *and* the base table. The point at which an index becomes profitable is best determined experimentally. The ORACLE SQL*PLUS User's Guide for example recommends indexing if the table has more than 'a few hundred' rows.

Query 12.2 'Get the details of customers who have outstanding
invoices dated before 1st Jan 1991'.

1 SELECT A.*
2 FROM CUS
3 WHERE C_NO IN
4 (SELECT C_NO
5   FROM INVOICE
6   WHERE INV_DATE < '1-jan-91') ;

Here, the index will probably not be useful. The query interpreter should decide not to use the index because the INVOICE table should first be scanned *on INV_DATE* to retrieve the required set of C_NOs. The CUS table rows will then be scanned to retrieve CUS rows. The INV_C_NO index does not contain the required kind of information. Only if the query interpreter decided to do a full join of CUS and INVOICE first would the INV_C_NO conceivably be of any use. This decision would only be wise if both tables were large and there was likely to be a high *hit rate* (proportion of rows accessed) on INVOICE due to the fact that many invoices were for dates before 1-jan-91. Of course it is unlikely the query interpreter will know this *a priori*.

12.3.3 Enforcing Uniqueness

Example 2

    1 CREATE UNIQUE INDEX CUS_C_NO
    2 ON CUS (C_NO) ;

The UNIQUE option will ensure that no two rows of the CUS table shall have the same value of C_NO. If you attempt to insert a new row with a duplicate value of C_NO, an error will result:

    1 INSERT INTO CUS
    2 VALUES (6, 'Mr', 'Jones', ...) ;

    'Error : DUPLICATE VALUE IN INDEX'

One should not over-estimate the powers of UNIQUE to support database integrity. Various types of primary key anomaly are *not* prevented by this option. For example, it is still possible to assign a customer *more than one* C_NO. It is still possible not to assign a customer a CUS record at all. It is still possible for a C_NO to be assigned to a customer that does *not exist*. UNIQUE really only prevents you from assigning two customers the same C_NO. One out of four.
   In the ANSI-86 and ISO 9075 standards, the UNIQUE option is specified in the CREATE TABLE command and in the latter, 'UNIQUE' can be replaced by 'PRIMARY KEY' (unless of course you want to specify a column or group of columns as unique and you have not chosen

that group of columns as the primary key i.e. it is a candidate key but is not used as a primary key).

The CREATE INDEX command does not appear in either standard, but it *does* appear in ORACLE, INGRES and dBASE IV with the syntax shown here.

12.3.4 Indexing on a Combination of Columns

Example 3

The syntax description shown above suggests that an index can be built out of more than one column. In example 3, it is desired to create an index on the primary key since it is expected that the rows will often be retrieved via the primary key. The primary key is a composite key consisting of INV_NO and PMT_NO. (See the definition of the PAYMENT table in the Appendix).

```
1 CREATE UNIQUE INDEX PMT_INV_NO_PMT_NO
2 ON PAYMENT (INV_NO, PMT_NO DESC) ;
```

The lefthand side of the index will notionally contain the concatenation of invoice and payment numbers with, for a given invoice number, the highest payment number first (because of the use here of the DESCending option).

12.3.5 Dropping Indexes

It might become necessary to remove an index, either as part of general 'housekeeping' duties to remove apparently unused indexes (the creator of the index can usually be found in the data dictionary), or in order to modify it (in which case you DROP it and reCREATE it). In either case, dropping the index will save space and speed up INSERTs, DELETEs and UPDATEs on the indexed column(s) and since it is unused it will not have any effect on queries. For example:

```
1 DROP INDEX INV_C_NO  ;
```

Appendix

Table Definitions

CUS

C_NO	TITLE	SNAME	INITS	STREET	CITY	POSTC	CRED_LIM	BALANCE
1	Mr	Sallaway	G.R.	12 Fax Rd	London	WC1	1000	42.56
2	Miss	Lauri	P.	5 Dux St	London	N1	500	200
3	Mr	Jackson	R.	2 Lux Ave	Leeds	LE1 2AB	500	510
4	Mr	Dziduch	M.	31 Low St	Dover	DO2 9CD	100	149.23
5	Ms	Woods	S.Q.	17 Nax Rd	London	E18 4WW	1000	250.1
6	Mrs	Williams	C.	41 Cax St	Dover	DO2 8WD		412.21

INVOICE

INV_NO	C_NO	INV_DATE	AMOUNT
940	1	5-DEC-90	26.2
1002	4	12-JAN-91	149.23
1003	1	12-JAN-91	16.26
1004	2	14-JAN-91	200
1005	3	20-JAN-91	510
1006	5	21-JAN-91	250.1
1017	6	22-JAN-91	412.21

PAYMENT

INV_NO	PMT_NO	PMT_DATE	AMOUNT
940	2	12-DEC-90	13
1005	1	14-JAN-91	510
1017	1	30-JAN-91	100
940	3	19-JAN-91	10

PRODUCT

PROD_NO	DESCR	QIS	MINQ	REORDQ	PRICE
1	Bat	10	5	10	12
2	Ball	5	5	20	2
3	Hoop	3	5	10	3
4	Net	2	5	10	20
5	Rope	1	10	10	6

DELIVERY

C_NO	PROD_NO	QTY	DEL_DATE
3	2	2	3-NOV-90
3	1	3	3-NOV-90
1	4	6	7-NOV-90
5	3	4	12-NOV-90
3	3	1	12-NOV-90

VIOLIN

STUD_NO	NAME	AGE
1	Fred	10
2	Sally	11
4	David	10

PIANO

STUD_NO	NAME	AGE
2	Jane	12
4	David	10
5	Zena	11

CELLO

STUD_NO	AGE	NAME
4	10	David
6	11	Josey

FLUTE

STUD	CNAME	AGE
7	Ashfak	12

CUST

CNO	NAME
1	Alan
2	Bill
3	Charles

PURCHASE

CNO	PRNO
1	a
1	b
2	a

PROD

PRNO	DESCR
a	Apple
b	Ball

GROUPS

TERM	GROUP_NO	MEMBER
1	1	1
1	1	2
1	1	3
1	2	4
1	2	5
1	2	6
2	10	3
2	10	2
2	1	5
2	1	7

CANDIDATE

CAND_NO	NAME	CONS_NO	PARTY	NO_OF_VOTES
1	Fred	1	Labour	100
2	Jim	1	Cons	120
3	Peter	1	Liberal	50
4	John	2	Labour	150
5	Mike	2	SLD	50
6	Jane	2	Cons	100
9	Sue	1	SDP	160
7	Mary	2	Green	150
8	Ulrike	1	Indep	150
10	U Li	3	Red Guards	150
21	Rosa	3	Simbianese	30
29	Patty	3	Simbianese	12
41	Astrid	3	Liberal	3
50	Gordon	3	Labour	160
52	Ben	1	Green	70

References

1. ISO TC97/SC21/WG3 and ANSI X3H2. (1987)
   ISO 9075 *Database Language SQL*.

2. Date C.J. (1987) *A Guide to the SQL Standard*.
   Addison-Wesley Publishing Company, Reading, Mass.

3. Date C.J. (1990) *An Introduction to Database
   Systems*, 5th edn. Addison-Wesley Publishing
   Company, Reading, Mass.

4. Lipschutz S. (1982) *Essential Computer Mathematics*.
   McGraw-Hill Book Company.

5. Clocksin W.F. & Mellish C.S. (1984) *Programming in
   Prolog*, pp. 233-244. Springer-Verlag, Berlin.

Index